Law for Professionals

The *Law for Professionals* book series contains publications in all fields of the law aimed at professionals and practitioners. The book series is dedicated to publish high quality books that provide in-depth insights into the workings and the practical functioning of the law, international organizations or regional legal frameworks.

The authors contributing to the book series are experienced legal professionals and practitioners whose expertise combines theory and practice.

Gianluca Rotino

Algoraceutics - Legal Perspectives on Artificial Intelligence in Drug Discovery and Development

Springer

Gianluca Rotino
Information Society Law Center (ISLC)
"Cesare Beccaria" Department of Legal Sciences, University of Milan
Milan, Italy

ISSN 2662-141X ISSN 2662-1428 (electronic)
Law for Professionals
ISBN 978-3-032-38536-9 ISBN 978-3-032-38537-6 (eBook)
https://doi.org/10.1007/978-3-032-38537-6

This Springer imprint is published by the registered company Springer Nature Switzerland AG
The registered company address is: Gewerbestrasse 11, 6330 Cham, Switzerland

To those who, faced with the machine's power to provide answers, keep what makes us human: the power to ask the questions.

Foreword

The emergence of artificial intelligence has profoundly transformed the relationship between technology and law.

What initially appeared to be a new computational tool has rapidly evolved into an autonomous layer of decision-making capable of influencing scientific research, economic organisation, public administration, healthcare and, increasingly, the exercise of legal judgement itself.

For scholars of legal informatics, this transformation represents not simply the arrival of another technological innovation, but the opening of an entirely new research paradigm.

The Information Society Law Center (ISLC) at the University of Milan was founded upon the conviction that technological change cannot be adequately understood through isolated legal disciplines.

Rather, it requires an interdisciplinary approach capable of integrating legal theory, computer science, regulatory studies, philosophy of technology, economics and public policy.

Our research has therefore consistently focused on the evolving interaction between digital technologies and legal systems, exploring how emerging computational architectures reshape fundamental legal concepts that have traditionally relied upon assumptions of human agency, transparency and accountability.

Artificial intelligence has brought these questions into particularly sharp focus.

The increasing autonomy of algorithmic systems challenges long-established legal categories concerning responsibility, causation, evidence, intellectual property, regulatory compliance and the protection of fundamental rights.

At the same time, the unprecedented capacity of machine learning systems to generate knowledge, support complex decisions and participate in highly regulated sectors requires legal scholarship to move beyond technology-specific regulation towards a broader reflection on the constitutional architecture of digital societies.

The pharmaceutical sector provides an especially valuable laboratory for observing these developments.

Drug discovery and development constitute one of the most heavily regulated scientific environments in contemporary society, where innovation, public health, industrial competition and fundamental rights converge.

When artificial intelligence becomes an active participant in this process, traditional legal assumptions begin to reveal their limitations. Questions that initially appear sector-specific rapidly acquire much broader theoretical significance.

Who bears responsibility when algorithmic systems substantially contribute to scientific decision-making? How should legal systems evaluate evidence generated by opaque computational models? Can explainability become a procedural requirement rather than merely a technical aspiration? How should intellectual property evolve when creativity increasingly emerges from human–machine interaction? What forms of governance are required when access to data and computational infrastructure becomes a decisive competitive advantage? Finally, how should regulators oversee technologies whose internal reasoning may remain only partially understandable even to their developers?

These are not exclusively pharmaceutical questions. They lie at the very heart of contemporary legal informatics. They concern the relationship between law and autonomous computation, between human oversight and algorithmic agency, between technological innovation and democratic accountability. They require scholars to reconsider fundamental legal concepts—including liability, proof, transparency, due process, market regulation and data governance—in light of computational systems that increasingly participate in activities once regarded as exclusively human.

It is precisely this perspective that aligns closely with the research agenda pursued within the Information Society Law Center. Across diverse domains—including artificial intelligence, cybersecurity, digital investigations, platform regulation, legal technology, algorithmic governance and digital rights—we seek to understand how computational systems transform legal institutions, and how legal systems, in turn, can preserve their normative legitimacy while adapting to technological change. Our objective is not merely to interpret existing regulation but to contribute to the development of conceptual frameworks capable of governing future technological transformations.

The present volume offers an illuminating contribution to this broader scholarly endeavour. By taking artificial intelligence in pharmaceutical research as its analytical focus, it opens a much wider discussion concerning the evolution of legal categories in the age of algorithmic decision-making. Its value therefore extends beyond pharmaceutical law. It invites legal scholars to engage with one of the defining challenges of our time: constructing legal frameworks that remain intellectually coherent while responding to increasingly autonomous computational systems operating across science, industry and public institutions.

At the ISLC, we believe that legal informatics must continue to serve precisely this function: not simply documenting technological innovation, but critically analysing its legal implications, identifying emerging normative tensions and contributing to the design of legal institutions capable of governing an increasingly algorithmic society. In this sense, the reflections developed throughout this volume resonate fully with the mission of our research centre and with the broader academic effort to understand how law itself is being reshaped by the digital transformation.

Information Society Law Center (ISLC),
Department of Legal Sciences "Cesare Beccaria"
University of Milan,
Milan, Italy

Giovanni Ziccardi
Paulina Kowalicka

Acknowledgements This book is the result of a path that crossed several disciplines and institutions, and it owes much to the people and the places that made that crossing possible.

My first thanks go to the Information Society Law Center (ISLC) of the University of Milan and to the Department of Legal Sciences 'Cesare Beccaria', for the intellectual environment in which this research took shape. The questions at the heart of this work were sharpened in the seminars and classrooms of the institutions where I had the privilege to study. Each taught me to read a problem from a different side, the legal, the scientific and the regulatory, and this monograph is an attempt to hold those perspectives together.

I am grateful to the colleagues and practitioners with whom I worked for nearly a decade in the advanced biopharma industry in Houston, where many of the ideas discussed in these pages were first tested against the reality of AI-driven drug discovery and clinical development.

I thank the editorial team at Springer Nature for their care and their patience in bringing this volume to publication.

Finally, and most importantly, I thank my family, for the time this book borrowed from them and for the support that gave it back to me.

In accordance with the policy of Springer Nature on the use of artificial intelligence, the author declares that generative artificial intelligence and large language model tools were used in a strictly assistive capacity, limited to language editing, formatting and the verification of bibliographic references. No artificial intelligence system is an author of this work or of any part of it. The author conceived the research, developed the analysis and verified the accuracy of every statement and citation, retaining full and exclusive responsibility for the content.

Competing Interests The author has no competing interests to declare that are relevant to the content of this manuscript.

Contents

About the Author

Gianluca Rotino is a qualified legal practioner and senior legal advisor with 20 years of executive and consulting experience at the intersection of law, life sciences and artificial intelligence. He holds a Master's Degree in Law from the University of Milan and is affiliated with its Information Society Law Center (ISLC). His training combines advanced programs in Artificial Intelligence at the University of Oxford (Saïd Business School) with specialized studies in Drug Discovery, Development and Commercialization at UC San Diego (Skaggs School of Pharmacy) and in GDPR, Clinical Trials and Medical Devices at the Scuola Superiore Sant'Anna of Pisa.

For nearly a decade he served as Chief Strategy and Innovation Officer and Board Director of Kiromic BioPharma (Houston, TX), a clinical-stage biotech operating a proprietary AI-driven target-discovery platform, where he defined the legal framework for AI applications in drug discovery and clinical trials. He currently advises pharmaceutical, biotech and ICT clients on AI Act, NIS2, MDR, GDPR and DORA compliance.

His publications include the chapter "Lo scenario internazionale" in Intelligenza artificiale generativa nella professione forense (Giuffrè, 2024), "Indicazioni operative dalla giurisprudenza" in "L'Avvocato Esteso" (Giuffrè, 2026) and the essay "Personal data in AI Driven drug discovery and development" (Ciberspazio e Diritto, 2024), which directly anticipates the themes addressed in the present monograph.

Abbreviations

AI	Artificial Intelligence
AIC	Marketing Authorization (Italy)
AIFA	Italian Medicines Agency
CDER	Center for Drug Evaluation and Research
CDMO	Contract Development and Manufacturing Organization
CHMP	Committee for Medicinal Products for Human Use
CVMP	Committee for Medicinal Products for Veterinary Use
DABUS	Device for the Autonomous Bootstrapping of Unified Sentience
DMA	Digital Markets Act (Regulation (EU) 2022/1925)
DSA	Digital Services Act (Regulation (EU) 2022/2065)
EC	European Commission
EEC	European Economic Community
EHDS	European Health Data Space (Regulation (EU) 2025/327)
EMA	European Medicines Agency
EPC	European Patent Convention
EPO	European Patent Office
EU	European Union
FDA	Food and Drug Administration
GAN	Generative Adversarial Network
GDPR	General Data Protection Regulation (Regulation (EU) 2016/679)
GPAI	General-Purpose Artificial Intelligence
HTS	High-Throughput Screening
ICMRA	International Coalition of Medicines Regulatory Authorities
IEC	International Electrotechnical Commission
ISO	International Organization for Standardization
IVDR	*In Vitro* Diagnostic Medical Devices Regulation (Regulation (EU) 2017/746)
LIME	Local Interpretable Model-agnostic Explanations
MDCG	Medical Device Coordination Group
MDR	Medical Devices Regulation (Regulation (EU) 2017/745)
ML	Machine Learning
OECD	Organisation for Economic Co-operation and Development
OJ	Official Journal of the European Union
PLD	Product Liability Directive (Directive (EU) 2024/2853)

PROCOVA	Prognostic Covariate Adjustment
QSAR	Quantitative Structure-Activity Relationship
SaMD	Software as a Medical Device
SHAP	SHapley Additive exPlanations
SMILES	Simplified Molecular-Input Line-Entry System
TFEU	Treaty on the Functioning of the European Union
USPTO	United States Patent and Trademark Office
XAI	Explainable Artificial Intelligence

Part I

Foundations: Artificial Intelligence and the Pharmaceutical Process

Introduction 1

Abstract

This introductory chapter frames the central problem of the book, namely the emergence of "algoraceutics," the structural integration of artificial intelligence into pharmaceutical discovery and development. Drawing on recent milestones (Isomorphic Labs' Drug Design Engine and the AI-supported candidates zasocitinib and rentosertib), it shows how AI has compressed the path from biological target to clinical testing from over a decade to a matter of months. It then sets out the three legal questions that organize the volume, asking who is the inventor when an algorithm designs the molecule, who is liable when an AI-designed product causes harm, and who owns the data and controls access to foundational models. The chapter advances the book's thesis that traditional legal categories, namely civil liability, intellectual property, competition law, and data protection, must be reworked rather than merely applied, and outlines the two-part structure that moves from technical and scientific context to legal analysis.

In February 2026, Isomorphic Labs unveiled its Drug Design Engine, a system that doubles the accuracy of molecular interaction predictions compared to AlphaFold 3 and forecasts small-molecule binding affinity better than gold-standard physicochemical computational methods, at a fraction of the time and cost. The company raised $600 million in March 2025 and sits at the center of strategic partnerships worth $3 billion with Eli Lilly and Novartis.[1] It is now preparing to enroll the first

[1] Isomorphic Labs (2026). Isomorphic Labs raised $600 million in March 2025 in a financing round led by Thrive Capital. Partnerships with Eli Lilly and Novartis, totaling $3 billion, were announced in January 2024; Novartis subsequently expanded the collaboration from three to six projects.

G. Rotino, *Algoraceutics - Legal Perspectives on Artificial Intelligence in Drug Discovery and Development*, Law for Professionals,
https://doi.org/10.1007/978-3-032-38537-6_1

patients in clinical trials for oncologic drugs designed entirely by artificial intelligence.

In parallel, zasocitinib (the candidate designed with algorithmic support by Nimbus Therapeutics, acquired by Takeda for $4 billion) is progressing through trials for plaque psoriasis with positive results from two pivotal studies reported in December 2025.[2] It is the most advanced candidate for what could become the first drug discovered with AI contribution to receive FDA approval. And rentosertib, the molecule discovered and designed entirely by an algorithmic generation system (Insilico Medicine), published positive Phase IIa results in June 2025 on idiopathic pulmonary fibrosis in Nature Medicine, with Phase IIb ongoing.[3]

What a contrast with the history of pharmaceutical science. What AI has compressed in 30 months, that is, from biological target to clinical testing, has historically required more than a decade. The case of PARP inhibitors illustrates the temporal compression we are witnessing: half a century from the discovery of the PARP enzyme in 1963 to therapeutic approval of the earliest inhibitors.[4] According to industry analyses, as of 2026 there are over 173 active clinical programs enabled by artificial intelligence in development.[5]

From these realities emerge three fundamental legal questions that this volume addresses.

- The first. Who is the inventor? If the Drug Design Engine designs the molecule and AlphaFold predicts the biological target, does the inventive activity belong to the algorithm, to the researcher, or to the entity that owns the AI model? The answer is not trivial. The categories of our patent tradition place inventiveness in human genius, in the capacity of the human mind to formulate a novel idea and translate it into a practical solution. Yet it remains to be established what the margin of human decision-making is when machine learning systems refine their own predictions over millions of prior iterations. This is the question that Chap. 7 addresses in detail.[6]
- The second. Who is liable for harm? If zasocitinib, designed with algorithmic support, causes an unforeseen adverse effect, the causal chain fragments between

[2] Zasocitinib (TAK-279), Takeda, positive Phase III results on plaque psoriasis reported on 18 December 2025 in two pivotal studies. Acquisition of Nimbus Therapeutics for $4 billion. FDA submission anticipated in fiscal year 2026.

[3] Xu et al. (2025). Phase III in China and Phase IIb in the United States scheduled from the fourth quarter of 2025.

[4] On the historical chronology, the PARP enzyme was discovered in 1963; PARP inhibitors (olaparib, rucaparib, niraparib) received FDA approval beginning in 2014. See Ashworth (2008).

[5] According to industry analyses, in 2026 there are more than 173 clinical programs enabled by AI in active development. See BCG (2023) and Axis Intelligence (2026).

[6] On the question of inventive activity in the context of AI, see EPO, Legal Board of Appeal, decisions J 8/20 and J 9/20 (DABUS case), 21 December 2021; Thaler v Vidal, US Court of Appeals for the Federal Circuit, 2022; IP High Court of Japan, January 2025; Swiss Federal Administrative Tribunal, decision B-2532/2024, 26 June 2025; USPTO, Revised Inventorship Guidance for AI-Assisted Inventions (November 2025).

the algorithm designer, the pharmaceutical company that develops it, and the platform itself that generated the molecular structure. Traditional categories of civil liability for defective products struggle to allocate responsibility when the algorithm's contribution to decision-making prevails over human contribution. The new Product Liability Directive of the European Union, which has just entered into force, must be read carefully to understand how it applies to a product whose defect lies in the quality of algorithmic prediction.[7] This question forms the core of Chap. 6.
- The third. Who owns the data and controls the market? Isomorphic Labs controls the foundational model for protein structure prediction and sits at the center of pharmaceutical value chains. Access to the Drug Design Engine could become an essential good whose denial constitutes abuse of dominant position under competition law. The data used to train these models comes from public genomic databases, from clinical trials, and from proprietary databases whose ownership is contested.[8] This intertwining of intellectual property, competition law, and data regulation is addressed in Chaps. 5 and 8.

The central thesis of this volume is as follows. Traditional legal categories (civil liability, intellectual property, competition law, data protection) prove inadequate to govern a process in which the algorithm's contribution to decision-making prevails over human contribution. The algoraceutical paradigm does not merely require applying existing rules to a new technology; it requires reworking the regulatory framework itself.

The neologism "algoraceutics" designates the intersection between artificial intelligence algorithms and the pharmaceutical process. It is not a metaphor. It describes an operational reality in which AI is no longer an external tool but a structural component of drug discovery and development. This volume intends to construct the legal foundations of this new space through critical reading of current regulations and emerging case law. The perspective is that of general legal theory, which privileges principles over a catalog of individual instruments.

If drug discovery had historically been structured as a sequential process in which the discovery phase was followed by the development phase, clinical testing, and finally commercialization, the algoraceutical paradigm tends to compress and integrate these phases.[9] The algorithm not only designs the target molecule but provides indications regarding pharmacokinetics, predicted toxicity, and probability of clinical success. The separation between the person who designs and the person who validates the product (between inventor and manufacturer) becomes blurred.

---

[7] Directive (EU) 2024/2853 of the European Parliament and of the Council of 23 October 2024 on liability for defective products, which replaces Directive 85/374/EEC. In force from 9 December 2024, with a transposition deadline for Member States until 9 December 2026. In particular art 4 on producer liability and the development-risk exception.

[8] On the doctrine of essential facility applied to AI models, see Mayer-Schönberger and Ramge (2018) and Rubinfeld and Gal (2017).

[9] Cockburn et al. (2018), introducing the concept of 'invention of a method of inventing'.

This volume is structured in two parts. Part I, comprising Chaps. 2, 3, and 4, provides the technical and scientific context necessary to understand the legal questions that follow. Chapter 2 reconstructs the evolution of artificial intelligence from its origins to contemporary foundational models. Chapter 3 examines in detail the application of AI in drug discovery and development processes, surveying the principal machine learning methodologies employed and documented successes. Chapter 4, finally, examines the limits and reliability margins of algorithms, addressing questions of transparency, verification, and validation in the regulatory context.

Part II, comprising Chaps. 5, 6, 7, 8, and 9, develops the legal dimensions. Chapter 5 addresses the European regulatory framework on artificial intelligence, from the Directive on the Liability of Sellers of Defective Products to Regulation (EU) 2024/1689 on Artificial Intelligence, analyzing how these instruments apply to the algoraceutical context.[10] Chapter 6 examines civil liability for harm caused by a pharmaceutical product designed with algorithmic contribution. Chapter 7 reconstructs the regime of intellectual property and patentability in the context of algorithmic drug discovery.[11] Chapter 8 addresses competition law and data protection issues, with particular attention to the role of AI platforms as managers of essential goods. Chapter 9 closes the volume with reflection on FDA and European Medicines Agency (EMA) regulation, as well as AIFA guidelines for Italy.

This volume is current as of spring 2026. The normative sources include Regulation (EU) 2024/1689, Directive (EU) 2024/2853 on the Liability of Sellers of Defective Products, the FDA Draft Guidance on AI in Drug Development (January 2025), the EMA Reflection Paper on the use of AI in the medicines lifecycle (September 2024),[12] and AIFA guidelines from May 2021.[13]

This volume occupies an interdisciplinary space between information technology law, pharmaceutical law, and industrial law. The ideal reader is the legal professional who must understand technological reality in order to construct adequate legal categories. Technical details are relegated to footnotes; the body of the text maintains the context necessary for legal analysis without descending into merely catalogical description of available tools. The field evolves with extraordinary speed; the editorial choice is to privilege principles over

[10] Regulation (EU) 2024/1689 of the European Parliament and of the Council of 13 June 2024, in particular art 6 on the classification of high-risk AI systems. The provisions on high-risk systems in Annex III apply from 2 August 2026, a deadline subsequently extended by Omnibus Regulation VII of March 2026 to 2 December 2027 for standalone high-risk systems and to 2 August 2028 for embedded systems.

[11] FDA, Considerations for the Use of Artificial Intelligence To Support Regulatory Decision-Making for Drug and Biological Products. Draft Guidance for Industry (January 2025); the final guidance is expected in the second quarter of 2026. FDA and EMA, Ten Guiding Principles of Good AI Practice in Drug Development (January 2026).

[12] EMA, Reflection Paper on the Use of Artificial Intelligence (AI) in the Medicinal Product Lifecycle (September 2024), final version adopted by CHMP and CVMP.

[13] AIFA, Guida alla presentazione della domanda di autorizzazione alla sperimentazione clinica che preveda l'utilizzo di sistemi di intelligenza artificiale (AI) o di machine learning (ML) (version 1.0, 24 May 2021).

enumeration of individual algorithmic tools, whose obsolescence is certain in the near term.[14]

It should be noted that this volume does not aim to provide technical advice to pharmaceutical researchers nor management advice to companies investing in algorithmic drug discovery. Its purpose is to construct the legal foundation for what we might call a "critical alliance" between legal professionals and scientists, in the awareness that law cannot disregard understanding of technological reality and that technology cannot develop undisturbed outside normative constraints and ethical principles.[15] In this sense, this volume is part of a collective effort at conceptual reworking that European and global legal institutions are undertaking.

The challenge facing legal professionals in the algoraceutical context is twofold. On the one hand, it is necessary to understand the functioning of technical tools at a sufficient level to assess their normative implications, without transforming legal analysis into a treatment of computer science or biochemistry. On the other, it is necessary to resist the temptation to mechanically apply existing categories to a phenomenon that puts their premises into question. Product liability presupposes a human manufacturer making conscious decisions; patentability presupposes inventive activity attributable to a subject possessed of intellect; competition law presupposes markets in which barriers to entry are identifiable and measurable. When the algorithm is the principal decision-maker, when the artificial intelligence model is the true "inventor," when access to a foundational model becomes the precondition for competing in the pharmaceutical market, each of these premises wavers.[16]

This volume proposes to address this wavering not with destructive criticism of existing categories, but with reconstruction that adapts them to the new paradigm. Algoraceutics is not a technological interlude destined to exhaust itself; it is a structural transformation of the pharmaceutical process that redefines relationships among enterprise, regulator, patient, and society. Law is called upon to govern this transformation, not to endure it.

One final observation deserves to be anticipated. Artificial intelligence applied to pharmaceuticals raises not only questions of private law and industrial law. It touches the public dimension of health, for algorithmic choices influence the selection of patients for clinical trials, the determination of drug prices, the evaluation of cost-effectiveness ratios that guide reimbursement decisions by national health systems. The algorithm that improves the measured efficacy of a drug affects its pricing and thus its accessibility to citizens. In this sense, algoraceutics is not merely a question of innovation law, but a question of the right to health. The pages that follow intend to provide the conceptual tools to address each of these dimensions.

---

[14] Teubner (2018).

[15] On producer liability in the context of products with integrated AI, see Pagallo (2013) and Van Fraassen (1980).

[16] On AlphaFold 2, Jumper et al. (2021); on AlphaFold 3, Abramson et al. (2024).

References

Abramson J, Adler J, Dunger J, Evans R, Green T, Pritzel A, Ronneberger O, Willmore L, Ballard AJ, Bambrick J, Bodenstein SW, Evans DA, Hung C-C, O'Neill M, Reiman D, Tunyasuvunakool K, Wu Z, Žemgulytė A, Arvaniti E, Beattie C, Bertolli O, Bridgland A, Cherepanov A, Congreve M, Cowen-Rivers AI, Cowie A, Figurnov M, Fuchs FB, Gladman H, Jain R, Khan YA, Low CMR, Perlin K, Potapenko A, Savy P, Singh S, Stecula A, Thillaisundaram A, Tong C, Yakneen S, Zhong ED, Zielinski M, Žídek A, Bapst V, Kohli P, Jaderberg M, Hassabis D, Jumper JM (2024) Accurate structure prediction of biomolecular interactions with AlphaFold 3. Nature 630:493–500

Ashworth A (2008) A synthetic lethal therapeutic approach: poly(ADP) ribose polymerase inhibitors for the treatment of cancers deficient in DNA double-strand break repair. J Clin Oncol 26(22):3785–3790

Axis Intelligence (2026) AI drug discovery 2026: 173 programs, FDA framework and market. https://axis-intelligence.com/ai-drug-discovery-2026-complete-analysis/. Accessed 7 June 2026

BCG (2023) Unlocking the potential of AI in drug discovery: current status, barriers and future opportunities. Boston Consulting Group. https://web-assets.bcg.com/86/e5/19d29e2246c7935e179db8257dd5/unlocking-the-potential-of-ai-in-drug-discovery-vf.pdf. Accessed 7 June 2026

Cockburn IM, Henderson R, Stern S (2018) The impact of artificial intelligence on innovation. NBER working paper no 24449

Isomorphic Labs (2026) The Isomorphic Labs Drug Design Engine unlocks a new frontier beyond AlphaFold. https://www.isomorphiclabs.com/articles/the-isomorphic-labs-drug-design-engine-unlocks-a-new-frontier. Accessed 7 June 2026

Jumper J, Evans R, Pritzel A, Green T, Figurnov M, Ronneberger O, Tunyasuvunakool K, Bates R, Žídek A, Potapenko A, Bridgland A, Meyer C, Kohl SAA, Ballard AJ, Cowie A, Romera-Paredes B, Nikolov S, Jain R, Adler J, Back T, Petersen S, Reiman D, Clancy E, Zielinski M, Steinegger M, Pacholska M, Berghammer T, Bodenstein S, Silver D, Vinyals O, Senior AW, Kavukcuoglu K, Kohli P, Hassabis D (2021) Highly accurate protein structure prediction with AlphaFold. Nature 596:583–589

Mayer-Schönberger V, Ramge T (2018) Reinventing capitalism in the age of big data. Basic Books, New York

Pagallo U (2013) The laws of robots: crimes, contracts, and torts. Springer, Dordrecht

Rubinfeld DL, Gal MS (2017) Access barriers to big data. Ariz Law Rev 59(2):339–381

Teubner G (2018) Digital personhood? The status of autonomous software agents in private law. Ancilla Iuris

Van Fraassen B (1980) The scientific image. Oxford University Press, Oxford

Winograd T. (1971) Procedures as a Representation for Data in a Computer Program for Understanding Natural Language, MIT AI Technical Report AITR-235.

Xu Z, Ren F, Wang P, Cao J, Tan C, Ma D, Zhao L, Dai J, Ding Y, Fang H, Li H, Liu H, Luo F, Meng Y, Pan P, Xiang P, Xiao Z, Rao S, Satler C, Liu S, Lv Y, Zhao H, Chen S, Cui H, Korzinkin M, Gennert D, Zhavoronkov A (2025) A generative AI-discovered TNIK inhibitor for idiopathic pulmonary fibrosis: a randomized phase 2a trial. Nat Med 31:2602–2610

From Artificial Intelligence to Algoraceutics: An Evolutionary Overview

2

Abstract

This chapter provides the technical and historical background required to follow the legal analysis in Part II. It surveys the evolution of artificial intelligence over 70 years, from the 1956 Dartmouth workshop through the two AI winters to machine learning, deep learning, and the post-2017 era of Transformers, foundation models, and generative systems. It clarifies the contested definition of artificial intelligence, including the operational notion adopted by Regulation (EU) 2024/1689, and explains the distinction between the symbolic approach, whose reasoning is transparent and reconstructible, and the subsymbolic approach, whose results are accurate but opaque, the technical root of the black box that recurs throughout the book. Searle's Chinese Room is recalled for its bearing on civil liability, where the absence of semantic understanding affects causation and the development-risk defense. The chapter then weighs the opportunities of AI in pharmaceutical research, namely compressed timelines and higher early-phase success rates, against its risks, namely opacity, data dependence, and market concentration. It closes by defining algoraceutics as a paradigm in which the algorithm increasingly replaces rather than assists human decision, posing autonomous problems of liability, intellectual property, and competition.

2.1 Premises

Artificial intelligence is not a recent technology. The idea of constructing machines capable of executing tasks that, if performed by humans, would require intelligence has accompanied scientific reflection for more than 70 years and has passed through phases of enthusiasm and disillusionment, each leaving behind a technical and conceptual legacy still operative today. What has changed, and what justifies the legal scholar's attention

G. Rotino, *Algoraceutics - Legal Perspectives on Artificial Intelligence in Drug Discovery and Development*, Law for Professionals,
https://doi.org/10.1007/978-3-032-38537-6_2

today, is not the theoretical ambition but the operational capacity of these systems. Systems that existed as prototypes confined to laboratories a few years ago now intervene directly in drug discovery and development, with implications for civil liability, intellectual property, and competition that existing law had not anticipated.

This chapter offers the evolutionary notes strictly necessary to understand the legal problems addressed in Part II of the volume. The selection of topics follows a functional criterion that we should declare at the outset to avoid misunderstanding the scope of the treatment. Every concept of artificial intelligence introduced here has a direct bearing on at least one legal question examined in the chapters that follow. The historical evolution is synthesized in its fundamental stages because without it the transition from the symbolic approach to the subsymbolic approach and its consequences for algorithmic transparency and patentability would remain incomprehensible. Searle's "Chinese Room" experiment is recalled as a conceptual premise that will find its full development in the analysis of civil liability. Where the connection with Part II is not evident, we have preferred to omit the material rather than burden the text.

2.2 The Problem of Definition

Defining artificial intelligence remains a controversial operation and in some respects circular. Over more than 70 years of debate, psychology, philosophy, neuroscience, computer science, and linguistics have proposed definitions rarely reconcilable with one another. As Sternberg observed, "there seem to be nearly as many definitions of intelligence as there are experts who have been asked to define it."[1] The term itself "artificial intelligence" has been considered an oxymoron, since it tends to juxtapose what is genuinely cognitive with what is mechanically reproduced, as though the adjective alone were sufficient to empty the noun of content.

Minsky's celebrated formulation, according to which artificial intelligence is "the science of making machines do things that would require intelligence if done by humans,"[2] grasps the fundamental intuition but locates the discipline in the territory of emulation of human cognitive capacities, with all the epistemological problems that derive from it. A different perspective, preferred by part of the literature, adopts an operational definition, that is, an entity is intelligent if it can pass the Turing Test.[3] Russell and Norvig have organized the entire debate into four approaches, distinguishing between systems that think or act in a human way and systems that think or act in a rational way.[4] The fourth perspective, that of the rational agent pursuing the best expected result given available information, has become the prevailing model in contemporary research.

[1] Russell and Norvig (2021) and Sternberg (1997).

[2] Minsky (1961).

[3] Turing (1950). The Turing Test, originally called the 'Imitation Game', proposes an operational criterion: a machine is intelligent if a human interrogator cannot distinguish it from a human interlocutor based solely on written responses.

[4] Russell and Norvig (2021), ch 1.

The concept of bounded rationality elaborated by Herbert Simon[5] offered a decisive correction to this approach. Since cognitive and informational resources are finite, the rational agent does not optimize in absolute terms but seeks a satisfactory solution within available constraints. The decision-maker, according to Simon's well-known metaphor, acts as a "satisficer," that is, someone who seeks a favorable solution rather than the ideal solution. This approach has a direct bearing on the legal problem of the due diligence required from a manufacturer employing AI systems in pharmaceutical research, a topic that will be examined in Chap. 6.

A more recent attempt to overcome the circularity of classical definitions is due to Kaplan and Haenlein, who proposed to understand AI as "the ability of a system to correctly interpret external data, learn from such data, and use such learning to achieve specific goals and tasks through flexible adaptation."[6] This definition has the merit of shifting emphasis from emulation of the human to the adaptive capacity of the system, drawing closer to the conception now prevailing in research.

The European legislator, for its part, adopted its own definition through Regulation (EU) 2024/1689, which qualifies the AI system as "an automated system designed to operate with varying levels of autonomy and that may exhibit adaptability after deployment and that, for explicit or implicit objectives, infers, from the input it receives, how to generate outputs such as predictions, content, recommendations or decisions that can influence physical or virtual environments."[7] This definition, intentionally broad and technologically neutral, is the normative reference point for the entire volume. It should be noted that the legislator deliberately avoided any reference to human intelligence as a parameter, preferring to anchor the notion to the functional autonomy of the system and its capacity to generate outputs that produce effects in the world.

2.3 From Origins to the First Winter: 1956–1974

The conventional birth of artificial intelligence as an autonomous discipline is situated in the summer of 1956, when John McCarthy, Marvin Minsky, Nathaniel Rochester, and Claude Shannon organized a workshop at Dartmouth College in New Hampshire.[8] The proposal accompanying the workshop formulated a working hypothesis as ambitious as it was, in retrospect, naive, namely that every aspect of learning and intelligence could be described with such precision as to permit its simulation on a machine. The participants estimated that a summer of work would be sufficient to achieve significant progress. History would demonstrate that 70 years have not sufficed to realize that ambition in its entirety, but the research

[5] Simon (1982). Simon rejected the idea of perfect rationality, arguing that 'the capacity of the human mind to formulate and solve complex problems is very small compared to the size of problems whose solution is required for objectively rational behavior in the real world'.

[6] Kaplan and Haenlein (2019).

[7] Regulation (EU) 2024/1689, art 3(1)(1).

[8] McCarthy et al. (1955). The workshop took place in the summer of 1956.

program that resulted has produced results that none of the founders could have predicted.

The first two decades produced results that seemed to confirm the initial optimism. Newell and Simon developed the Logic Theorist, capable of proving theorems of propositional logic.[9] Programs like ELIZA simulated conversations in natural language with surprising results for the time.[10] SHRDLU (Winograd 1971) demonstrated the possibility of understanding commands referring to a simplified world of geometric blocks. These programs, however, functioned in restricted and artificial domains. The available computational capacity was insufficient to handle problems of real complexity, and generalization, the capacity to transfer competence acquired in one domain to different problems, proved an insurmountable obstacle with the techniques of the era. The Lighthill Report of 1973[11] crystallized the criticism, and the consequent withdrawal of British public funding inaugurated what the historiography of the discipline calls the "first winter" of AI.

2.4 Expert Systems, Connectionism and the Second Winter: 1974–1993

The recovery of the 1980s was driven by two distinct currents. On the one hand, expert systems (Knowledge-Based Systems) found industrial and medical application. These systems codified the knowledge of human specialists in formal if-then rules, and an inference engine applied such rules to derive conclusions from new facts. MYCIN, developed at Stanford University, diagnosed bacterial infections and suggested antibiotic therapies with accuracy comparable to that of specialist physicians.[12] For the legal scholar of algorithmic pharmaceutics, expert systems are significant because they constitute the first case in which software participates in a medical-pharmaceutical decision-making process, posing in embryonic form the problem of liability for system error. If MYCIN suggests an incorrect antibiotic therapy, who is responsible? The programmer who coded the rules? The expert physician whose knowledge was translated into code? The clinician who followed the recommendation? These questions, which in the 1980s might have seemed academic, have become central to the debate on liability for algoraceutical products.

On the other hand, the mid-1980s saw a renaissance of artificial neural networks. The work of Rumelhart, Hinton, and Williams on the backpropagation algorithm[13] demonstrated that multilayer networks could learn internal representations of data, solving the problem that Minsky and Papert had identified in 1969 for single-layer networks. This current, termed connectionism, proposed an alternative model to the symbolic approach. Knowledge is not coded in explicit rules but is distributed in the

[9] Newell and Simon (1956).

[10] Weizenbaum (1966).

[11] Lighthill (1973).

[12] Feigenbaum (1977). On liability for error of the expert system in medical practice, see Chap. 6.

[13] Rumelhart et al. (1986).

weights of connections between nodes, in a manner analogous, albeit simplified, to the functioning of biological neural networks. Connectionism thus introduced, without its proponents fully measuring the implications, the problem of algorithmic opacity that would become central to the legal debate in subsequent decades.

Despite the progress, the late 1980s and early 1990s brought a second slowdown. Expert systems proved fragile in the face of unforeseen situations and the maintenance of rules became prohibitively costly as the complexity of the domain grew. The neural networks of the time, limited by computational power and data scarcity, could not scale toward complex problems. The "second winter" of AI, between 1987 and the early 1990s, was less dramatic than the first but sensibly slowed funding and academic interest.

2.5 Machine Learning and the Data Turn: 1993–2017

The subsequent recovery was not due to a theoretical breakthrough but to the convergence of three material factors: the exponential increase in computational power (particularly through GPUs, originally designed for video game graphics and proving ideal for the parallel computing required by neural networks), the availability of large volumes of digitized data, and the refinement of machine learning algorithms. Machine learning, in Mitchell's now classical definition, designates a program that "learns from experience E with respect to a class of tasks T and measure of performance P if its performance on tasks in T, as measured by P, improves with E."[14] In less formal terms, these are systems that extract regularities from data without being explicitly programmed for the specific task.

Deep Blue's victory against Garry Kasparov in 1997[15] had a strong media impact but was, from a technical standpoint, the last great triumph of the approach based on computational brute force. The true breakthrough manifested in the following decade, when statistical learning methods began systematically to prevail over those founded on explicit rules.

The turning point is generally identified in 2012, when the convolutional neural network of Krizhevsky, Sutskever, and Hinton won the ImageNet competition with an error margin drastically lower than any previous method.[16] This result demonstrated that deep neural networks (deep learning), provided with sufficient computational power and training data, could achieve performance superior to humans in visual recognition tasks. As LeCun, Bengio, and Hinton synthesized in a foundational contribution to Nature, deep learning enables the discovery of representations of data at multiple levels of abstraction, where each level transforms the representation of the previous level into a more abstract and composite representation.[17]

[14] Mitchell (1997), p. 2.

[15] Deep Blue defeated world champion Garry Kasparov on 11 May 1997. The system could evaluate 200 million positions per second but operated with tree-search methods, not machine learning.

[16] Krizhevsky et al. (2017). The original work was presented at NIPS 2012.

[17] LeCun et al. (2015).

Three families of machine learning algorithms merit mention for their relevance in the pharmaceutical context. Supervised learning, in which the system learns from pairs of known inputs and outputs, forms the basis of predictive models of toxicity and biological activity. Unsupervised learning, which identifies latent structures in unlabeled data, enables clustering of molecules by properties and discovery of patient subpopulations. Reinforcement learning, in which the agent learns through rewards and penalties derived from interaction with the environment, finds application in optimization of molecular structures and planning of chemical syntheses. Each of these families poses differentiated legal problems in terms of transparency, human control, and attribution of liability for error, as will be seen in Chaps. 5 and 6.

2.6 Foundation Models, Generative AI and Large Language Models: 2017–2026

The period after 2017 produced a qualitative transformation in artificial intelligence, with direct repercussions on the pharmaceutical sector and, consequently, on the legal framework that is the subject of this volume.

In 2014, Goodfellow and colleagues introduced Generative Adversarial Networks (GANs), an architecture in which two neural networks, a generator and a discriminator, compete with one another. The generator produces synthetic data, and the discriminator evaluates it.[18] GANs have found application in the de novo generation of pharmacological molecules, opening a legal frontier.[19]

In 2017, the Transformer architecture, introduced by Vaswani and colleagues,[20] radically renewed the treatment of natural language. The attention mechanism at the base of the Transformer enables the model to weight the relative importance of each element in a sequence with respect to the others, overcoming the limitations of recurrent networks in managing long-range dependencies. From this architecture derive large language models (LLMs), such as GPT-3[21] and its successors, capable not only of comprehending and generating text but of executing tasks for which they were not specifically trained, a property that the literature has termed "emergent capabilities" and which surprised even the researchers themselves.

These developments fall within the broader concept of the foundation model,[22] that is, models pre-trained on enormous corpora of data, subsequently adaptable to specific tasks through fine-tuning. Foundation models represent a structural shift with respect to traditional AI, in which each application required a model built from scratch. A single model, trained once at massive scale, is specialized for diverse

[18] Goodfellow et al. (2014).

[19] On the potential and limitations of GANs in generating pharmacological molecules, see Chap. 4, Sect. 4.2, where the case is examined from the perspective of opacity and chain of liability.

[20] Vaswani et al. (2017).

[21] Brown et al. (2020). GPT-3 was the first model to demonstrate emergent capabilities on tasks not predicted during training.

[22] Bommasani et al. (2021).

applications, from text generation to prediction of protein structures, from musical composition to molecular design.[23] The significance of this change for law has not yet been fully appreciated by legal scholarship, but its implications cut across the topics of liability (who is responsible for error, the provider of the base model or the party who adapted it?), intellectual property (whose are the training data? whose is the generated output?), and competition (who controls the foundation models controls access to the market?).

The most significant case for this volume is AlphaFold. Developed by DeepMind, the system addressed the problem of predicting the three-dimensional structure of proteins from the amino acid sequence, a problem open for 50 years in structural biology. AlphaFold 1 participated in the CASP13 competition in 2018, surpassing all competitors, but the decisive result came with AlphaFold 2, which won CASP14 in 2020 with an accuracy score that the scientific community deemed equivalent to resolving the problem.[24] In October 2024, Hassabis and Jumper received the Nobel Prize in Chemistry precisely for AlphaFold's results in protein structure prediction.[25] AlphaFold 3, presented in 2024,[26] draws closer to an integrated computational understanding of cell biochemistry.

The significance of AlphaFold for algorithmic pharmaceutics is twofold. On the operational plane, knowledge of the three-dimensional structure of the biological target is the prerequisite for rational drug design, and AlphaFold renders this knowledge available in hours rather than years of X-ray crystallography.[27] On the legal plane, AlphaFold poses with clarity the three fundamental questions of the volume, namely, who is the inventor of the predicted structure?[28] Who is liable for damage if the prediction is erroneous and leads to synthesis of a toxic compound? Who may access the training data and on what terms? The transition from academic research to industrial commercialization has already occurred. Isomorphic Labs, a company founded by Demis Hassabis as a spin-off of DeepMind, concluded in 2024 collaboration agreements with Eli Lilly and Novartis valued at over 3 billion dollars.[29] The algoraceutical paradigm is no longer a prospect but an industrial fact.

Generative artificial intelligence applied to chemistry and molecular biology is, as of 2026, a rapidly expanding field that merits autonomous attention. Systems

---

[23] For a significant example of biological foundation model, see the ESM 3 model (98 billion parameters, trained on 2.78 billion proteins) developed by Meta; Hayes et al. (2025). ESM 3 designed de novo a fluorescent protein with 58% sequence identity relative to known variants.

[24] Jumper et al. (2021).

[25] The prize was shared with David Baker for computational protein design. NobelPrize.org (2024).

[26] Abramson et al. (2024).

[27] Ren et al. (2023). First documented case of using a protein structure predicted by AlphaFold to identify a pharmacological inhibitor (CDK20, hepatocellular carcinoma), with discovery completed in 30 days.

[28] On the question of the algorithmic inventor, the US Supreme Court refused certiorari on 2 March 2026 in Thaler v Vidal (USPTO), definitively confirming that an AI system (in this case, DABUS) cannot be recognized as an inventor under the US Patent Act. The issue is examined in detail in Chap. 7.

[29] On Isomorphic Labs, see Chap. 1.

based on diffusion architectures or language models adapted to chemistry generate candidate molecules that exist in no known database, navigating autonomously a chemical space whose vastness (estimated at 10^{60} pharmacologically relevant molecules) exceeds any possibility of human exploration or even enumeration. This generation occurs in a digital space that is not a passive archive but an operational environment, where the AI designs, evaluates, and optimizes compounds without direct human intervention. It is in this space, as will be seen in Chap. 3, that the question of the inventor (Chap. 7) and the causal nexus in damage (Chap. 6) emerges with greater urgency. When the entire path from biological target to candidate molecule unfolds *in silico*, the reconstruction of the causal chain and the identification of the human inventive contribution become legal problems of first magnitude.

2.7 The Distinction Between Symbolic and Subsymbolic Approaches

Throughout the entire history of artificial intelligence runs a distinction that the legal scholar must know because it bears directly on transparency, explainability, and patentability of systems.[30]

Symbolic and Subsymbolic: Two Modes of Representing Knowledge

The symbolic approach may be imagined as an annotated legal dictionary in which the meaning of each concept is written explicitly and the relationship between concepts is fixed by rules that the operator can read. A symbolic system that qualifies a contract as a lease does so by applying a definition written by a human, and the path leading to the conclusion is traceable step by step. The reasoning of the algorithm is, from this perspective, transparent reasoning, verifiable by the interpreter and retraced in the grounds of a decision called upon to review its outcome.[31]

The subsymbolic approach operates in the opposite manner. Knowledge is not written in readable rules but is distributed in millions of numerical parameters that calibrate automatically during training. The system learns statistical

(continued)

[30] The distinction is functional to understanding the different profiles of liability and patentability examined in Part II. A symbolic system produces reasoning that is reconstructible and, in principle, explainable; a subsymbolic system produces accurate but opaque results. This difference underlies the problem of algorithmic transparency (Chap. 5, art 13 AI Regulation) and patentable describability (Chap. 7).

[31] The reference treatment of the classical symbolic approach is Russell and Norvig (2021), ch 8, where first-order logic is presented as the elective language for declarative knowledge representation. On the philosophical premise of the separation between symbolic manipulation and semantic understanding, see Sect. 2.8 of this chapter, dedicated to the Chinese Room experiment.

(continued)
correlations between input and output without the operator being able to consult a dictionary of rules. When the legal scholar asks the system why a particular molecule was classified as potentially toxic, the answer does not exist in readable form, since the system knows the result without knowing the reasons that produced it. This asymmetry between derivable result and unknown reason is the technical foundation of the notion of black box upon which the analyses of Part II will develop.[32]

The symbolic approach, dominant from the Dartmouth Workshop through the 1980s, conceives intelligence as manipulation of symbols according to explicit rules. Systems based on knowledge are its most mature expression. A knowledge base codes facts and relations, an inference engine applies logical rules to derive new conclusions. The reasoning is reconstructible step by step. Rule-based systems, like MYCIN, operate with chains of if-then rules whose application can be traced and justified. In principle, a symbolic system can explain why it has reached a particular conclusion, and this characteristic renders it compatible, at least at first approximation, with the requirements of transparency and reasoning that law traditionally demands of decision-making processes of relevance.

The subsymbolic approach, of which neural networks and deep learning are the prevalent expressions, proceeds in radically different fashion. Knowledge is not coded in explicit rules but is distributed in the millions (or billions) of parameters that the neural network calibrates during training. The system learns representations of data at increasing levels of abstraction, and the reasoning leading from input to output is not reconstructible in terms comprehensible to humans. This intrinsic opacity, the so-called "black box," is the trait that distinguishes modern AI systems from any preceding technology and that poses law unprecedented problems in terms of transparency (Article 13 of the AI Regulation), of proof of the causal nexus in civil liability (Chap. 6), and of sufficiency of description in a patent application (Chap. 7).[33]

In contemporary practice, the two approaches are not mutually exclusive. Many pharmaceutical applications combine symbolic components (for representation of biochemical knowledge) with subsymbolic components (for prediction and generation). So-called "neuro-symbolic" systems attempt to conjoin the accuracy of deep learning with the explainability of logical reasoning. This hybridization further complicates legal analysis, since different parts of the same system may present differing degrees of transparency, raising the question whether the explainability requirements of the AI Regulation must be satisfied by the system as a whole or component by component.

---

32 The manifesto of the contemporary subsymbolic paradigm is LeCun et al. (2015), where the authors describe learning of distributed representations as an irreversible overcoming of rule-based systems. On the procedural fallout of the black-box structure, see Chap. 4, Sect. 4.2, infra, and, for the recourse to explainability tools in judicial proceedings, Chap. 4, Sect. 4.6, infra.

33 Goodman and Flaxman (2017) and Pasquale (2015).

2.8 The "Chinese Room" and the Boundary Between Simulation and Understanding

A thought experiment elaborated in 1980 by philosopher John Searle merits recall in this context for its argumentative bearing in Part II of the volume.[34]

Searle imagines a person locked in a room who receives Chinese ideograms through a window. The person does not know Chinese but has a manual of instructions, written in English, that specifies which ideogram to produce in response to each input. An external observer, a native Chinese speaker, judges the responses appropriate and concludes that the person in the room understands Chinese. However, the person in the room understands nothing, because he follows formal rules without accessing the semantic meaning of the symbols he manipulates. Searle's argument thus establishes a distinction between syntax and semantics, namely a system can manipulate symbols according to formal rules (syntactic operation), producing results that appear intelligent, without for that reason understanding the content of what it produces (semantic comprehension). The Chinese Room remains, in this sense, a "mere simulator."

The relevance of this experiment for this volume is not epistemological but legal.[35] If an AI system in pharmaceutical research operates as the Chinese Room, manipulating molecular data according to statistical rules without "understanding" the underlying biology, the consequences on the plane of liability are immediate. Who is responsible when the result is erroneous? The system lacks intentionality, lacks awareness of error, cannot foresee the consequences of its output beyond the objective function for which it was trained. This absence of semantic comprehension becomes a central argument in the construction of the causal nexus and in the analysis of the development risk defense, as will be seen in Chap. 6. If the machine does not understand, one must ask whether it can truly "know" the state of the art and technique at the moment of placing the product on the market and thus whether the defense, as traditionally constructed, is suited to govern algoraceutical damage.

2.9 Risks and Opportunities of AI in the Pharmaceutical Sector

Before proceeding to the definition of the concept of algoraceutics, it is appropriate to dwell on the risks and opportunities that artificial intelligence brings to the pharmaceutical sector, since it is these risks, declined in legal terms, that constitute the object of Part II.

On the side of opportunities, the data available in 2026 are eloquent. The average time for bringing a drug from discovery to regulatory approval has historically been around

[34] Searle (1980).

[35] See Chap. 6, where the distinction between syntactic manipulation and semantic understanding is examined as an argument in the construction of the causal link between algorithmic action and harm.

10–15 years, with an average estimated cost of 2.6 billion dollars and an overall success rate that rarely exceeds 10%. AI promises to compress each of these parameters. Companies like Insilico Medicine have brought molecules entirely designed by AI to Phase II of clinical trials in timeframes that traditional pharmaceuticals would consider unrealistic.[36] Success rates in Phase I of AI-generated compounds, according to the most recent data, range between 80% and 90%, against a historical average of 52%. The number of pharmaceutical programs employing AI in at least one stage of the process has exceeded 170 units in active clinical development.[37]

On the side of risks, critical issues are specular and touch directly on categories of law. The first is algorithmic opacity, already evoked in the previous paragraph. A deep learning system that identifies a pharmaceutical target or generates a candidate molecule produces a result whose genesis is not reconstructible in terms comprehensible to humans, with evident implications for proof of the causal nexus and the transparency required by the AI Regulation.[38] The second is data dependence, that is, the quality of the output is a function of the quality and representativeness of the training data, and historically imbalanced clinical datasets by gender, ethnicity, or age group can propagate and amplify discrimination with consequences for drug safety. The third is market concentration, that is, the computational resources, proprietary data, and expertise necessary to train and employ models are concentrated in a small number of organizations, creating barriers to entry and potential anticompetitive effects that Chap. 8 will examine.

To these critical issues a transversal element concerning regulation itself is added. The process of adopting general and sectoral normative frameworks, still in the phase of consolidation, must account for the balancing between compliance costs, which inevitably reflect drug prices and thus weigh on patients and health systems, and the need not to leave a sector so sensitive without rules, relying solely on market self-regulation. The AI Regulation represents the first systematic attempt to govern this equilibrium in the European context, but its application to the pharmaceutical sector, as will be seen in Chap. 5, raises specific questions that the legislator has not resolved explicitly.[39]

---

[36] Positive results from Phase IIa on rentosertib (INS018_055), the first drug entirely designed by AI to complete a randomized clinical trial with favorable outcomes, were published in June 2025; Xu et al. (2025).

[37] The most recent data, updated to the first quarter of 2026, indicate 173 programs in active clinical development; IntuitionLabs (2026).

[38] Regulation (EU) 2024/1689, recital 47 and art 6, which classifies as high-risk AI systems intended to be used as safety components of a product or that are themselves products governed by EU harmonization legislation listed in Annex I. Software used as a medical device (pursuant to Regulation (EU) 2017/745) falls within this category. On 2 February 2025 the prohibitions on systems with unacceptable risk entered into force; on 10 July 2025 the AI Office published the code of practice for general-purpose AI models (arts 53–55), which entered into force on 2 August 2025.

[39] On 14 January 2026 the FDA and EMA jointly published the Guiding Principles of Good AI Practice in Drug Development, ten principles applicable to the entire medicinal product lifecycle, from discovery to pharmacovigilance. EMA and FDA, 'Guiding Principles of Good AI Practice in Drug Development' (14 January 2026), https://www.ema.europa.eu, accessed 7 June 2026.

2.10 Toward Algoraceutics

The evolutionary notes traced thus far converge on one point: artificial intelligence has achieved an operational maturity that renders it no longer an external aid to the pharmaceutical process but a structural component of it. The convergence between machine learning algorithms, availability of digitized biological and chemical data, and unprecedented computational power has created a new paradigm, which this volume designates with the term "algoraceutics."[40]

Algoraceutics is not the mere application of AI to the pharmaceutical sector, just as computer law was not the mere application of the computer to law. It is the emergence of a process in which the algorithm does not assist human decision but, to an increasing extent, replaces it. The algorithm identifies biological targets, generates candidate molecules, predicts their toxicity, optimizes synthesis, and selects patients for clinical trials. In each of these phases, the creative and decisional contribution of the algorithm poses to law questions that the following chapters will analyze in detail. As has been observed for artificial intelligence in general, it is a matter of the "invention of a method of invention," a technology that has revolutionized the very manner of inventing and that for this reason has an impact extending through the entire lifecycle of the product, from conception to commercialization.

The themes, moreover, are of difficult separation, being profoundly interconnected with one another. The opacity of the algorithm, for example, besides having autonomous significance under the profile of transparency (Chap. 5), bears on proof of the causal nexus in product liability (Chap. 6) and on sufficiency of description in a patent application (Chap. 7). The algoraceutical datum, which Chap. 8 will analyze as a possible essential facility, is at the same time the prerequisite for training algorithms (Chaps. 3 and 4) and the subject of fundamental rights to protection of personal data. This interconnection is not a defect of the treatment but a structural character of the matter, and the volume addresses it by choosing an expository order that proceeds from the technical-scientific context (Part I) to the legal profiles (Part II), with cross-references where necessary.

Chapter 3 will describe how AI intervenes in each stage of the process of drug discovery and development, with the state of the art as of 2026. Chapter 4 will examine the limitations and profiles of reliability of the algorithms employed, organizing them not by technical taxonomy but by legal relevance, namely opacity, bias, reliability, and decision-making autonomy. On these bases, Part II will address the European normative framework (Chap. 5), civil liability (Chap. 6), intellectual property (Chap. 7), competition and data (Chap. 8), and the regulatory ecosystem (Chap. 9).

[40] The neologism 'algoraceutics', coined by the Author, designates the intersection between artificial intelligence algorithms and the pharmaceutical process, understood not as a mere technological application but as a paradigm that poses autonomous legal problems of liability, intellectual property, and competition.

References

Abramson J, Adler J, Dunger J, Evans R, Green T, Pritzel A, Ronneberger O, Willmore L, Ballard AJ, Bambrick J, Bodenstein SW, Evans DA, Hung C-C, O'Neill M, Reiman D, Tunyasuvunakool K, Wu Z, Žemgulytė A, Arvaniti E, Beattie C, Bertolli O, Bridgland A, Cherepanov A, Congreve M, Cowen-Rivers AI, Cowie A, Figurnov M, Fuchs FB, Gladman H, Jain R, Khan YA, Low CMR, Perlin K, Potapenko A, Savy P, Singh S, Stecula A, Thillaisundaram A, Tong C, Yakneen S, Zhong ED, Zielinski M, Žídek A, Bapst V, Kohli P, Jaderberg M, Hassabis D, Jumper JM (2024) Accurate structure prediction of biomolecular interactions with AlphaFold 3. Nature 630:493–500

Bommasani R, Hudson DA, Adeli E et al (2021) On the opportunities and risks of foundation models. Stanford Center for Research on Foundation Models

Brown TB, Mann B, Ryder N, Subbiah M, Kaplan JD, Dhariwal P, Neelakantan A, Shyam P, Sastry G, Askell A, Agarwal S, Herbert-Voss A, Krueger G, Henighan T, Child R, Ramesh A, Ziegler DM, Wu J, Winter C, Hesse C, Chen M, Sigler E, Litwin M, Gray S, Chess B, Clark J, Berner C, McCandlish S, Radford A, Sutskever I, Amodei D (2020) Language models are few-shot learners. In: Advances in neural information processing systems 33. Curran Associates, Red Hook, pp 1877–1901

Feigenbaum EA (1977) The art of artificial intelligence: themes and case studies of knowledge engineering. In: Proceedings IJCAI-77, pp 1014–1029

Goodfellow IJ, Pouget-Abadie J, Mirza M, Xu B, Warde-Farley D, Ozair S, Courville A, Bengio Y (2014) Generative adversarial nets. In: Advances in neural information processing systems 27. Curran Associates, Red Hook, pp 2672–2680

Goodman B, Flaxman S (2017) European Union regulations on algorithmic decision-making and a "right to explanation". AI Mag 38(3):50–57

Hayes T, Rao R, Akin H, Sofroniew NJ, Oktay D, Lin Z, Verkuil R, Tran VQ, Deaton J, Wiggert M, Badkundri R, Shafkat I, Gong J, Derry A, Molina RS, Thomas N, Khan YA, Mishra C, Kim C, Bartie LJ, Nemeth M, Hsu PD, Sercu T, Candido S, Rives A (2025) Simulating 500 million years of evolution with a language model. Science 387:850–858

IntuitionLabs (2026) AI applications in the drug development pipeline. https://intuitionlabs.ai/articles/ai-drug-development-pipeline. Accessed 7 June 2026

Jumper J, Evans R, Pritzel A, Green T, Figurnov M, Ronneberger O, Tunyasuvunakool K, Bates R, Žídek A, Potapenko A, Bridgland A, Meyer C, Kohl SAA, Ballard AJ, Cowie A, Romera-Paredes B, Nikolov S, Jain R, Adler J, Back T, Petersen S, Reiman D, Clancy E, Zielinski M, Steinegger M, Pacholska M, Berghammer T, Bodenstein S, Silver D, Vinyals O, Senior AW, Kavukcuoglu K, Kohli P, Hassabis D (2021) Highly accurate protein structure prediction with AlphaFold. Nature 596:583–589

Kaplan A, Haenlein M (2019) Siri, Siri, in my hand: who's the fairest in the land? On the interpretations, illustrations, and implications of artificial intelligence. Bus Horiz 62(1):15–25

Krizhevsky A, Sutskever I, Hinton GE (2017) ImageNet classification with deep convolutional neural networks. Commun ACM 60(6):84–90

LeCun Y, Bengio Y, Hinton G (2015) Deep learning. Nature 521:436–444

Lighthill J (1973) Artificial intelligence: a general survey. In: Artificial intelligence: a paper symposium. Science Research Council, London

McCarthy J, Minsky M, Rochester N, Shannon CE (1955) A proposal for the Dartmouth summer research project on artificial intelligence, 31 August 1955. Reprinted in AI Magazine 27(4):12–14 (2006)

Minsky M (1961) Steps toward artificial intelligence. Proc IRE 49(1):8–30

Mitchell TM (1997) Machine learning. McGraw-Hill, New York

Newell A, Simon H (1956) The logic theory machine: a complex information processing system. IRE Trans Inf Theory 2(3):61–79

NobelPrize.org (2024) The Nobel Prize in Chemistry 2024. https://www.nobelprize.org/uploads/2024/10/press-chemistryprize2024-3.pdf. Accessed 7 June 2026

Pasquale F (2015) The black box society. Harvard University Press, Cambridge

Ren F, Ding X, Zheng M, Korzinkin M, Cai X, Zhu W, Mantsyzov A, Aliper A, Aladinskiy V, Cao Z, Kong S, Long X, Liu BHM, Liu Y, Naumov V, Shneyderman A, Ozerov IV, Wang J, Pun FW, Polykovskiy DA, Sun C, Levitt M, Aspuru-Guzik A, Zhavoronkov A (2023) AlphaFold accelerates artificial intelligence powered drug discovery: efficient discovery of a novel CDK20 small molecule inhibitor. Chem Sci 14:1443–1452

Rumelhart DE, Hinton GE, Williams RJ (1986) Learning representations by back-propagating errors. Nature 323:533–536

Russell S, Norvig P (2021) Artificial intelligence: a modern approach, 4th edn. Pearson, Hoboken

Searle JR (1980) Minds, brains, and programs. Behav Brain Sci 3(3):417–457

Simon HA (1982) Models of bounded rationality. MIT Press, Cambridge

Sternberg RJ (1997) The concept of intelligence and its role in lifelong learning and success. Am Psychol 52(10):1030–1037

Turing AM (1950) Computing machinery and intelligence. Mind 59:433–460

Vaswani A, Shazeer N, Parmar N, Uszkoreit J, Jones L, Gomez AN, Kaiser Ł, Polosukhin I (2017) Attention is all you need. In: Advances in neural information processing systems 30. Curran Associates, Red Hook, pp 5998–6008

Weizenbaum J (1966) ELIZA: a computer program for the study of natural language communication between man and machine. Commun ACM 9(1):36–45

Xu Z, Ren F, Wang P, Cao J, Tan C, Ma D, Zhao L, Dai J, Ding Y, Fang H, Li H, Liu H, Luo F, Meng Y, Pan P, Xiang P, Xiao Z, Rao S, Satler C, Liu S, Lv Y, Zhao H, Chen S, Cui H, Korzinkin M, Gennert D, Zhavoronkov A (2025) A generative AI-discovered TNIK inhibitor for idiopathic pulmonary fibrosis: a randomized phase 2a trial. Nat Med 31:2602–2610

Artificial Intelligence in the Process of Drug Discovery and Development

3

Abstract

This chapter moves from the conceptual history of Chap. 2 to the operational reality of how artificial intelligence intervenes in drug discovery and development. It frames the pharmaceutical process as the interaction of three spaces, chemical, biological, and digital, and shows how modern AI inverts their traditional order, so that decisions taken in the digital space now precede and direct work in the laboratory. It surveys, by legal relevance rather than technical taxonomy, the principal applications, namely generative models and guided screening in the preclinical phase; quantitative structure-activity relationships and protein structure prediction, including AlphaFold and its limits; AI in clinical development, patient stratification, and adaptive trial design; quality control and pharmacovigilance; and intelligent robotics that formulate hypotheses and run experiments autonomously. Drawing on the state of the art as of 2026 and on cases such as Insilico Medicine, Exscientia, Recursion, and Isomorphic Labs, it identifies three structural traits, velocity, concentration, and opacity, that condition the legal analysis of Part II and motivate the questions of liability, inventorship, and competition examined there.

3.1 Introduction

The previous chapter traced the evolution of artificial intelligence from its origins to the algoraceutical paradigm.[1] This chapter shifts the analysis from the historical-conceptual plane to the operational plane, that is, how AI concretely intervenes in the phases of drug discovery and development and with what degree of autonomy.

[1] The neologism 'algoraceutics' was introduced in Chap. 2 to designate the intersection between artificial intelligence algorithms and the pharmaceutical process. In this chapter the term is used in

G. Rotino, *Algoraceutics - Legal Perspectives on Artificial Intelligence in Drug Discovery and Development*, Law for Professionals,
https://doi.org/10.1007/978-3-032-38537-6_3

The pharmaceutical process, commonly designated in international contexts as Drug Discovery and Development,[2] traverses a series of concatenated stages that lead from the identification of a biological target to the submission of an application for market authorization. Each of these stages today employs algorithmic tools whose complexity and autonomy increase in a non-linear fashion. The survey that follows makes no claim to technical completeness; it selects applications based on their legal relevance, that is, their capacity to generate questions of liability, intellectual property, or competition that will be examined in Part II.

3.2 The Three Spaces: Chemical, Biological, and Digital

The pharmaceutical discovery process is conventionally understood as a series of nested operations within three distinct spaces, each operating according to its own logic. The chemical space comprises the set of all possible molecular structures synthesizable by human chemistry, defined by the rules of molecular stability and synthetic feasibility. The biological space encompasses living organisms, their cellular and molecular mechanisms, and the network of interactions that govern biological processes. The digital space is the computational environment in which data flows and algorithms construct models, predictions, and simulations. The algoraceutical paradigm does not simply juxtapose these three spaces; it establishes systematic bridges between them such that decisions made in the digital space reshape the trajectory through the chemical and biological spaces.

Traditionally, the pharmaceutical researcher operated primarily within the chemical and biological spaces. The chemist synthesized molecules within the constrained set of synthesis routes known to him; the pharmacologist tested their biological activity in assays and animal models. The digital tools available were supportive and derivative: they visualized structures already conceived by human intuition, performed statistical analyses on data already gathered by experiment, and supplied calculations that the human mind could not execute at reasonable cost. The researcher remained the protagonist.

The entry of modern AI into drug discovery inverts this relationship. The digital space now precedes and directs movement through the chemical and biological spaces. Before a molecule is synthesized, before an experiment is conducted, the algorithm has already constructed a probabilistic landscape of what compounds are likely to succeed, what structures are worth exploring, and what measurements will most efficiently narrow the search space. The chemist and pharmacologist become

its operative sense, to describe how AI concretely intervenes in the phases of drug discovery and development.

[2]The process is commonly designated in the international context as Drug Discovery and Development (DD&D). The preference for 'Discovery and Development' over 'Research and Development' reflects the specificity of the pharmaceutical sector, where the path from target identification to commercialization includes phases (clinical trial, regulatory review) that exceed the traditional concept of R&D.

operators who execute decisions made in the digital space rather than authors of the inquiry itself.

This inversion has profound consequences for every layer of the legal analysis that follows. If the decision emerges from an algorithmic process operating in the digital space, questions of responsibility, prediction, knowledge, and causality must be reformulated.

3.3 The Preclinical Phase and the Role of AI

Drug discovery in the strict sense unfolds across the preclinical phase, which encompasses target identification, compound screening, and lead optimization. This phase is traditionally the most protracted and resource-intensive segment of drug development, commonly spanning 7–10 years before a compound is deemed ready for clinical testing. The bottleneck has consistently been the size of the chemical space that humans and traditional methods can explore.[3]

Classical high-throughput screening (HTS)[4] tests thousands of compounds against a given biological target, recording which exhibit activity above a defined threshold. The process is essentially brute force: synthesize or procure large libraries of small molecules, expose them to a target, and measure response. A typical HTS campaign tests 100,000 to 500,000 compounds,[5] a vast number by historical standards yet infinitesimal against the estimated 10^{60} theoretical structures within synthetically accessible chemical space.[6] The hit rate, that is, the fraction of compounds showing measurable activity, typically ranges from 0.1% to 2%, meaning the researcher obtains thousands of candidates, nearly all of which must be discarded through iterative cycles of chemical modification and retesting.

AI reshapes this process by shifting from brute-force enumeration to guided exploration. Generative models[7] trained on known bioactive compounds learn pat-

[3] On druggability, see Hopkins and Groom (2002). The concept designates the capacity of a biological target to be therapeutically modulated through drugs.

[4] Bajorath (2011). High-throughput screening (HTS) employs robotics, data-processing software, and liquid-handling devices to conduct millions of tests.

[5] The 'digital space', as here understood, designates the set of data generated, collected, and processed by computational systems employed in drug discovery and development. This space is fed by a constant feedback circuit: databases generate the data that train algorithms, algorithms produce results that populate databases, in a cycle in which human oversight is progressively reduced. Chapter 8 will analyze the algoraceutic datum, understood as the output of this circuit, from the perspective of competition law and possible framing as an essential facility.

[6] Computer-aided drug design (CADD) has a history of more than 40 years. On 5 October 1981 Fortune magazine, in an article titled 'Next Industrial Revolution: Designing Drugs by Computer at Merck', proclaimed computational drug design 'the next industrial revolution'. See Van Drie (2007).

[7] Recurrent neural networks (RNN), associated with the molecular libraries of the ChEMBL database, have demonstrated effectiveness in de novo molecule generation; Öztürk et al. (2018).

terns in molecular structure correlated with activity. These patterns allow the algorithm to propose novel candidates predicted to bind the target with high affinity, without requiring synthesis and testing of intermediate compounds. The compression is substantial. Where classical HTS might require 9 years and hundreds of millions of dollars to identify a lead candidate, an AI-guided screen can accomplish this in months.

The technical mechanisms vary. Generative adversarial networks (GANs)[8] learn to synthesize novel molecular structures by competing against a discriminator that evaluates whether generated compounds are chemically realistic.[9] Variational autoencoders (VAEs) compress the representation of known active compounds into a learned vector space, permitting interpolation and traversal to discover new regions likely to contain activity. Transformer-based language models treating SMILES strings,[10] linearized representations of molecular structure, as tokens can generate new structures conditional on target binding predictions. Reinforcement learning frameworks allow an agent to explore the chemical space by learning a policy that maximizes expected binding affinity while remaining within a region of drug-like properties.[11] Each approach encodes the algorithm's implicit theory of which molecular features matter; each is opaque[12] regarding why any particular proposal is made.

3.4 Molecular Design and Structure Prediction

The design of molecular structures and prediction of their biological outcomes constitute the heart of algoraceutical practice. Two domains merit particular attention for their legal consequences: structure-activity relationships and the prediction of protein structures.

Structure-activity relationships (SARs) traditionally derive from empirical observation. A researcher synthesizes compounds and measures their properties; patterns emerge inductively from the data. Modern AI inverts this. Rather than observing activity in structures already made, quantitative structure-activity relationship (QSAR) models learn statistical associations between molecular

[8] Goodfellow et al. (2014) and Méndez-Lucio et al. (2020).

[9] On the difference between classical GANs and RANC architectures, with particular regard to the role of reinforcement learning in constraining the generator to predefined pharmacological objectives, see Popova et al. (2018). The first pharmacological candidate generated with this type of architecture and brought to preclinical trial is documented in Zhavoronkov et al. (2019), relating to the Insilico Medicine case and the DDR1 kinase inhibitor.

[10] The chemical space comprises approximately 10^{60} pharmacologically relevant molecules; Bohacek et al. (1996); see also Polishchuk et al. (2013).

[11] Mayr et al. (2016) and Pu et al. (2019).

[12] The foundational work on this architecture is Goodfellow et al. (2014), p. 2672. On the specific opacity of generative models and the recourse to explainability tools in judicial proceedings, see Chap. 4, Sect. 4.6, infra.

descriptors[13] and activity, then use these associations to predict activity in compounds not yet synthesized. The model becomes a surrogate for experiment. A compound can be evaluated *in silico*, that is, purely in computation, without being made or tested.

This substitution appears simple but carries profound consequences. First, the QSAR model is not a theory of biological mechanism; it is a statistical association learned from finite historical data. When the QSAR model predicts that a novel structure will bind a target, it does not explain why, only that similar compounds in the training set have done so. The prediction rests on an assumption that the structure lies in a region of chemical space sufficiently similar to the training data that linear or non-linear extrapolation is reliable. Many AI-generated candidates do lie in such regions. But compounds proposed in regions distant from training data, or in structural classes not previously explored, carry higher uncertainty that the model does not transparently quantify.

Second, the training data itself[14] embeds the history of human chemical exploration. The set of compounds known to be active against a given target reflects which chemists attempted which synthetic routes, which scaffolds were pursued, which regions of chemical space happened to attract research investment. An algorithm trained on this biased sample inherits the bias. The model will reliably propose candidates resembling historical successes but may miss entire classes of structures discoverable by exploration of neglected regions.

Third, once QSAR predictions guide the experimental campaign, success becomes partially self-fulfilling. Compounds predicted to be active are synthesized and tested; compounds predicted to be inactive are not, so their actual activity remains unknown. The training data for the next iteration of the model becomes biased toward compounds the algorithm already selected. Feedback loops of this character have not been systematically studied in drug discovery, yet they alter the statistical foundation on which the algorithm rests.

The second major domain is protein structure prediction, a problem of extraordinary impact. Proteins are synthesized as linear chains of amino acids; they then fold into three-dimensional structures that determine function. For decades, determining the structure required years of work and substantial resources: X-ray crystallography, nuclear magnetic resonance, cryo-electron microscopy. The structure-function relationship itself remained largely opaque; knowing the sequence did not reveal the structure reliably.[15]

---

[13] The acronym ADMET designates the parameters of absorption, distribution, metabolism, excretion, and toxicity; Cheng et al. (2012).

[14] Open-access databases that allow investigation of chemical space are numerous. Among the most relevant: PubChem (National Center for Biotechnology Information), ChEMBL (European Bioinformatics Institute), DrugBank (University of Alberta), and ChemDB (University of California, Irvine). These databases associate chemical compounds with their respective biological targets and constitute the training material for AI algorithms employed in drug discovery.

[15] The Chematica program (subsequently called Synthia), developed by B A Grzybowski. See Szymkuć et al. (2016) and Klucznik et al. (2018).

AlphaFold, developed by DeepMind and trained on structures in the Protein Data Bank, changed this fundamentally. AlphaFold 2[16] accepts an amino acid sequence as input and outputs a three-dimensional structure with remarkable accuracy, often exceeding the precision of experimental methods. The achievement is extraordinary for drug discovery because the structure of a protein target determines which compounds can bind it. AlphaFold has made it possible to predict how a drug candidate will interact with its target before synthesis.[17]

Yet this power conceals a significant limitation that legal analysis must confront. AlphaFold is a structure prediction system; it does not explain mechanism. It predicts where atoms will be located but not why they arrive there, not how the structure changes under cellular conditions, not how the protein's function emerges from its geometry. Moreover, AlphaFold's predictions are probabilistic; the confidence scores assigned to different regions of the predicted structure vary widely. A region predicted with high confidence may be experimentally well-described; a region of low confidence may be dangerously misleading. Current AlphaFold versions cannot predict how mutations alter structure, how ligand binding affects structural stability, or how the structure changes over time. These limitations matter for liability. A drug designed to bind a target protein on the assumption that an AlphaFold prediction is reliable across these conditions may fail in clinical testing or cause unexpected toxicity.

The integration of AlphaFold with QSAR models and binding affinity predictions yields a powerful but opaque pipeline. A molecule is proposed, its structure predicted, its binding affinity estimated, and the binding pose, that is, the three-dimensional configuration in which it contacts the target, inferred, all without experimental measurement. Each step introduces uncertainty; the uncertainties propagate forward without explicit quantification.

3.5 Clinical Development and AI

The transition from preclinical research to clinical trials represents a regulatory and scientific boundary.[18] Preclinical work occurs largely outside the regulatory perimeter; clinical work is heavily supervised by health authorities and ethics boards. AI enters clinical development in several contexts, some of which raise novel legal problems.

Patient selection and stratification constitute one domain.[19] Clinical trials[20] recruit subjects who meet eligibility criteria; these are typically defined by demographic and

[16] Jumper et al. (2021). AlphaFold 2 won the CASP14 competition in 2020 with a median GDT score of 92.4 out of 100.

[17] Abramson et al. (2024).

[18] DiMasi et al. (2016).

[19] The BRCA2 gene, discovered in 1994, codes for a protein whose mutation is associated with the development of breast, ovarian, prostate, and pancreatic carcinoma; Ashworth (2008).

[20] The database ClinicalTrials.gov (US National Registry of Clinical Studies) collects over 434,000 trials conducted in 50 American states and 221 nations. The European Clinical Trials Register enumerates over 42,000 studies and the EMA approves approximately 4000 trials every year; US National Library of Medicine (2026).

clinical variables such as age, disease severity, prior treatment history. Traditional trials recruit broadly and then analyze outcomes separately for prespecified subgroups. Modern trials increasingly employ AI[21] to predict which patients are most likely to benefit from the experimental drug, stratifying enrollment accordingly. The predicted benefit[22] derives from learned associations between patient characteristics and drug response, not from mechanistic understanding. A patient whose features resemble responders in historical data is predicted to respond; whether they will depends on predictions of associations, not on knowledge of why the drug works.

This practice carries legal implications. If the algorithm's predictions are incorrect, if the association between patient features and response does not hold in the trial population, the subjects enrolled may be those least likely to benefit. The researcher's duty to minimize harm and maximize benefit, central to research ethics, becomes dependent on the algorithm's accuracy. Moreover, the algorithm learns from historical trial data, which may have been generated in populations not representative of the current trial. Bias in historical data propagates forward.[23]

Trial design itself is subject to algorithmic optimization.[24] Adaptive trial designs[25] adjust enrollment, dosing, and subject allocation based on interim data, maximizing the probability of demonstrating efficacy while minimizing the sample size needed. AI assists in this optimization, proposing which subjects to enroll, what dosages to test, which biomarkers to measure, all chosen to maximize the likelihood that the trial will reach its endpoint. Such designs have legitimate appeal, since they can reduce sample size and accelerate approval,[26] but they carry a hidden cost. A trial designed to maximize the probability of success, conditional on interim data, may

[21] The algorithm ALICE (ArtificiaL Intelligence ClassifiEr) was presented at the European Society for Medical Oncology (ESMO) in 2020. Trained through whole-genome sequencing data from the International Cancer Genome Consortium (ICGC), ALICE enables increased precision in selecting patients eligible for PARP inhibitor therapy. Retrospective analysis demonstrated that use of this algorithm increases Median Overall Survival (MOS) by 18 months, achieved in significantly less time than would have been necessary without AI support. Deep Lens is a company based in Ohio (USA) that uses AI to accelerate oncology clinical trials. Its VIPER platform (Visual Intelligence Platform for Enhanced Recruitment) automates the patient-screening process from diagnosis to qualified enrollment, acquiring genomic, EMR (electronic medical records), and pathological data. In a documented case study, VIPER identified over 1000 patients, 58 of whom with the specific genetic mutation, 20 qualified for the study, with one patient fully enrolled in 4 weeks, compared to an average of 12 months for oncology trials.

[22] The MOS (Median Overall Survival) parameter for PARP inhibitors ranges between 16.6 and 22.1 months. The 18-month increase achieved through algorithmic patient selection brings life expectancy near or beyond the indicative threshold of 'out of danger'. This result has direct repercussions on pharmacoeconomics, drug pricing, and access to therapies. In the Netherlands, in 2018, it was estimated that 3100 annual deaths from breast cancer produce a loss of 26,000 years of life and 65,000 years lost to disability; Vondeling et al. (2018).

[23] On the inheritance of bias from historical training data, see Sect. 3.4 of this chapter, supra.

[24] Babel et al. (2021).

[25] The concept of 'digital twin' applied to clinical trials provides for the creation of a computational replica of the patient; Björnsson et al. (2020).

[26] Unlearn.AI, founded in 2017 in San Francisco, developed the TwinRCT system. The FDA granted breakthrough device designation in 2023. In 2025 TwinRCT technology obtained EMA

be less likely to detect unexpected harms or to identify important subgroups for which the drug is ineffective. The optimization is transparent regarding its objective[27] but opaque regarding its tradeoffs.[28]

3.6 Quality Control and Pharmacovigilance

Quality control (QC/QA) is an essential process in pharmaceutical manufacturing that involves numerous tests to assure the conformity of each batch and traditionally requires frequent manual intervention. This latter aspect guides AI applications, whose objective is to reduce manual intervention to the maximum extent, as such intervention constitutes a source of non-conformity.[29] Quality standards are established through good manufacturing practices (GMP),[30] guidelines issued by regulatory bodies that specify the parameters to follow in laboratory, clinical, and manufacturing settings so that conformity is achieved and assured.

The introduction of the Quality-by-Design approach, which requires quality to be integrated from the design phase onward, has found in AI a natural implementation tool. Systems based on artificial neural networks are used to monitor critical processes, such as lyophilization, controlling temperature, drying parameters, and final product quality. The combination of intelligent technologies and knowledge-based systems makes it possible to create expert systems for comprehensive quality management, supporting complex decisions or reducing human interference in the process.

A significant consideration must be raised for the legal analyst. If it is true that human interference in processes is a source of possible non-conformity, the moment of quality control represents one of the essential checkpoints in which it is possible to review the automated process. The introduction of intelligent systems of increasing complexity and autonomy reduces the possibility of error but, at the same time,

---

qualification for use as primary analysis in Phase 2 and 3 trials with continuous outcomes; the FDA (CDER) confirmed alignment with the EMA evaluation.

[27] On the construction of synthetic control arms and the transition from external to within-experimental design, see Thorlund et al. (2020). On the European regulatory framework, see EMA, Reflection Paper on Establishing Efficacy Based on Single-Arm Trials Submitted as Pivotal Evidence in a Marketing Authorization Application (2022). For systematic analysis, see Chap. 9, Sect. 9.3, infra.

[28] Recognition of the methodological limitations of the digital twin by the developers themselves is documented in Schuler et al. (2022), where it is noted that the variance reduction produced by PROCOVA is conditioned on the quality of the historical data used to construct the prognostic covariate. On the probative relevance of the digital twin under Article 9(4) of Directive (EU) 2024/2853, see Chap. 6, Sect. 6.6.4, infra.

[29] ICH Guideline Q8(R2), Pharmaceutical Development (2009); Yu et al. (2014).

[30] Good Manufacturing Practices (GMP) standards ensure that quality and safety levels of the entire process are guaranteed from production of the investigational compound (Investigational Medicinal Product, IMP, in EMA terminology) through commercialization. See Delegated Regulation (EU) 2017/1569 of the Commission, establishing the principles and guidelines of good manufacturing practice for experimental medicinal products for human use.

reduces the possibility of integrating human review and control into the operational cycle.[31] AI improves process quality precisely by restricting the spaces in which humans could validate its functioning, and this is not an accidental contradiction but the very structure of algorithmic autonomy. This paradox traverses the entire volume and will find its legal analysis in Chaps. 5 and 6.

In the post-commercialization phase, pharmacovigilance employs AI systems to monitor adverse events. Databases such as FAERS (FDA Adverse Event Reporting System) in the United States and EudraVigilance in the European Union collect reports of suspected adverse reactions, and algorithms employing natural language processing and pattern recognition analyze data flows to identify risk signals that traditional surveillance might not detect. AI also makes it possible to integrate data from heterogeneous sources, including wearable medical devices and electronic medical records. The integration of this data raises, however, questions regarding personal data protection and treatment proportionality that will be examined in Chap. 5.

The regulatory approval process for drugs is itself subject to AI applications. Regulatory authorities, foremost among them the FDA and the EMA, confront registration dossiers whose complexity has grown exponentially; the evaluation of a single dossier may require analysis of tens of thousands of pages of preclinical and clinical data. AI tools are employed to automate data review, identify inconsistencies in datasets presented, and verify dossier conformity to regulatory requirements. The EMA published in 2023 a work plan on the use of AI in pharmaceutical regulation,[32] recognizing that the agency itself must equip itself with algorithmic competencies in order to evaluate products whose development was guided by algorithms. There thus emerges a novel symmetry, namely AI that generates the drug and AI that evaluates it, with the risk that the opacities of the first system propagate to the second and that human control is reduced to supervision of algorithmic processes that interact with one another.[33]

A complementary aspect concerns the management of recalls and market withdrawals. When a pharmacovigilance signal indicates an unforeseen risk,

[31] The increasing automation of drug discovery and development raises a cross-cutting legal question that runs through the whole of Part II: when the chain from target identification to candidate molecule unfolds in silico, with human intervention progressively reduced to a supervisory function, do the traditional notions of 'human control' on which the civil-liability regime is founded and the requirement of 'inventive activity' on which patent law is founded maintain their adequacy? The question is not rhetorical; the answer conditions the entire structure of Part II.

[32] EMA and CHMP, Qualification Opinion for Prognostic Covariate Adjustment (PROCOVA) (EMADOC-1700519818-907465, adopted 15 September 2022, published 20 September 2022), qualifying the method as suitable for use as primary analysis in Phase 2 and 3 trials with continuous outcomes. For US alignment, see FDA and CDER, Statistical Review of the PROCOVA Methodology (2022).

[33] In September 2024 the CHMP and CVMP of the EMA adopted the Reflection Paper on the Use of Artificial Intelligence in the Lifecycle of Medicines. The EMA and FDA have also identified ten common principles for the use of AI in drug development, published jointly in 2024. See EMA, AI in the Lifecycle of Medicines: Multi-Annual AI Workplan 2023–2028 (2023); EMA and FDA, Guiding Principles of Good AI Practice in Drug Development (2024).

response speed is critical. AI makes it possible to correlate in real time reports from geographically dispersed sources, identifying patterns that would be invisible to manual analysis. This capacity has immediate legal consequence. If the manufacturer possesses an AI system capable of detecting a risk signal in advance of traditional methods and does not employ it, the failure to adopt it may affect the evaluation of post-commercialization diligence. The topic connects to the broader question of omissive liability for the failure to adopt AI that will be examined in Chap. 6.

3.7 State of the Art as of 2026

As of 2026, the application of artificial intelligence to drug discovery and development is no longer an experimental prospect but a consolidated industrial fact. The available data permit us to sketch a picture that, while subject to rapid evolution, exhibits already well-defined structural features.

The number of pharmaceutical programs employing AI in at least one phase of the process has exceeded 170 units in active clinical development.[34] The success rate in Phase I of AI-generated compounds oscillates between 80 and 90%, against a historical average of 52%. Global investment in the sector has experienced exponential growth, from 300 million dollars in 2018 to 5.2 billion in 2020, to estimates ranging between 15 and 20 billion by 2025.[35] AI, which in 2018 represented less than 0.2% of R&D expenditure in the pharmaceutical industry, today absorbs a significant and rapidly expanding share.

Several cases illustrate with particular clarity the maturity reached by the paradigm. Insilico Medicine[36] is the first drug discovery company built entirely on AI to have brought a molecule into Phase II clinical testing. The compound INS018_055, designed by generative algorithms for the treatment of idiopathic pulmonary fibrosis, entered Phase I in June 2023 and Phase II in December of that year. The time from target nomination to clinical testing was approximately

[34] The success rate in Phase I of AI-generated compounds oscillates, according to the most recent data (2025), between 80% and 90%, against a historical average of 52%. By 2026, the number of AI-discovered drugs in clinical trials has exceeded 173 (94 in Phase I, 56 in Phase II, 15 in Phase III); first complete regulatory approvals are anticipated for 2026–2027. See IntuitionLabs (2026).

[35] According to a 2020 survey, the investment of major pharmaceutical companies in AI, in the United States alone, reached $5.2 billion, growing from just over $300 million in 2018, an 18-fold increase in 2 years, rising from 0.18% to 3.25% of the sector's global R&D spending. By 2025, estimates place AI investment in drug discovery between $15 and $20 billion globally; GlobalData (2025).

[36] Insilico Medicine was founded in 2014. INS018_055 (rentosertib), a first-in-class TNIK inhibitor, entered Phase I in June 2023 and Phase IIa in December 2023. The Phase IIa results, published in Nature Medicine in June 2025, showed an average improvement of 98.4 mL in forced vital capacity at the highest dose versus −20.3 mL for placebo. It is the first drug in which both target and molecule were identified and designed by generative AI. See Xu et al. (2025) for the Phase IIa results and Zhavoronkov et al. (2019) for the DDR1 case.

30 months, against a historical average of over 4 years. The case demonstrates that the temporal compression promised by algoraceutics is not theoretical but operational.

Exscientia,[37] founded at Oxford in 2012, was the first company to bring a molecule entirely designed by AI into clinical testing. The compound DSP-1181, a serotonin receptor 5-HT1A agonist for the treatment of obsessive-compulsive disorder, reached clinical nomination in just 12 months, against an average of approximately 4.5 years. In 2022 Exscientia raised over 1 billion dollars and was listed on NASDAQ. The case is significant not only for temporal compression but for its business model. The company operates as a platform that collaborates with traditional pharmaceutical companies, supplying AI-generated candidates for clinical testing.

BenevolentAI[38] has developed a drug discovery platform based on knowledge graphs and deep learning. Beyond the already cited case of baricitinib,[39] its compound BEN-2293 entered Phase II for atopic dermatitis in 2023. The BenevolentAI model is particularly interesting for the legal analyst as it rests on a knowledge graph that connects biomedical data from heterogeneous sources, bringing into sharp focus the question of ownership and legality of the aggregation of data belonging to different subjects.

Recursion Pharmaceuticals[40] represents a different model, founded on the combination of automated robotics, high-content microscopy, and deep learning. The platform generates over 2.5 million cellular images per week, used to train models that identify correlations between chemical perturbations and phenotypic responses. In 2023 Recursion entered into an agreement with NVIDIA worth 50 million dollars to integrate generative AI models into its own pipeline. The interest of the case lies in the volume of data generated and in the question, analyzed in Chap. 8, of who controls access to datasets of this magnitude.

Zasocitinib,[41] developed by Nimbus Therapeutics with the support of AI platforms for molecular design, reached Phase III for the treatment of psoriasis in 2024. Nimbus ceded the rights to Takeda for 4 billion dollars, marking one of the largest acquisitions in the field of AI-guided drug discovery. The case illustrates how AI-assisted design can generate value through licensing rather than direct commercialization, with implications for the competitive structure of the market.

---

[37] In November 2024 Recursion Pharmaceuticals completed the acquisition of Exscientia for $688 million (all-stock transaction); the combined company operates under the name Recursion. See Bender and Cortés-Ciriano (2021).

[38] BEN-2293 (pan-Trk inhibitor for atopic dermatitis) reached the primary safety endpoint in Phase IIa (April 2023) but failed secondary efficacy endpoints; development was discontinued. The company reoriented to BEN-8744 (PDE10 inhibitor for ulcerative colitis). See Richardson et al. (2020).

[39] Drug repurposing means the reuse of a drug already approved for a different therapeutic indication; Ashburn and Thor (2004). Richardson et al. (2020).

[40] Recursion Pharmaceuticals was founded in 2013 in Salt Lake City. Recursion Pharmaceuticals, SEC filing, Form 10-K (2023).

[41] Zasocitinib (TAK-279) is a TYK2 inhibitor; the rights were ceded to Takeda in 2023. Nimbus Therapeutics, press release (11 December 2022); Takeda, SEC filing (2023).

Isomorphic Labs,[42] a spin-off of DeepMind, announced in 2024 collaboration agreements with Eli Lilly and Novartis with a combined value exceeding 3 billion dollars. In February 2026 the company presented its Drug Design Engine (IsoDDE),[43] which integrates protein structure prediction with modeling of drug interactions in a single framework. The Isomorphic Labs case is paradigmatic of market concentration. A company that controls the foundational model for protein structure prediction places itself at the center of the value chain of drug discovery, with the power to condition competitors' access to an instrument that has become indispensable. The question will be analyzed in Chap. 8 from the perspective of the essential facilities doctrine.

The picture that emerges from this survey highlights three structural traits that condition the legal analysis of Part II. The first is velocity. The temporal compression of drug discovery reduces the period during which scientific knowledge forms on which the development-risk exemption rests, raising the question whether the "state of scientific and technical knowledge" referred to in Article 7(e) of Directive 85/374/EEC should be evaluated with reference to algorithmic knowledge available at the moment of market introduction. The second is concentration. A limited number of platforms control foundational models, datasets, and pipelines, with risks for competition and market access. The third is opacity. The deep learning systems that generate molecular candidates, predict structures, and design syntheses operate as black boxes whose genesis is not reconstructible,[44] with direct implications for transparency, proof of causal nexus, and patent specification.

3.8 Intelligent Robotics and Research Automation

AI applications in drug discovery and development encounter robotics at the point where laboratory automation reaches a degree of autonomy such as to transform the robot from an executive tool into a system capable of formulating hypotheses and conducting the scientific process without human intervention.

The most significant case is that of EVE, a robot scientist equipped with artificial intelligence developed by the University of Cambridge.[45] EVE was designed to automate the early-stage drug design phase, with the capacity to test 10,000 compounds per day. Its functioning does not stop at massive sampling. EVE randomly

[42] Isomorphic Labs, founded in 2021 by Demis Hassabis as a spin-off of DeepMind, announced in 2024 agreements with Eli Lilly and Novartis for over 3 billion dollars. In March 2025 the company raised $600 million (round led by Thrive Capital); in February 2026 it presented its Drug Design Engine (IsoDDE), which doubles the accuracy of AlphaFold 3 in predicting protein-ligand interactions. As of 2026, Isomorphic Labs is preparing the first clinical trials with molecules designed through its platform.

[43] On the resulting market concentration, see Chap. 8.

[44] On the legal implications of algorithmic opacity in drug discovery, see Chap. 5 (art 13 AI Regulation, transparency obligations) and Chap. 6 (proof of causal link and product liability). On the patentability of algorithmic invention, see Chap. 7.

[45] Williams et al. (2015).

selects a subset of the molecular library, identifies compounds that pass the first test, retests each hit multiple times to reduce the false-positive rate, and uses statistical and machine learning algorithms to predict new structures with potentially higher scores. In 2018 EVE discovered that triclosan, a component of toothpaste, could be repurposed in the treatment of drug-resistant malaria. In 2022 it was reported that EVE had found a solution to the "replicability crisis" in scientific research, automating verification of replicability and making serendipitous discoveries during the process.

EVE's predecessor was ADAM, developed in 2009 by the Universities of Aberystwyth and Cambridge,[46] described as "the first machine to independently discover new scientific knowledge." ADAM formulated hypotheses autonomously and conducted experiments in complete autonomy. The trajectory from ADAM to EVE marks the passage from proof of principle to operation at industrial scale. The declared ambition of the developers is the combination of AI with robots used for synthesis, to navigate reaction space in a completely automatic manner, without any human intervention either upstream or downstream of the investigation chain.

The legal significance of these applications is multifaceted. First, the robot scientist that formulates hypotheses and conducts experiments in autonomy poses with the utmost clarity the problem of inventorship. If EVE discovers a potential drug, who is the inventor under patent law? The question is not substantially different from that posed by the DABUS case, which will be examined in Chap. 7. Second, the robot scientist that operates without human supervision poses the problem of liability for error. If the compound selected by EVE proves toxic, does the causal chain trace back to the algorithm programmer, the robot designer, the manager of the molecular library, the pharmaceutical company that employed the system? The intertwining of algorithmic and robotic components further complicates the reconstruction of the causal nexus, as the error may originate indifferently in software, hardware, or their interaction.

A further profile concerns the relationship between AI and animal testing. AI presents itself as constituting an alternative to mandatory *in vivo* testing, as recognized by the FDA Modernization Act 2.0.[47] The construction of *in silico* models[48] capable of predicting toxicity in a manner equivalent to animal testing could make the latter no longer necessary, at least for certain categories of drugs. This prospect raises, however, a question deserving of reflection. The AI systems employed in

---

[46] King et al. (2009).

[47] H.R. 2617, FDA Modernization Act 2.0, signed on 29 December 2022, ends an 84-year federal mandate for mandatory animal testing in toxicity studies, allowing drug developers to use alternatives (including in silico AI-based models) when effectively available. The law does not completely prohibit animal testing but recognizes computational alternatives as an equivalent validation method. This reform was made possible precisely by the advancement of AI applications.

[48] The FDA Modernization Act 2.0 expressly recognizes 'non-animal testing methods' including 'cell-based assays, organ chips, microphysiological systems, computer modeling'. The explicit inclusion of computer modeling in the federal rule marks the legislative recognition of the validity of in silico models, with consequences for the construction of the development-risk exception examined in Chap. 6, Sect. 6.4.

drug discovery process data that derive, in part, from validations in animal models conducted in jurisdictions with different ethical standards. A system trained on data from experiments conducted in countries where animal protection is less rigorous incorporates, in its own parameters, results obtained under conditions that the European legal system would consider unacceptable. The question is whether and how the law ought to take account of the ethical provenance of training data, a topic that connects animal protection to the discipline of data and algorithmic transparency.

The evolution of intelligent robotics applied to drug discovery is inscribed in the broader trend toward Smart Lab and Smart Factory that traverses the pharmaceutical industry. The convergence of robotic automation, AI, and the Internet of Things promises laboratories in which the entire process, from formulation of hypothesis to compound synthesis to experimental verification, occurs without human intervention. Industry invests in this direction because automation reduces errors, accelerates timelines, and enables continuous operation. But the progressive expulsion of the human operator from the operational cycle poses a problem that transcends any single application. If no human being participates in the decision-making chain that has led to the selection of the compound, the legal categories founded on human conduct, from negligence to due diligence, from foreseeability to inventive activity, lose their empirical referent. Chapters 6 and 7 will address this problem in their respective domains of civil liability and intellectual property.

The survey conducted in this chapter confirms the initial assumption. Artificial intelligence is no longer an external aid to the pharmaceutical process but a structural component of it, intervening in every phase with an increasing degree of autonomy. This observation is the foundation of Part II of the volume. The legal problems that algoraceutics poses, from the European regulatory framework to civil liability, from intellectual property to competition, do not arise from the application of a technology to an industrial sector, but from the transformation of the discovery and development process itself. AI does not assist the process; increasingly, it determines it.[49] Chapter 4 will examine the limits and reliability profiles of the algorithms employed, organizing them by legal relevance; Part II will analyze their consequences.

References

Abramson J, Adler J, Dunger J, Evans R, Green T, Pritzel A, Ronneberger O, Willmore L, Ballard AJ, Bambrick J, Bodenstein SW, Evans DA, Hung C-C, O'Neill M, Reiman D, Tunyasuvunakool K, Wu Z, Žemgulytė A, Arvaniti E, Beattie C, Bertolli O, Bridgland A, Cherepanov A, Congreve M, Cowen-Rivers AI, Cowie A, Figurnov M, Fuchs FB, Gladman H, Jain R, Khan YA, Low CMR, Perlin K, Potapenko A, Savy P, Singh S, Stecula A, Thillaisundaram A, Tong C, Yakneen S, Zhong ED, Zielinski M, Žídek A, Bapst V, Kohli P, Jaderberg M, Hassabis D, Jumper JM (2024) Accurate structure prediction of biomolecular interactions with AlphaFold 3. Nature 630:493–500

Ashburn TT, Thor KB (2004) Drug repositioning: identifying and developing new uses for existing drugs. Nat Rev Drug Discov 3:673–683

[49] See Part II, Chaps. 5–9, infra.

Ashworth A (2008) A synthetic lethal therapeutic approach: poly(ADP) ribose polymerase inhibitors for the treatment of cancers deficient in DNA double-strand break repair. J Clin Oncol 26(22):3785–3790

Babel A, Taneja R, Mondello Malvestiti F, Monaco A, Donde S (2021) Artificial intelligence solutions to increase medication adherence in patients with non-communicable diseases. Front Digit Health 3:669869

Bajorath M (2011) Chemoinformatics and computational chemical biology. Humana Press, New York

Bender A, Cortés-Ciriano I (2021) Artificial intelligence in drug discovery: what is realistic, what are illusions? Drug Discov Today 26(2):511–524

Björnsson B, Borrebaeck C, Elander N, Gasslander T, Gawel DR, Gustafsson M, Jörnsten R, Lee EJ, Li X, Lilja S, Martínez-Enguita D, Matussek A, Sandström P, Schäfer S, Stenmarker M, Sun XF, Sysoev O, Zhang H, Benson M (2020) Digital twins to personalize medicine. Genome Med 12:4

Bohacek RS, McMartin C, Guida WC (1996) The art and practice of structure-based drug design: a molecular modeling perspective. Med Res Rev 16(1):3–50

Cheng F, Li W, Zhou Y, Shen J, Wu Z, Liu G, Lee PW, Tang Y (2012) admetSAR: a comprehensive source and free tool for assessment of chemical ADMET properties. J Chem Inf Model 52(11):3099–3105

DiMasi JA, Grabowski HG, Hansen RW (2016) Innovation in the pharmaceutical industry: new estimates of R&D costs. J Health Econ 47:20–33

GlobalData (2025) Artificial intelligence (AI) in drug discovery. Pharma Intelligence Center. https://www.globaldata.com/store/report/ai-in-drug-discovery-theme-analysis/. Accessed 7 June 2026

Goodfellow IJ, Pouget-Abadie J, Mirza M, Xu B, Warde-Farley D, Ozair S, Courville A, Bengio Y (2014) Generative adversarial nets. In: Advances in neural information processing systems 27. Curran Associates, Red Hook, pp 2672–2680

Hopkins AL, Groom CR (2002) The druggable genome. Nat Rev Drug Discov 1:727–730

IntuitionLabs (2026) AI applications in the drug development pipeline. https://intuitionlabs.ai/articles/ai-drug-development-pipeline. Accessed 7 June 2026

Jumper J, Evans R, Pritzel A, Green T, Figurnov M, Ronneberger O, Tunyasuvunakool K, Bates R, Žídek A, Potapenko A, Bridgland A, Meyer C, Kohl SAA, Ballard AJ, Cowie A, Romera-Paredes B, Nikolov S, Jain R, Adler J, Back T, Petersen S, Reiman D, Clancy E, Zielinski M, Steinegger M, Pacholska M, Berghammer T, Bodenstein S, Silver D, Vinyals O, Senior AW, Kavukcuoglu K, Kohli P, Hassabis D (2021) Highly accurate protein structure prediction with AlphaFold. Nature 596:583–589

King RD, Rowland J, Oliver SG, Young M, Aubrey W, Byrne E, Liakata M, Markham M, Pir P, Soldatova LN, Sparkes A, Whelan KE, Clare A (2009) The automation of science. Science 324(5923):85–89

Klucznik T, Mikulak-Klucznik B, McCormack MP, Lima H, Szymkuć S, Bhowmick M, Molga K, Zhou Y, Rickershauser L, Gajewska EP, Toutchkine A, Dittwald P, Startek MP, Kirkovits GJ, Roszak R, Adamski A, Sieredzińska B, Mrksich M, Trice SLJ, Grzybowski BA (2018) Efficient syntheses of diverse, medicinally relevant targets planned by computer and executed in the laboratory. Chem 4(3):522–532

Mayr A, Klambauer G, Unterthiner T, Hochreiter S (2016) DeepTox: toxicity prediction using deep learning. Front Environ Sci 3:80

Méndez-Lucio O, Baillif B, Clevert D-A, Rouquié D, Wichard J (2020) De novo generation of hit-like molecules from gene expression signatures using artificial intelligence. Nat Commun 11:10

Öztürk H, Özgür A, Ozkirimli E (2018) DeepDTA: deep drug-target binding affinity prediction. Bioinformatics 34(17):i821–i829

Polishchuk PG, Madzhidov TI, Varnek A (2013) Estimation of the size of drug-like chemical space based on GDB-17 data. J Comput Aided Mol Des 27(8):675–679

Popova M, Isayev O, Tropsha A (2018) Deep reinforcement learning for de novo drug design. Sci Adv 4(7):eaap7885

Pu L, Naderi M, Liu T, Wu H-C, Mukhopadhyay S, Brylinski M (2019) eToxPred: a machine learning-based approach to estimate the toxicity of drug candidates. BMC Pharmacol Toxicol 20:2

Richardson P, Griffin I, Tucker C, Smith D, Oechsle O, Phelan A, Rawling M, Savory E, Stebbing J (2020) Baricitinib as potential treatment for 2019-nCoV acute respiratory disease. Lancet 395(10223):e30

Schuler A, Walsh D, Hall D, Walsh J, Fisher C (2022) Increasing the efficiency of randomized trial estimates via linear adjustment for a prognostic score. Int J Biostat 18(2):329–356

Szymkuć S, Gajewska EP, Klucznik T, Molga K, Dittwald P, Startek M, Bajczyk M, Grzybowski BA (2016) Computer-assisted synthetic planning: the end of the beginning. Angew Chem Int Ed 55(20):5904–5937

Thorlund K, Dron L, Park JJH, Mills EJ (2020) Synthetic and external controls in clinical trials: a primer for researchers. Clin Epidemiol 12:457–467

US National Library of Medicine (2026). ClinicalTrials.gov. https://clinicaltrials.gov. Accessed 7 June 2026

Van Drie JP (2007) Computer-aided drug design: the next 20 years. J Comput Aided Mol Des 21(10-11):591–601

Vondeling GT, Menezes GL, Dvortsin EP, Jansman FGA, Konings IR, Postma MJ, Rozenbaum MH (2018) Burden of early, advanced and metastatic breast cancer in the Netherlands. BMC Cancer 18:262

Williams K, Bilsland E, Sparkes A, Aubrey W, Young M, Soldatova LN, De Grave K, Ramon J, de Clare M, Sirawaraporn W, Oliver SG, King RD (2015) Cheaper faster drug development validated by the repositioning of drugs against neglected tropical diseases. J R Soc Interface 12(104):20141289

Xu Z, Ren F, Wang P, Cao J, Tan C, Ma D, Zhao L, Dai J, Ding Y, Fang H, Li H, Liu H, Luo F, Meng Y, Pan P, Xiang P, Xiao Z, Rao S, Satler C, Liu S, Lv Y, Zhao H, Chen S, Cui H, Korzinkin M, Gennert D, Zhavoronkov A (2025) A generative AI-discovered TNIK inhibitor for idiopathic pulmonary fibrosis: a randomized phase 2a trial. Nat Med 31:2602–2610

Yu LX, Amidon G, Khan MA, Hoag SW, Polli J, Raju GK, Woodcock J (2014) Understanding pharmaceutical quality by design. AAPS J 16(4):771–783

Zhavoronkov A, Ivanenkov YA, Aliper A, Veselov MS, Aladinskiy VA, Aladinskaya AV, Terentiev VA, Polykovskiy DA, Kuznetsov MD, Asadulaev A, Volkov Y, Zholus A, Shayakhmetov RR, Zhebrak A, Minaeva LI, Zagribelnyy BA, Lee LH, Soll R, Madge D, Xing L, Guo T, Aspuru-Guzik A (2019) Deep learning enables rapid identification of potent DDR1 kinase inhibitors. Nat Biotechnol 37:1038–1040

Algorithmic Limits and Reliability: The Legal Knot

4

Abstract

This chapter reorganizes the technical limits of pharmaceutical AI not as a taxonomy of algorithms but as four categories of legal relevance, namely opacity, bias, reliability, and decision-making autonomy. It distinguishes epistemic, structural, and intentional opacity and links them to the transparency duty of Article 13 of Regulation (EU) 2024/1689 and to proof of causation; it analyses data, selection, and algorithmic bias and their bearing on defectiveness under Directive (EU) 2024/2853 and on Article 10 of the AI Regulation; it examines reliability and the reproducibility crisis, including algorithmic risk scores and the development-risk defense; and it sets out a tool-assistant-agent scale of autonomy that conditions both liability and inventorship. A concluding section develops an original thesis, that post-hoc explainability techniques (SHAP, LIME, saliency maps), when used not as regulatory compliance but as evidence in civil proceedings, constitute a tertium genus probatorio, to be assessed as scientific evidence and coordinated with the presumption of defectiveness. The chapter thus supplies the technical-legal groundwork for Part II.

4.1 Introduction: From Technical Catalog to Legal Relevance

The preceding chapter illustrated how artificial intelligence intervenes at every stage of the drug discovery and development process.[1] That survey reveals that the predominant approach is based on deep learning and deep neural networks,

[1] For the description of the phases of the process and AI applications in each phase, see Chap. 3.

G. Rotino, *Algoraceutics - Legal Perspectives on Artificial Intelligence in Drug Discovery and Development*, Law for Professionals,
https://doi.org/10.1007/978-3-032-38537-6_4

architectures that produce highly accurate results but whose decision-making process is opaque, not reconstructible in terms comprehensible to humans. It is conceivable that an operational chain from target discovery through clinical development could be entirely guided by these tools, in which human intervention reduces to authorization of the input and procedural supervision of the output.

This observation lies at the root of the legal problems that Part II addresses. This chapter does not propose a technical taxonomy of algorithms, which would be foreign to the aims of this volume, but organizes the limits and reliability profiles of pharmaceutical AI systems according to four categories of legal relevance: opacity, bias, reliability, and decision-making autonomy. For each, the chapter identifies the technical problem, illustrates a concrete case from the pharmaceutical sector, and previews the implications for the chapters of Part II.

It is useful to provide an essential map of the algorithms employed in the sector, which does not claim to substitute for the technical literature but rather furnishes the legal reader with the minimum coordinates necessary to follow the analysis that follows. The AI algorithms used in algorithmic pharmaceutics are classified, as a first approximation, along two axes.[2] The first axis distinguishes the learning modality: supervised learning, in which the model learns from pairs of labeled data (for example, molecules classified as toxic or non-toxic); unsupervised learning, in which the model identifies latent structures in unlabeled data (for example, clustering of molecules by similar chemical properties); and reinforcement learning, in which the model optimizes a strategy through trial and error in a simulated environment (for example, navigation of chemical space in search of molecules with optimal properties).

The second axis distinguishes the function of the model, namely discriminative models that classify or predict (for example, a model that predicts whether a molecule will be toxic), while generative models produce new data (for example, a network that generates molecules with desired properties). The intersection of the two axes produces the typology of systems actually employed. Supervised-discriminative systems, such as convolutional neural networks (CNN) used in predicting molecular properties, are among the most accurate and among the least interpretable.[3] Generative systems, such as generative adversarial networks (GAN), produce new molecules but through a doubly opaque process, in which two neural networks interact with one another without any intermediate step being reconstructible.

[2] The classification adopted here follows the functional distinction among supervised learning (the model learns from labeled input-output pairs), unsupervised learning (the model identifies structures in unlabeled data), and reinforcement learning (the model optimizes an objective function through trial and error). To these three categories is added the distinction between discriminative models (that classify or predict) and generative models (that produce new data). For systematic treatment, see Russell and Norvig (2021), pts IV–V, and Goodfellow et al. (2016), chs 5, 14, 20.

[3] Convolutional neural networks (CNN), widely used in molecular property prediction, operate through layers of filters that extract features at progressively higher levels of abstraction. A CNN model with millions of parameters produces accurate results in toxicity classification, but the logical path from input to classification is not reconstructible. By contrast, a decision tree produces readable rules of the type 'if molecular weight exceeds X and logP exceeds Y, the compound is toxic'. The trade-off between accuracy and interpretability is documented; Rudin (2019).

To these fundamental categories is added a further distinction, relevant for the analysis that follows: the distinction between static models and adaptive models. A static model, once trained, does not modify its parameters during use, meaning its predictions are an exclusive function of the original training data. An adaptive model updates its parameters based on new data it receives during deployment, learning from operational experience. In the pharmaceutical context, this distinction is legally relevant because an adaptive model can modify its behavior after the drug is placed on the market, raising specific problems of liability (Chap. 6) and continuous surveillance (Chap. 5). Directive 2024/2853 has incorporated this specificity by including the product's capacity to continue learning among the elements for assessing defectiveness.

The legal relevance of this taxonomy does not reside in the technical classification per se, but in the fact that each type of algorithm corresponds to a different legal risk profile. A discriminative model that incorrectly predicts the safety of a compound generates a product-liability problem; a generative model that autonomously produces a new molecule generates an inventorship problem; a model trained on non-representative data generates an algorithmic-discrimination problem. The synoptic Table 4.1 maps these correspondences.

4.2 Opacity and the Black Box

The opacity of AI systems based on deep neural networks is the feature that distinguishes these systems from any previous technology employed in the pharmaceutical sector. A traditional system, based on explicit rules, produces reconstructible reasoning, namely one can trace the logical path from input to conclusion. A deep neural network, trained on millions or billions of parameters, produces accurate output but the how and why remain inaccessible. The system functions as a black box, namely it receives data as input, returns a result, but the intermediate process

Table 4.1 Technical limits and their legal implications in Part II

Technical limit	Problem in algorithmic pharmaceutics	Legal implication in Part II
Opacity (black box)	Unexplainable output: the network generates a molecule but cannot justify why	Chap. 5 (art 13 AI Reg, transparency); Chap. 6 (proof of causation); Chap. 7 (patentability, description)
Bias in data and algorithm	Non-representative clinical datasets; objective function that penalizes subpopulations	Chap. 5 (art 10 AI Reg, dataset quality); Chap. 6 (defective product due to discrimination)
Reliability and reproducibility	Predictions of toxicity or efficacy not verifiable; training data not reproducible	Chap. 6 (development-risk defense); Chap. 9 (FDA credibility framework)
Decision-making autonomy	The algorithm does not assist but decides: identifies targets, generates molecules, selects patients	Chap. 6 (liability attribution); Chap. 7 (inventorship)

is not reconstructible in terms that a human operator, an expert, or a judge can understand.

It is useful to distinguish three forms of opacity.[4] Epistemic opacity derives from the intrinsic complexity of the model, namely even with complete access to the parameters, the deep neural network operates through mathematical transformations that humans cannot reduce to a chain of comprehensible reasoning. Structural opacity depends on the architecture chosen, given that some architectures (such as decision trees) are intrinsically more interpretable than others (such as deep convolutional networks), but the most accurate in the pharmaceutical context are also the least interpretable. Intentional opacity is that deliberately maintained by the supplier to protect trade secrets, namely the source code, the model weights, and the training data are made accessible neither to the user nor to the regulator, except to the extent required by law.

Each form poses distinct legal problems. Epistemic opacity concerns the transparency requirement of Article 13 of the AI Regulation,[5] in the sense that if the system is intrinsically non-interpretable, the transparency requirement cannot be satisfied by technical documentation alone, but requires additional tools whose suitability is contested. Structural opacity concerns the trade-off between accuracy and explainability,[6] namely the supplier who chooses the most accurate model (and therefore least interpretable) makes a choice that has consequences for proving causation in the event of harm. Intentional opacity concerns the balance between the supplier's right to protection of trade secrets and the right of the user (and regulator) to understand how the system makes its decisions. This balance is at the heart of the tension between Chapter 4 of Regulation (EU) 2024/1689 (obligations of suppliers) and the protection of industrial property.[7]

In the pharmaceutical sector, the three forms of opacity accumulate and reinforce one another. Consider the case of a toxicity prediction system based on a deep

---

[4] The distinction among epistemic opacity (impossibility of understanding the model's internal reasoning), structural opacity (complexity of architecture), and intentional opacity (trade secret) is functional to legal analysis, as each type poses distinct problems in terms of transparency (Chap. 5), proof (Chap. 6), and patent description (Chap. 7). The tripartition recalls, though it does not coincide with, the distinction proposed by Burrell (2016).

[5] Regulation (EU) 2024/1689, art 13, on the requirement of transparency and provision of information to users. The requirement imposes that high-risk AI systems be designed and developed in such a way as to ensure sufficiently transparent functioning to enable deployers to interpret the system's output and use it appropriately.

[6] The distinction between explainability (capacity to reconstruct the model's decision-making process) and interpretability (possibility of intuitively understanding functioning) is relevant to the transparency requirement of art 13 AI Regulation and to the adequacy of description in a patent application (Chap. 7); Barredo Arrieta et al. (2020).

[7] For clarifications on the interaction between Regulation (EU) 2024/1689 and Regulations (EU) 2017/745 (MDR) and 2017/746 (IVDR), with specific regard to medical software with integrated AI components, see AIB 2025-1/MDCG 2025-6, Interplay between the Medical Devices Regulation (MDR) and In vitro Diagnostic Medical Devices Regulation (IVDR) and the Artificial Intelligence Act (AIA) (June 2025). The document clarifies that the obligations of the AI Regulation apply in a complementary, not substitutive, manner with respect to MDR/IVDR requirements.

neural network, developed by a company that makes neither the model weights nor the training data accessible, namely the system is epistemically opaque (the model's complexity prevents reconstruction of the reasoning), structurally opaque (the chosen architecture maximizes accuracy at the expense of interpretability), and intentionally opaque (the supplier protects its competitive advantage). The regulator and judicial authority are faced with a system whose functioning is inscrutable under all three profiles.

What Article 13 of Regulation (EU) 2024/1689 Prescribes

Article 13 of the AI Regulation imposes on suppliers of high-risk AI systems, a category into which systems employed in pharmaceutical research and clinical trials fall, a transparency obligation whose target is often misunderstood. The recipient is not the patient or data subject, but rather the downstream user, namely the professional deployer who employs the system in their own supply chain. To these subjects the supplier must provide instructions for use which, pursuant to paragraph 3, shall indicate the identity and contact details of the supplier, the characteristics and limitations of the system, the expected level of accuracy, robustness and cybersecurity, the circumstances of intended use and reasonably foreseeable misuse, the measures for human oversight, and the expected useful life and maintenance necessary over the system's lifecycle.[8]

The systematic meaning of this provision resides in the fact that Article 13 regulates the product *ex ante* as a requirement for access to the single market and does not itself provide the procedural proof of causation in the civil-liability judgment. Its possible violation merges into the general regime of Directive (EU) 2024/2853, where it can integrate one of the indices of defectiveness that can be valued by the judge pursuant to Article 7. Confusing the two dimensions, regulatory and procedural, leads to the recurring misunderstanding that formal compliance with the AI Regulation would be sufficient per se to exclude the supplier's civil liability. On the second dimension, that of explainability employed as a tool of proof in court, we shall return systematically in Sect. 4.6 of this chapter.[9]

[8] Regulation (EU) 2024/1689, art 13. Recital 72 clarifies that the supplier's transparency obligation is functional to the effective exercise of the human oversight provided by Article 14 by the deployer, so that operating instructions are not mere documentary compliance but the operational safeguard of human control over the system. On the dogmatic meaning of the requirement, see Finocchiaro (2023), pp. 87–92, where transparency is reconstructed as a 'condition of possibility' of accountability of the professional user.

[9] On the distinction between regulatory product requirement and judicial proof of the causal link, which the text invokes as the key to reading Article 13, see Comporti (1965), pp. 214 ff., and, with specific reference to the AI Regulation, Pardolesi and Arnaudo (2023), where it is observed that formal compliance with Article 13 is not per se decisive, in that it may at most establish a presumption of correct information to the deployer, without excluding the separate finding of the defect relevant under product liability.

The GAN/RANC Case as an Example of Multi-level Opacity

Generative adversarial networks (GAN), widely employed in the de novo generation of pharmacological molecules,[10] offer a paradigmatic example of multi-level opacity. In a GAN, the generator produces candidate molecules and the discriminator evaluates them; both are deep neural networks, each opaque for reasons of its own. The final output, the selected molecule, is the result of an iterative process in which two black boxes interact with one another. The level of opacity is not simply doubled, it is qualitatively different, because no point in the process is reducible to a single model analyzable in isolation.

Consider the following scenario. The generator produces an apparently perfect molecule, which passes all the predictive filters imposed by the discriminator and achieves a high safety score. The molecule advances in development, passes preclinical and clinical phases, and is placed on the market. In the post-commercialization pharmacovigilance phase, the molecule proves toxic due to a mechanism not contemplated in the discriminator's feature set. The legal question is immediate, namely who is responsible? The programmer of the generator, who produced the molecule? The supplier of the training data for the discriminator, whose data did not contain information on that toxic mechanism? The pharmaceutical company that placed the compound on the market based on the algorithm's safety score?

This scenario illustrates how opacity is not only an epistemological problem but also an evidentiary problem, namely in the causal chain leading from the training data to the toxic molecule, no link is reconstructible.[11] Proving causation, which in the civil-liability regime falls on the injured party (except for the reversals provided by Directive 2024/2853), becomes practically impossible when the entire process is shrouded in a double black box. Chapter 6 will examine how the new directive addresses this specificity and whether the disclosure mechanisms provided by the AI Regulation are sufficient to rebalance the informational asymmetry between supplier and injured party.

Finally, it should be observed that the techniques of Explainable AI (XAI), developed to render opaque models interpretable, do not solve the problem.[12] The most widely used tools (SHAP, LIME, attention maps) provide local approximations, namely they indicate which input features most influenced a specific prediction, but

[10] For the technical description of GANs and RANC architectures, see Chap. 3, Sect. 3.4. The example developed here is inspired by the risk profiles actually encountered in the pharmacological literature on AI-assisted de novo generation.

[11] The problem of the chain of liability in the GAN is structurally different from that which arises for a monolithic system. In a single system, the producer is identifiable; in a GAN, the output is the product of interaction between two autonomous networks, each potentially developed and trained by different subjects, on different datasets. Chapter 6 will examine how Directive 2024/2853 addresses this specificity.

[12] The most widely used Explainable AI (XAI) techniques include SHAP (SHapley Additive exPlanations), LIME (Local Interpretable Model-agnostic Explanations), and attention-map analysis. These techniques provide approximate and local explanations, not a complete reconstruction of the decision-making process. Their reliability as an evidentiary tool is disputed; Rudin (2019) and Ghassemi et al. (2021).

do not reconstruct the decision-making process in its entirety. A post-hoc explanation is not equivalent to intrinsic transparency. In the legal context, the distinction is relevant, namely a judge or expert who receives a SHAP explanation is not accessing the model's reasoning, but a simplified and potentially misleading representation. The confidence placed in XAI techniques risks generating an illusion of understanding that aggravates, rather than solves, the problem of opacity.

4.3 Bias in Data and Algorithms

An AI system is only as reliable as the data on which it is trained. In the pharmaceutical context, the problem of bias assumes a particularly grave dimension, because algorithmic error not only produces an unjust decision but can produce a defective drug for an entire subpopulation. Three forms of bias merit attention for their legal implications, namely data bias, selection bias, and algorithmic bias.

4.3.1 Data Bias

Clinical datasets used to train predictive models reflect the characteristics of populations historically overrepresented in clinical trials, namely predominantly adults, males, of Caucasian ethnicity.[13] A model trained on this data may systematically underperform when applied to women, ethnic minorities, pediatric or geriatric populations. The underrepresentation is not accidental but the product of decades of recruitment practices that privileged more easily enrollable populations and those less subject to biological variability.[14] AI does not create bias, but inherits it, amplifies it, and crystallizes it in its own parameters.[15]

The legal implication is direct. If a drug developed with AI exhibits adverse effects in a population underrepresented in the training dataset, data bias becomes a relevant element in assessing product defectiveness pursuant to Directive 2024/2853.[16] The regulation introduces a significant criterion with Article 7,

[13] Bias in clinical datasets is a documented problem, as the underrepresentation of women, ethnic minorities, and pediatric populations in historical trials is transmitted to predictive models trained on that data; Obermeyer et al. (2019). The study demonstrated that an algorithm widely used in the US healthcare system systematically discriminated against African American patients, assigning them a lower risk score under equal clinical conditions.

[14] In the context of oncology clinical trials, historical data show that women represent less than 40% of participants and ethnic minorities less than 20%, despite the incidence of some diseases being higher in these populations. An AI model trained on this data replicates and amplifies the underrepresentation; US Food and Drug Administration (2022).

[15] For an updated review on strategies for bias mitigation in healthcare AI, with attention to disparities in diagnosis and therapeutic outcomes among demographic groups, see Chinta et al. (2025).

[16] Directive 2024/2853, art 7(2)(c): the capacity of the product to continue learning after distribution is an element for the evaluation of defectiveness. The reference directly affects pharmaceutical AI systems that update their models with new data after market placement. The rule introduces a dynamic criterion for the evaluation of defectiveness, which does not crystallize at the moment of market placement but evolves with the product.

paragraph 2, letter c), which includes among the elements for assessing defectiveness the product's capacity to continue learning after distribution. A pharmaceutical AI system that updates its models with post-commercialization data from a population that replicates the non-representative composition of the dataset would amplify rather than correct the original bias, creating a legal problem that merges with the regime of liability for discrimination and defectiveness.

Article 10 of the AI Regulation addresses the problem from the regulatory perspective, imposing on suppliers of high-risk systems requirements for dataset quality that include representativeness and the absence of bias.[17] The formulation of the rule is, however, cautious, namely datasets must be "sufficiently representative" and "as far as possible, free from errors." These formulas, understandably dictated by awareness of practical limitations, leave the supplier a margin of discretion that can translate into non-uniform application. In the pharmaceutical sector, where the composition of the dataset directly determines the safety of the drug for entire subpopulations, the "as far as possible" should be interpreted in light of the precautionary principle and the specific obligations deriving from sector-specific regulation.

4.3.2 Selection Bias

Selection bias manifests itself when the available data are not representative of reality. Public databases in pharmaceutical chemistry contain predominantly information on molecules already studied and on known chemical classes.[18] An algorithm for de novo generation trained on this data tends to produce molecules structurally similar to those already existing, penalizing the discovery of genuinely new structures. The chemical space explored by AI is as broad as the chemical space documented in the training data; the latter is an infinitesimal fraction of the total chemical space.

Selection bias has a dual legal relevance. From the competition perspective (Chap. 8), it consolidates the position of those holding large proprietary databases,[19] namely whoever has broader and more diverse datasets produces models less affected by bias and therefore more competitive, creating a barrier to entry for

---

[17] Regulation (EU) 2024/1689, art 10, on requirements for the quality of training, validation, and test datasets. Paragraph 2 specifies that datasets must be 'relevant, sufficiently representative and, to the extent possible, free from errors and complete with regard to the intended purpose'. Paragraph 3 requires that datasets take into account the characteristics or elements specific to the geographical, contextual, behavioral, or functional setting in which the high-risk AI system is intended to be used.

[18] Selection bias occurs when the available data are not representative of the real population. In the pharmaceutical context, public databases (PubChem, ChEMBL) contain predominantly data on molecules already studied, creating a bias toward known chemical classes and penalizing the discovery of genuinely new structures; Mendez et al. (2019).

[19] Competition among operators in access to training data is examined in Chap. 8. Selection bias reinforces the position of proprietary database holders, because whoever has broader and more diverse data produces models less affected by bias and therefore more competitive. This dynamic can configure a relevant barrier to entry within the meaning of competition law.

operators who do not have comparable data. From the intellectual property perspective (Chap. 7), it raises the question of the novelty of the generated output, in the sense that if the algorithm is systematically conditioned to produce molecules similar to those known, is the output truly "new" in the sense required by patent law? The question is all the more pertinent when the algorithm operates as an agent, generating molecules without a specific input from the human operator.

4.3.3 Algorithmic Bias

Algorithmic bias is distinguished from data bias in that it emerges from the model's structure or objective function. An algorithm for de novo generation optimized to maximize the docking score (binding affinity to the target) may systematically produce molecules with high affinity but poor safety profile, because the objective function does not include toxicity parameters. Similarly, an algorithm optimized for average efficacy across a population may systematically underperform on specific subgroups. In the pharmaceutical sector, algorithmic discrimination is not an abstract problem, namely a model that underestimates a compound's toxicity in a subpopulation produces a defective drug for that subpopulation.

The choice of the objective function is, ultimately, a choice of the designer. It is the designer who decides which parameters the model must optimize and which it can neglect. This choice, apparently technical, has direct legal consequences, namely a model that does not include renal toxicity among the optimization parameters and that produces a drug that is nephrotoxic for a vulnerable subpopulation configures a case in which bias is inscribed in the system's design, not in the data. Responsibility, in this case, cannot be attributed to data quality but to the design choice. Article 10 of the AI Regulation, focused on dataset quality, does not explicitly cover this profile, which remains subject to the supplier-liability regime examined in Chap. 6.

4.4 Reliability and Reproducibility

The question of the reliability of pharmaceutical algorithms articulates into two profiles, namely the reliability of the predictive model and the reliability of the data on which it is trained. Both profiles have a specific legal implication, which concerns first the development-risk defense (Chap. 6) and second the regulatory framework for the credibility of AI models (Chap. 9).

The DeepTox Case and the Problem of the Risk Score

DeepTox, as illustrated in the preceding chapter, predicts molecular toxicity from 2500 predefined toxicophore features.[20] Its reliability depends on the completeness of the feature set, namely a toxicity mediated by a mechanism not contemplated in

[20] On DeepTox, see Chap. 3, Sect. 3.3; Mayr et al. (2016).

the set systematically escapes the model. The system won the Tox21 Data Challenge in 2014, demonstrating superior performance to all conventional methods, but this relative excellence does not eliminate the structural limitation, namely the model is only as reliable as its set of features is complete, and no set can be complete with respect to the totality of toxicological mechanisms.

The PrOCTOR system (Predicting Odds of Clinical Trial Outcomes using Random forest) illustrates a different aspect of the same problem.[21] PrOCTOR predicts the probability of a compound's success in clinical phases based on 48 structural and pharmacological features. In a retrospective study it demonstrated 78% accuracy in predicting success in Phase I. The data is significant but raises a precise legal question, namely when a manufacturer uses an algorithmic risk score to decide to advance a compound into clinical development and that compound proves harmful, is the risk score part of the "state of scientific and technical knowledge" for purposes of the development-risk defense?

Consider the following scenario, namely a manufacturer uses the low-risk score provided by DeepTox to place a molecule on the market, qualifying it as a safe medicinal product; in the pharmacovigilance phase, the molecule proves toxic for a mechanism not foreseen by the model. Can the company invoke the development-risk defense, provided by Article 11, letter e), of Directive 2024/2853,[22] based on the fact that the algorithm, at the time of commercialization, was unable to detect that toxicity? The answer depends on the legal qualification of the "state of scientific and technical knowledge," namely does the score of a deep learning algorithm, trained on a necessarily incomplete set of features, integrate the "state of knowledge"? Or does the "state of knowledge" also include awareness of the model's limitations and therefore the fact that the manufacturer knew (or should have known) that the safety prediction was necessarily incomplete?

The Draft Guidance of the FDA of January 2025 addressed the question by introducing a seven-criterion framework of credibility for AI models.[23] The criteria include model validation, transparency of training data, robustness of predictions, management of uncertainty, reproducibility, data governance, and continuous monitoring of performance. The framework has no binding force in the European legal order, but represents the most advanced reference for evaluating the reliability of AI models in the pharmaceutical field. Chapter 6 and Chapter 9 will examine,

[21] Gayvert et al. (2016). For an updated scoping review of AI in clinical-trial risk assessment (142 studies, 2013–2024), see Teodoro et al. (2025).

[22] The development-risk exception, provided by art 11(1)(e) of Directive 2024/2853, permits the producer to escape liability by proving that 'the state of scientific and technical knowledge at the moment when the product was placed on the market or put into service did not permit the defect to be discovered'. The question whether the score of a deep learning algorithm, trained on a necessarily incomplete set of features, integrates the 'state of knowledge' is examined in Chap. 6.

[23] FDA, Considerations for the Use of Artificial Intelligence To Support Regulatory Decision-Making for Drug and Biological Products, Draft Guidance (January 2025). The seven-criterion credibility framework includes: (1) model validation; (2) transparency of training data; (3) robustness of predictions; (4) uncertainty management; (5) reproducibility; (6) data governance; (7) continuous monitoring of performance. Chapter 9 examines the framework in detail.

respectively, whether and how this framework can impact the assessment of the defense in European law and the construction of a regulatory system of model credibility.[24]

The Reproducibility Crisis and Its Transmission to Models

A less obvious but no less insidious problem concerns the reproducibility of training data. The so-called reproducibility crisis in scientific research[25] transmits directly to AI models, in the sense that if the training data is not reproducible, the model's prediction inherits the error. In the pharmaceutical sector, where algorithmic decisions impact patient safety, the reliability of prediction depends on the quality of upstream data, and the quality of upstream data is systematically inferior to what the scientific community had supposed. Data from Amgen (11% of preclinical studies reproducible) and Bayer (25% of results consistent with literature) suggest that a significant portion of the data on which pharmaceutical AI models are trained rests on fragile foundations.

This effect is amplified by the stratification of the digital space,[26] where the results of one model feed the training of the next in a feedback loop that can propagate and consolidate original errors. The phenomenon, known in the computer science literature as model collapse, manifests itself when models trained on data generated by other models progressively lose the capacity to represent the actual distribution of data. In the pharmaceutical context, stratification can produce a particularly pernicious effect, namely a predictive model that inherits an error from a prior model can produce an incorrect safety prediction on which another model bases its own decisions, in a chain of self-feeding errors that escapes empirical verification.

Model robustness, understood as stability of predictions as input data varies, becomes an essential requirement whose verification becomes increasingly difficult the more complex the model is. A robust model produces stable predictions even with moderate variations in input; a fragile model produces radically different predictions for minimal variations, without the user being able to distinguish one case from another. In the pharmaceutical context, model fragility can translate into an oscillation of the toxicity score that renders the clinical decision aleatoric. The question of robustness will be examined in Chap. 9 in the context of the regulatory framework for model credibility.

---

[24] On the front of transatlantic regulatory convergence, see EMA and FDA, Guiding Principles of Good AI Practice in Drug Development (2025), which establishes shared principles for the credibility, transparency, and governance of AI models employed in drug development. The document is also referred to in Chap. 3.

[25] The so-called reproducibility crisis in scientific research has been documented in numerous studies. A survey published in Nature in 2016 found that 70% of researchers attempted without success to reproduce experiments of others and more than 50% failed to reproduce their own. In the pharmaceutical sector, Amgen reported the ability to reproduce only 6 of 53 landmark preclinical studies (11%); Bayer achieved results consistent with the published literature in only 25% of cases; Baker (2016) and Begley and Ellis (2012).

[26] On digital-space stratification, see Chap. 3; on model collapse, Shumailov et al. (2024).

4.5 Decision-Making Autonomy

The final profile concerns the degree of autonomy of the algorithm in the decision-making process. It is possible to distinguish three levels.[27] At the first level, AI operates as a tool, namely it executes a specific task under the direction of the human operator, who provides the input, evaluates the output, and decides whether and how to use it. At the second level, AI operates as an assistant, namely it proposes solutions, selects options, filters results, reducing human intervention but leaving the final decision to the human. At the third level, AI operates as an agent, namely it autonomously identifies the biological target, generates candidate molecules, selects patients for the trial, in a closed loop where human intervention reduces to procedural supervision.

The survey of the preceding chapter shows that algorithmic pharmaceutics is situated, as of 2026, predominantly between the second and third levels. Self-driving laboratories, de novo generation platforms, and digital twin systems for clinical trials operate with degrees of autonomy that existing legal frameworks had not contemplated. The robot EVE,[28] developed at Cambridge University, illustrates the "agent" level in its most developed form, namely the system integrates hypothesis generation, experimental design, physical execution of the experiment, and analysis of results, autonomously identifying compounds with pharmacological activity. In 2015, EVE identified a compound already approved as an antiparasitic (triclosan) with activity against the malaria parasite, without human intervention going beyond definition of the biological target and supervision of the protocol.

AlphaFold exemplifies the same phenomenon in the domain of structural prediction,[29] namely the system autonomously generates the three-dimensional structure of a protein from the amino acid sequence alone, without human intervention in the prediction phase. The human contribution is situated in the training phase (data selection, architecture choice) and in the validation phase (comparison with experimental data). The molecule or structure generated is the product of a process in which human contribution can be null or marginal in the operational phase, though it was determinative in the preparatory phase. This temporal dissociation between human contribution and algorithmic output lies at the root of the inventorship problem examined in Chap. 7.

Qualifying the level of autonomy has immediate implications for two fundamental questions. The first concerns liability. Article 14 of the AI Regulation imposes human oversight of high-risk systems,[30] but oversight presupposes the supervisor's

[27] The tool-assistant-agent scale recalls the taxonomy of automation levels adopted in other sectors. The most direct parallel is with the SAE (Society of Automotive Engineers) scale for autonomous vehicles, which distinguishes six levels from 0 (no automation) to 5 (complete automation). In the pharmaceutical context, the qualification of the autonomy level determines the applicable liability regime (see Chap. 6).

[28] EVE (Every Versatile Explorer); in 2015 it autonomously identified triclosan, an approved antiparasitic, as active against the malaria parasite. Williams et al. (2015).

[29] Jumper et al. (2021).

[30] Regulation (EU) 2024/1689, art 14, on human oversight of high-risk AI systems. Paragraph 1 requires that systems be designed and developed in such a way that they can be effectively supervised by natural persons during the period of use. Paragraph 4 specifies that oversight must enable

capacity to understand and, if necessary, correct the system's output. In pharmaceutical practice, the human supervisor can verify procedural compliance but not, in most cases, the substantive correctness of the output of a deep neural network.[31] A computational chemist can verify that the generated molecule respects basic chemical constraints (stability, synthesizability), but cannot reconstruct the logical path that led the model to generate that specific molecule rather than another. Oversight becomes formal rather than substantive, namely the supervisor certifies procedural compliance but cannot guarantee the correctness of algorithmic reasoning. Chapter 6 will examine the consequences of this asymmetry for the attribution of liability.

The second question concerns inventorship.[32] If AI operates as a tool, the inventive contribution remains fully human, namely the operator conceives the idea, directs the research, interprets the results, and the system executes. If AI operates as an agent, the generated molecule is the product of a process in which human contribution can be null or marginal in the creative phase. The digital space described in the preceding chapter is the environment in which AI generates and evaluates compounds autonomously; it is in this space that the question of inventorship arises with the greatest urgency. Chapter 7 will examine the question in light of the DABUS case law and the revised USPTO guidance of November 2025, which qualifies AI as a "laboratory tool" even when its contribution exceeds that of the human operator.

The four profiles here examined are not independent; they interweave and reinforce one another. An opaque and autonomous system operating on bias-affected data produces results whose reliability is not verifiable and whose correctness is not guaranteed for all populations. Opacity prevents identification of bias; bias compromises reliability; the system's autonomy withdraws the process from the human control that could, in theory, intercept the error. It is on this convergence of technical limitations that the legal problems of Part II take root, namely the European regulatory framework (Chap. 5), civil liability (Chap. 6), intellectual property (Chap. 7), competition and data (Chap. 8), and the regulatory ecosystem (Chap. 9).

The treatment that follows proceeds from the awareness that the pharmaceutical algorithm is neither infallible nor neutral. Its limitations, here organized into categories of legal relevance, are the raw material of the analysis that Part II will conduct with the tools proper to law, namely civil liability for the harm that the algorithm

---

the supervisor to fully understand the capabilities and limitations of the system and to decide, in any particular situation, not to use the high-risk AI system or otherwise to disregard, cancel, or reverse its output.

[31] The requirement for human oversight (art 14 AI Regulation) conflicts in certain applications with the technical characteristics of certain generative models. Specifically, when a language model generates medical hypotheses in real time at the inference stage, the supervisory obligation becomes operationally problematic: the supervisor would need to evaluate not only whether the output is appropriate, but also to understand the model's reasoning process, which, for neural networks, remains largely opaque. This creates a gap between regulatory obligation and technical feasibility.

[32] On the distinction between 'tool' and 'autonomous system' in the pharmaceutical context, see Marchetti (2022). The author notes that the classification depends not on technical architecture alone, but on the degree of autonomy in decision-making related to the pharmaceutical product lifecycle.

contributes to produce, intellectual property for the invention that the algorithm contributes to generate, competition for the market that the algorithm contributes to redefine, regulation for the framework of rules that must govern a process in which human decision is progressively replaced by algorithmic decision.

4.6 Procedural Use of Explainability: SHAP, LIME and Saliency Maps as a Tertium Genus Probatorio

4.6.1 Regulatory Explainability and Procedural Explainability

Explainability circulates in the legal literature of the past decade in two distinct acceptations that warrant separating with clarity. The first is regulatory and derives from recital 71 of the General Data Protection Regulation, which speaks of a "right to obtain an explanation" of the automated decision affecting the subject and has consolidated with Article 13 of the AI Regulation, which imposes on suppliers of high-risk systems an obligation of transparency toward downstream users. In this acceptation, explainability serves an *ex ante* administrative judgment of compliance, namely it is a product requirement, not proof of a harmful fact. The second acceptation, developed in application practice from 2020 onward, concerns instead the use of the same explanation techniques as a means of proof in a civil-liability judgment. The difference is not terminological but functional. In the first case, the explanation serves to demonstrate to the regulator that the model meets certain procedural requirements; in the second, it serves to demonstrate to the judge that in a single decision of the model a specific variable was underweighted or overweighted, with causal consequences on harm. Ignoring the distinction produces doctrinal confusion and leads to the recurring misunderstanding that compliance with the AI Regulation would be sufficient to exclude the manufacturer's civil liability.[33]

4.6.2 Technical Taxonomy: SHAP, LIME and Saliency Maps

The explainability techniques now consolidated in pharmaceutical research reduce to three principal families. The first are Shapley attributions, in their unified formulation proposed by Lundberg and Lee in 2017 and abbreviated SHAP, which assign to each input variable a numerical value corresponding to its marginal contribution to the prediction, in conformity with the axioms of efficiency, symmetry, nullity, and additivity proper to cooperative game theory. The second consists of the model-agnostic local explanations of Ribeiro, Singh and Guestrin, known as LIME, which approximate the behavior of any model in the neighborhood of the instance of interest through an interpretable linear model. The third is formed by saliency maps,

[33] On the distinction between regulatory explainability, an ex ante requirement of administrative compliance, and procedural explainability as a means of proof in civil-liability proceedings, see Wachter et al. (2017) and Edwards and Veale (2017).

typically employed with convolutional networks, which highlight in histological or molecular images the regions to which the network assigns the greatest weight in producing its own decision.[34]

Each of these techniques presents limitations that the legal professional must understand before according them evidentiary value. SHAP attributions depend on the reference distribution with which marginal counterfactuals are calculated, given that changing the distribution changes the ranking of variables, which requires explicit justification of the choice. LIME explanations are subject to instability on minimal perturbations of the instance of interest, which can generate significantly different explanations with the model unchanged. Saliency maps, finally, present the well-known pathology of saliency-map confounding, whereby image regions with high visual contrast attract the attribution independently of their actual contribution to the decision. To these limitations is added a transversal consideration, which crosses all three families, in that the statistical weight attributed to a variable does not coincide with its causal relevance in the physical world, because high correlation in the model can derive from spurious associations present in the training data.[35]

4.6.3 Admissibility in Italian Civil Procedure

In the transition from laboratory to courtroom, SHAP attributions, LIME and saliency maps must be qualified as scientific evidence. Italian law does not know a preliminary admissibility test analogous to that which US case law developed first with the Frye case in 1923 and then with the Daubert decision in 1993, but entrusts the evaluation of the reliability of scientific evidence to the prudent assessment of the judge pursuant to Article 116 of the code of civil procedure. The American experience provides, however, a useful decalogue for structuring the reliability judgment, namely empirical verifiability of the technique, peer review, known error rate, standards of application, and acceptance in the relevant scientific community. Applied to explainability techniques, these criteria yield differentiated results. SHAP and LIME readily exceed the first four parameters, thanks to a solid theoretical foundation and widespread use in industrial practice, while saliency maps remain more fragile on the plane of stability.[36]

The relationship with Article 2697 of the civil code merits in turn a clarification. Explainability techniques do not formally shift the burden of proof, which remains

[34] On the techniques recalled in the text, see Lundberg and Lee (2017) for SHAP, Ribeiro et al. (2016) for LIME, and Simonyan et al. (2014) for saliency maps.

[35] Regulation (EU) 2024/1689, art 13. The transparency obligation extends to the limitations and risks of the AI system.

[36] On the admissibility of scientific evidence, see Frye v United States, 293 F 1013 (DC Cir 1923), and Daubert v Merrell Dow Pharmaceuticals Inc., 509 US 579 (1993); in Italian civil procedure the reliability assessment is entrusted to the judge under Article 116 of the code of civil procedure. On scientific evidence, see Taruffo (2005).

on the injured party for the demonstration of causation and harm, but operate on the material plane by facilitating its discharge. They link with the presumption of defectiveness of Article 10, paragraph 4, of Directive 2024/2853, in the sense that they enable the injured party to reach the threshold of "sufficient allegation" necessary to activate the presumption, given that once a SHAP map is produced that identifies the underweighted variable, the judge can deem the hypothesis of the defect plausible and reverse the burden of proof onto the manufacturer, who to exonerate itself must demonstrate either the methodological inconsistency of the attribution or the causal irrelevance of the identified variable. Article 9 of the same Directive, in turn, assures the injured party access to the technical file necessary to concretely perform the calculation of attributions and shall be coordinated in Italian procedural law with Article 210 of the code of civil procedure on documentary production, and, where necessary, with conservatory seizure ex Article 670.[37]

4.6.4 Court-Appointed Expert Consultation on Pharmaceutical Algorithmic Models

When the judge appoints an expert for court-appointed expert consultation on a pharmaceutical algorithmic system, a problem opens that Italian procedural practice has not yet addressed with any systematicity. The retained expert must possess combined competencies difficult to locate in a single person, namely pharmaceutical chemistry, machine learning theory, inferential statistics, and evidentiary law. The practical impossibility of finding figures so complete pushes the judge toward the appointment of a panel of experts, a solution already practiced in case law concerning complex medical liability and permitted by Article 191 of the code of civil procedure. The panel must be required to document, in the expert opinion, the choice of reference distribution used for the attributions, verification of the stability of explanations on random perturbations, comparison between alternative techniques, and, where available, correlations with evidence of a biological nature. Any simplification of this probative package exposes the expert to the risk of civil liability toward the parties ex Article 64 of the code of civil procedure, and also to disciplinary liability before their professional order. On the deontological plane, the expert is called to expressly declare the reliability limitations of the techniques employed, without presenting SHAP attributions or saliency maps as if they were direct proof of causation, in order to enable the judge a conscious evaluation.[38]

[37] Article 2697 of the civil code; on the presumption of defectiveness and on the disclosure of evidence, Articles 10 and 9 of Directive (EU) 2024/2853, coordinated in Italian procedural law with Articles 210 and 670 of the code of civil procedure. On burden of proof and presumptions in the new product-liability regime, see Pardolesi and Arnaudo (2023) and Wendehorst (2020).

[38] On the appointment of a panel of experts, Article 191 of the code of civil procedure; on the consultant's liability toward the parties, Article 64 of the code of civil procedure. On scientific evidence and its assessment, see Taruffo (2005).

4.6.5 Systematic Thesis: Explainability as a Tertium Genus Probatorio

The reconstruction proposed above permits the formulation of a systematic thesis. Procedural explainability, differently from regulatory explainability, is neither mere administrative compliance nor free proof in the traditional sense of civil process. It constitutes a tertium genus probatorio, connoted by the combination of three elements, namely rigorous mathematical foundation, replicability of the calculation procedure, and the structurally contestable nature of attributions. The judge who employs it must evaluate it as any scientific evidence, taking into account the methodological limitations proper to each technique, and integrate it into the comprehensive probative reasoning in coordination with the presumption of defectiveness of Directive 2024/2853. The concrete applications of this thesis will be developed in Chap. 6, where Sect. 6.6.4 on the "Digital Twin" case and Sect. 6.6.5 on the "Alfa SHAP" case illustrate two typical scenarios of judicial employment of explainability; Chap. 9, in turn, examines the relationship with European regulatory governance and proposes a public register of models as a tool of *ex ante* transparency and *ex post* evidentiary facilitation.[39]

References

Baker M (2016) 1,500 scientists lift the lid on reproducibility. Nature 533:452–454

Barredo Arrieta A, Díaz-Rodríguez N, Del Ser J, Bennetot A, Tabik S, Barbado A, García S, Gil-López S, Molina D, Benjamins R, Chatila R, Herrera F (2020) Explainable artificial intelligence (XAI): concepts, taxonomies, opportunities and challenges toward responsible AI. Inf Fusion 58:82–115

Begley CG, Ellis LM (2012) Raise standards for preclinical cancer research. Nature 483:531–533

Burrell J (2016) How the machine "thinks": understanding opacity in machine learning algorithms. Big Data Soc 3(1)

Chinta SV, Wang Z, Palikhe A, Zhang X, Kashif A, Smith MA, Liu J, Zhang W (2025) AI-driven healthcare: a review on ensuring fairness and mitigating bias. PLOS Digit Health 4(5):e0000864

Comporti M (1965) Esposizione al pericolo e responsabilità civile. Morano, Napoli

Edwards L, Veale M (2017) Slave to the algorithm? Why a "right to an explanation" is probably not the remedy you are looking for. Duke Law Technol Rev 16:18–84

Finocchiaro G (2023) Intelligenza artificiale e diritto. Un'introduzione. Giappichelli, Torino

Gayvert KM, Madhukar NS, Elemento O (2016) A data-driven approach to predicting successes and failures of clinical trials. Cell Chem Biol 23(10):1294–1301

Ghassemi M, Oakden-Rayner L, Beam AL (2021) The false hope of current approaches to explainable artificial intelligence in health care. Lancet Digit Health 3(11):e745

Goodfellow I, Bengio Y, Courville A (2016) Deep learning. MIT Press, Cambridge

Jumper J, Evans R, Pritzel A, Green T, Figurnov M, Ronneberger O, Tunyasuvunakool K, Bates R, Žídek A, Potapenko A, Bridgland A, Meyer C, Kohl SAA, Ballard AJ, Cowie A, Romera-Paredes B, Nikolov S, Jain R, Adler J, Back T, Petersen S, Reiman D, Clancy E, Zielinski M, Steinegger M, Pacholska M, Berghammer T, Bodenstein S, Silver D, Vinyals O, Senior AW,

[39] See Chap. 6, Sects. 6.6.4–6.6.5, and Chap. 9.

Kavukcuoglu K, Kohli P, Hassabis D (2021) Highly accurate protein structure prediction with AlphaFold. Nature 596:583–589
Lundberg SM, Lee S-I (2017) A unified approach to interpreting model predictions. In: Advances in neural information processing systems 30. Curran Associates, Red Hook, pp 4765–4774
Marchetti L (2022) Intelligenza artificiale e farmaci: il ruolo della sorveglianza umana. In: Finocchiaro G (ed) Diritto e intelligenza artificiale. Giappichelli, Torino, pp 189–215
Mayr A, Klambauer G, Unterthiner T, Hochreiter S (2016) DeepTox: toxicity prediction using deep learning. Front Environ Sci 3:80
Mendez D, Gaulton A, Bento AP, Chambers J, De Veij M, Félix E, Magariños MP, Mosquera JF, Mutowo P, Nowotka M, Gordillo-Marañón M, Hunter F, Junco L, Mugumbate G, Rodriguez-Lopez M, Atkinson F, Bosc N, Radoux CJ, Segura-Cabrera A, Hersey A, Leach AR (2019) ChEMBL: towards direct deposition of bioassay data. Nucl Acids Res 47(D1):D930
Obermeyer Z, Powers B, Vogeli C, Mullainathan S (2019) Dissecting racial bias in an algorithm used to manage the health of populations. Science 366(6464):447–453
Pardolesi R, Arnaudo L (2023) Ecce robot. Sulla responsabilità dei sistemi adulti di intelligenza artificiale. Danno e responsabilità 2023(4):409–417
Ribeiro MT, Singh S, Guestrin C (2016) "Why should I trust you?": explaining the predictions of any classifier. In: Proceedings of the 22nd ACM SIGKDD international conference on knowledge discovery and data mining. ACM, New York, pp 1135–1144
Rudin C (2019) Stop explaining black box machine learning models for high-stakes decisions and use interpretable models instead. Nat Mach Intell 1:206–215
Russell S, Norvig P (2021) Artificial intelligence: a modern approach, 4th edn. Pearson, Hoboken
Shumailov I, Shumaylov Z, Zhao Y, Papernot N, Anderson R, Gal Y (2024) AI models collapse when trained on recursively generated data. Nature 631:755–759
Simonyan K, Vedaldi A, Zisserman A (2014) Deep inside convolutional networks: visualizing image classification models and saliency maps. In: Workshop at the international conference on learning representations
Taruffo M (2005) La prova scientifica nel processo civile. Riv Trim Dir Proc Civ 59:1079–1111
Teodoro D, Naderi N, Yazdani A, Zhang B, Bornet A (2025) A scoping review of artificial intelligence applications in clinical trial risk assessment. NPJ Digit Med 8:486
US Food and Drug Administration (2022) Drug trials snapshots summary report. https://www.fda.gov/drugs/drug-approvals-and-databases/drug-trials-snapshots. Accessed 7 June 2026
Wachter S, Mittelstadt B, Floridi L (2017) Why a right to explanation of automated decision-making does not exist in the General Data Protection Regulation. Int Data Privacy Law 7(2):76–99
Wendehorst C (2020) Strict liability for AI and other emerging technologies. J Eur Tort Law 11(2):150–180
Williams K, Bilsland E, Sparkes A, Aubrey W, Young M, Soldatova LN, De Grave K, Ramon J, de Clare M, Sirawaraporn W, Oliver SG, King RD (2015) Cheaper faster drug development validated by the repositioning of drugs against neglected tropical diseases. J R Soc Interface 12(104):20141289

Part II

Legal and Regulatory Perspectives on the Algoraceutical Drug

The European Regulatory Framework: From the AI Act to the Machinery Regulation

5

Abstract

This chapter reconstructs the European regulatory framework that, in 2026, governs the use of artificial intelligence in the pharmaceutical domain. The analysis rests on three pillars. The Artificial Intelligence Act (Regulation (EU) 2024/1689) introduces a risk-based architecture whose application to drug discovery is complicated by the absence of an explicit classification of pharmaceutical AI, a gap filled indirectly through the medical-device route and through regulatory practice. The reformed Product Liability Directive (Directive (EU) 2024/2853) extends strict liability to software and AI, recognizes the safety implications of continuous learning, and alleviates the claimant's burden of proof where algorithmic opacity makes causation excessively difficult to establish. The Machinery Regulation (Regulation (EU) 2023/1230) completes the picture for AI incorporated into automated laboratories. The chapter examines the withdrawal of the proposed Artificial Intelligence Liability Directive and the residual role of Article 2050 of the Italian civil code, proposes a functional tripartition of pharmaceutical AI by level of risk, and surveys the technical standards and guidance that translate these obligations into practice.

5.1 Introduction: From *de iure condendo* to *de iure condito*

Between 2023 and 2026, the regulatory landscape on artificial intelligence underwent substantial transformation. Until 2023, the regulatory landscape was characterized by legislative proposals not yet finalized and partial, fragmented regulation.

G. Rotino, *Algoraceutics - Legal Perspectives on Artificial Intelligence in Drug Discovery and Development*, Law for Professionals,
https://doi.org/10.1007/978-3-032-38537-6_5

Regulation (EU) 2024/1689, which entered into force on August 1, 2024,[1] represents the first systematic European attempt to govern AI on a generalist basis, articulated on a risk-based approach that identifies four levels of regulatory intervention. Simultaneously, Directive 2024/2853, which replaces Directive 85/374/EEC after 40 years of application,[2] extended the scope of civil liability for product defect to software and AI, creating a liability scheme that prior legislation did not contemplate.

The Proposed Directive on civil liability related to artificial intelligence (COM(2022) 496 final), initially announced as a cornerstone of a comprehensive strategy, was withdrawn in February 2025 with subsequent confirmation in the Council in October 2025.[3] This development compelled the European legal system to reconfigure itself, with the result that Directive 2024/2853 absorbed parts of the withdrawn proposal, while other issues remain unresolved. The Machinery Regulation (Regulation (EU) 2023/1230), applicable from January 20, 2027, completes the framework with specific disciplines for AI systems incorporated into physical products. In Italy, the withdrawal of the directive has brought Article 2050 of the civil code on liability for hazardous activities back to the fore, already indicated by the MISE expert group in 2019 as the reference norm for damages caused by AI. On March 13, 2026, the EU Council adopted the negotiation position on amendments to the AI Regulation (the Digital Omnibus on AI), extending timelines for autonomous high-risk systems to December 2, 2027 and for incorporated systems to August 2, 2028, with simplification measures for small and medium enterprises. The Council and the European Parliament subsequently reached a provisional agreement on these timelines on 7 May 2026. The interaction between the various European and national regulatory sources constitutes the guiding thread of the analysis that follows.

This chapter examines three regulatory pillars governing European algoraceutics in 2026: the AI Regulation in its application to drug discovery systems and patient selection; Directive 2024/2853 in its reformed discipline of liability for product defect; the Machinery Regulation in its overlap with automated laboratories. The analysis proceeds with particular attention to original gaps in the regulatory framework, first and foremost the absence of explicit classification of pharmaceutical AI in Annex III of the AI Regulation, and the manner in which such gaps have progressively narrowed through regulatory practice and embryonic jurisprudence.

---

[1] Regulation (EU) 2024/1689 of the European Parliament and of the Council of 13 June 2024 laying down harmonized rules on artificial intelligence (*Artificial Intelligence Act*), OJ L, 2024/1689, 12 July 2024. The Regulation entered into force on 1 August 2024 (Art. 113).

[2] Directive (EU) 2024/2853 of the European Parliament and of the Council of 23 October 2024 on liability for defective products and repealing Council Directive 85/374/EEC, OJ L, 2024/2853, 18 November 2024. It entered into force on 8 December 2024, with transposition due by 9 December 2026.

[3] Proposal for a Directive on adapting non-contractual civil liability rules to artificial intelligence (*AI Liability Directive*), COM(2022) 496 final, 28 September 2022. The withdrawal was announced in the Commission Work Program 2025, COM(2025) 45 final, 11 February 2025, and subsequently formalized (OJ C, 2025). See Sect. 5.4 below.

It is worth recalling that, as of 2023, the near-total absence of explicit references to AI applications in the pharmaceutical sector in Annex III of the proposed AI Regulation. This observation proved well founded. The initial programmatic gap was filled not through direct inclusion, but through the mechanism of qualifying pharmaceutical AI as software medical device (SaMD) or artificial intelligence as a medical device (AIaMD) under Regulation (EU) 2017/745, which determines the application of obligations provided for high-risk systems where the AI is integrated into the device. This transversal solution, on one hand, ensures a degree of regulatory protection, while on the other amplifies legal uncertainty regarding correct classification of AI applications that do not fully meet the criteria for medical devices, finding themselves in a zone of ambiguous qualification. A step forward in rationalizing this zone is represented by the joint document MDCG 2025-6/AIB 2025-1, published in June 2025, which outlines the interplay between the Medical Devices Regulation, the *In Vitro* Diagnostic Medical Devices Regulation and the AI Act, clarifying that the AI Act complements, and does not replace, the medical device framework.

5.2 The Regulation on Artificial Intelligence (Regulation (EU) 2024/1689)

5.2.1 Structure and Risk-Based Approach

The AI Regulation adopts a risk-based approach that differentiates regulatory obligations according to the level of risk that the AI system poses. Four levels structure the entire architecture, articulated in prohibited practices, high-risk systems, limited-risk systems, and minimal-risk systems. This articulation reflects the conviction that uniform regulation would be inadequate, since the cost of compliance grows exponentially with decreasing tolerance for risk, with direct consequences on drug prices.

The Regulation additionally adopts a broad and technology-neutral definition of an AI system,[4] intended to incorporate future technological developments without requiring legislative reform. Determinative for the pharmaceutical domain is the principle of coordination with sector-specific legislation, whereby where more specific sectoral regulation exists (such as Regulation 2017/745 for medical devices), the general Regulation does not apply to the same aspects.[5]

[4] Art. 3(1), Regulation (EU) 2024/1689 (definition of an 'AI system'); see also recital 12.

[5] On the relationship with sectoral Union law, see Art. 2 and recital 64, Regulation (EU) 2024/1689; for medical devices, Regulation (EU) 2017/745 (MDR).

5.2.2 Prohibited AI Practices and Algoraceutical Applications

Article 5 of the AI Regulation prohibits four categories of practices. The first two prohibit forms of subliminal manipulation and exploitation of vulnerabilities specific to vulnerable populations; the third prohibits social credit scoring in certain contexts; the fourth prohibits real-time mass biometric surveillance systems in public spaces. In the pharmaceutical context, violation of prohibition (b) is theoretically possible were a patient recruitment system for clinical trials that exploited psychological vulnerabilities of subjects suffering from chronic conditions (depression, chronic pain) to induce them to participate in a potentially risky study to fall under the prohibition.[6] In practice, this scenario remains marginal in contemporary pharmaceutical research, where algorithmic systems remain internal to selection processes and do not interface directly with patient persuasion.

5.2.3 High-Risk Systems: Classification of Algoraceutical Applications

Article 6 of the AI Regulation classifies as high-risk those AI systems that fall within the categories listed in Annex III. Annex I, Section A, references Regulation 2017/745 (medical devices) with a cross-reference that in appearance should have resolved the question of algorithmic pharmaceutics.[7] Reality is more complex. The AI Regulation classifies medical devices (SaMD) as high-risk only to the extent they fall into the category of "brand new devices," that is, medical devices entirely novel for which no prior history of clinical use exists. This formulation creates a regulatory gap particularly relevant to drug discovery.

The strategy for filling the gap has been recourse to the SaMD (Software as Medical Device) paradigm and, more recently, AIaMD (AI as Medical Device). According to this interpretation, an AI model for identifying pharmacological targets, if employed to guide decisions affecting patient safety in the clinical context, falls within the definition of medical device. However, the vast majority of traditional drug discovery algorithms do not fall under such definition because they are internal research tools, not direct interfaces with patients.[8] The ambiguity has generated a *de facto* bifurcation, whereby identical algorithms are classified differently depending on their context of use.

---

[6] Art. 5, Regulation (EU) 2024/1689 (prohibited AI practices); the exploitation of the vulnerabilities of specific groups is addressed in Art. 5(1)(b).

[7] Art. 6 and Annex I, Section A, Regulation (EU) 2024/1689: medical devices governed by Regulation (EU) 2017/745 enter the high-risk regime through Art. 6(1) and the harmonization legislation listed in Annex I, rather than through Annex III.

[8] Joint guidance MDCG 2025-6/AIB 2025-1, *Interplay between the Medical Devices Regulation and the In Vitro Diagnostic Medical Devices Regulation and the Artificial Intelligence Act*, 19 June 2025, accessed 7 June 2026.

We propose a functional classification of algoraceutical applications into three categories. The first, identification of biological targets and prediction of molecular properties, falls into a zone of regulatory marginality, insofar as the product is informational, not directly applied to patients. The second, de novo molecular design through generative models, remains in a broad "gray zone," since it produces candidate molecules not present in databases and for which no "history of use" in the traditional sense exists. The third, patient stratification for enrollment in clinical trials and pharmacovigilance, is clearly high-risk insofar as the output directly impacts clinical safety. This tripartition is not purely theoretical, since the consequences for compliance, liability, and documentation are significant.

The unresolved tension concerns the median category. A generative model (GAN or diffusion) that produces candidate molecules on the basis of desired biological properties is technically a high-risk system? Would the ensuing obligations be proportionate relative to the benefit? And who, in the chain of command, should bear the weight of compliance, the pharmaceutical company that uses the model, the supplier of the model (e.g., a computational AI company), or the provider of the training dataset? On these questions the European legislator provided no explicit answers, delegating to regulatory practice the task of defining the boundaries.

5.2.4 Requirements for High-Risk Systems

For systems classified as high-risk, the Regulation imposes eight categories of requirements. The first is risk management.[9] The provider must conduct a preliminary risk analysis, identify known and foreseeable risks, implement mitigation measures, and maintain post-distribution feedback mechanisms. In drug discovery, this means independent biological and chemical validation of generated molecules, tracking of erroneous predictions and the ability to revert to previous versions of the model.

The second requirement is data quality.[10] Training data must be representative of the population for which the system is intended, subject to quality control and corrected for known bias. In the pharmaceutical research context, the requirement directly invests the problem of bias in clinical datasets examined in Chap. 4, Sect. 4.3, since historically imbalanced datasets for gender, ethnicity, and age transmit their distortions to predictive models, with consequences for the safety and predicted efficacy of drugs in underrepresented subpopulations. The formulation of Article 10 ("sufficiently representative" and "to the extent possible, free from errors") leaves providers a margin of discretion that, in the pharmaceutical sector, should be interpreted restrictively in light of the precautionary principle.

Third, technical documentation.[11] The provider must compile a technical file that describes the system, the algorithms, the data, the performance metrics, the results

[9] Art. 9, Regulation (EU) 2024/1689 (risk-management system).

[10] Art. 10, Regulation (EU) 2024/1689 (data and data governance).

[11] Art. 11 and Annex IV, Regulation (EU) 2024/1689 (technical documentation).

of the conformity assessment. For deep learning systems, this documentation immediately confronts the problem of opacity, namely how one documents the genesis of a molecule generated by a GAN if the generator provides no transparent justifications? The provider's temptation is to circumscribe documentation to "macro-characteristics" (input, output, aggregate metrics), omitting the detailed trace of internal decisions, which in turn compromises the verifiability of conformity.

Fourth, logging and recording.[12] Systems must record operational data, particularly where human-in-the-loop cycles are foreseen. In the pharmaceutical context, logging becomes a determinative element for subsequent reconstruction of causality in the event of harm, such that if the chemist followed or rejected the algorithmic suggestion, this trace is essential both to exonerate the provider and to attribute responsibility to the user.

Fifth, transparency and information to users.[13] The system must function with "sufficient transparency" and users must be "duly informed" of its nature and limitations. This generic formulation was a point of contention in legislative negotiations. For deep learning models, "sufficient transparency" remains an elastic concept; a provider could maintain that furnishing aggregated accuracy metrics is sufficient, while the pharmaceutical user might require explanations at the level of individual predictions. The tension between normative operability and accountability requirements remains unresolved. As highlighted in Chap. 4, Sect. 4.2, explainable artificial intelligence techniques provide local approximations that do not amount to intrinsic model transparency.

Sixth, human oversight.[14] The system must be designed so that natural persons are able to understand the output and intervene. In the pharmaceutical context, this entails that the chemist or biologist using the system can understand the rationale of the algorithmic recommendation. But where the system is opaque (an uninterpretable deep neural network), human oversight becomes a legal fiction; the person understands aggregate performance metrics but not the specific reasons for the individual prediction. This contradiction, already examined in Chap. 4, Sect. 4.5, with the paradox of formal rather than substantive oversight, is among the most significant of algoraceutical regulation.

Seventh, accuracy, robustness and cybersecurity.[15] The provider must ensure appropriate levels of accuracy (where technically feasible), robustness to unexpected inputs, protection from cyberattacks. In drug discovery, accuracy is measured in the rate of false positives (molecules predicted active that are not) and false negatives (molecules predicted inactive that could have been useful), with tolerances varying depending on the discovery stage.

---

[12] Art. 12, Regulation (EU) 2024/1689 (record-keeping and automatic logging).

[13] Art. 13, Regulation (EU) 2024/1689 (transparency and provision of information to deployers).

[14] Art. 14, Regulation (EU) 2024/1689 (human oversight).

[15] Art. 15, Regulation (EU) 2024/1689 (accuracy, robustness and cybersecurity).

5.2.5 Obligations of Providers and Users

The Regulation articulates responsibility on a fundamental distinction between provider and user. The provider is the person who develops the AI system and places it on the market; the user is the person who uses it according to instructions for use. This distinction is far from merely formal in the pharmaceutical context.[16] A large multinational that develops machine learning models internally is a provider and responsible for conformity; a small or medium enterprise that uses a drug discovery platform (e.g., Insilico Medicine, Exscientia) is a user and responsible for conformity with the regime of use. The legal consequences are differentiated. The provider is responsible for the intrinsic conformity of the product; the user is responsible for appropriate use and proper human supervision.

Algorithmic pharmaceutics generates a significant bifurcation in this regard. The training dataset is provided (e.g., molecular structures and biological activity data from public or proprietary databases), the model is provided (architecture, neural weights), but the specific training for a particular class of molecules could be conducted by the user. If the training constitutes a "substantial modification" in the sense of Article 8, paragraph 2, of Directive 2024/2853, the user becomes in all respects the manufacturer of the modified system and assumes its responsibility. The question is decisive for current industrial practice, where retraining on proprietary datasets is the norm rather than the exception. Chapter 6 will examine the consequences of this qualification on the chain of responsibility.

5.2.6 General-Purpose AI Models (GPAI)

Articles 51–56 of the Regulation are dedicated to general-purpose AI models, defined as models "that are capable of competently performing a wide range of distinct tasks with minimal adaptation." The threshold of systemic risk is set at 10 to the 25th FLOP (floating-point operations).[17] In the pharmaceutical context, a generative diffusion model or a large language model fine-tuned for chemistry that reaches this threshold becomes subject to specific requirements, including model transparency, ability to follow explicit instructions, mechanisms for preventing misuse.

The principal actors in this space are research laboratories with significant computational resources, among which DeepMind (Alphabet), Isomorphic Labs, Recursion Pharmaceuticals operate with models that likely reach the systemic threshold. For these players, the Regulation requires the drafting of codes of conduct specifying how to address risks of misuse (e.g., accelerated design of biological weapons, or generation of intentionally toxic molecules). The Code of

[16] Arts. 3(3) and 3(4), Regulation (EU) 2024/1689 (definitions of 'provider' and 'deployer'); the corresponding obligations are set out in Arts. 16 and 26 respectively.

[17] Art. 51, Regulation (EU) 2024/1689; the threshold of 10^{25} floating-point operations triggering the presumption of systemic risk is laid down in Art. 51(2). See also Arts. 52–55 and Annex XIII.

Practice for GPAI models, published in final version on July 10, 2025 and approved by the Commission on August 1, 2025, has made these obligations concrete in three chapters devoted to transparency, copyright and security.[18]

5.2.7 Governance, Oversight and Sanctions

The governance of the AI Regulation is entrusted to the European AI Office, established at the Commission with functions of coordination, competency development and complaint receipt. Operational oversight is devolved to national regulators, who in the pharmaceutical field include, in Italy, AIFA (for medicinal aspects) and AGCM (for competition aspects). In Italy, with Law No. 132 of 23 September 2025, the legislator adopted the first national regulatory framework on artificial intelligence, designating the ACN and AgID as competent authorities and providing sector-specific provisions on healthcare, labor and public administration.[19] Administrative sanctions calibrate the severity of the violation, providing for up to 35 million euros or 7% of global turnover for violations of absolute prohibitions; up to 15 million or 3% for violations of high-risk system requirements. In the pharmaceutical context, the sanction could also include withdrawal from the market of the drug developed with non-compliant AI assistance, with significant economic consequences. On the jurisprudential front, the Court of Justice of the European Union received in November 2024 the first request for a preliminary ruling on the AI Regulation (Case C-806/24, District Court of Sofia), concerning the provisions on automated decision-making in Article 86, paragraph 1, a signal of embryonic future jurisprudential development.

5.3 The Directive on Liability for Damage Caused by Defective Products (Directive (EU) 2024/2853)

5.3.1 From the Repealed Directive 85/374 to the New Regime

Directive 85/374/EEC dominated civil liability for defective products for 40 years in Europe. Its historical innovation was the introduction of strict liability (liability without fault), whereby the manufacturer is liable for harm deriving from a product defect regardless of any negligence or intent. This shift rests on a structural informational asymmetry, since the manufacturer knows the manufacturing processes and

[18] *General-Purpose AI Code of Practice*, published 10 July 2025 and endorsed by the Commission and the AI Board on 1 August 2025; it comprises three chapters, on transparency, copyright, and safety and security. See Arts. 53 and 56, Regulation (EU) 2024/1689. Accessed 7 June 2026.

[19] On national governance, see Art. 70, Regulation (EU) 2024/1689; in Italy, legge 23 settembre 2025, n. 132 (*Gazzetta Ufficiale* n. 223 of 25 September 2025; in force 10 October 2025) designates AgID and ACN as competent authorities. Administrative penalties are governed by Art. 99 of the Regulation.

the risks of a technology in a manner incomparable to the consumer. In the context of pharmaceutical AI, this asymmetry is even more pronounced, since a consumer (patient) has no access to the training data, algorithms, or performance metrics of the system that generated the drug she takes.

Directive 2024/2853 maintains the foundation of strict liability but introduces three substantial transformations. The first widens the concept of product to explicitly include software. The second introduces presumptions of defectiveness when the manufacturer has not observed regulatory requirements. The third limits the development risk defense, the historic loophole that allowed the manufacturer to escape liability by demonstrating that the defect was unknown at the time of commercialization. In the algoraceutical context, this last change is radical.

5.3.2 Software and AI as "Product"

Article 4 of Directive 2024/2853 explicitly expands the notion of product to include software.[20] Simultaneously, the definition of "component" designates an article that can be incorporated into another article and exercise autonomous or auxiliary functions. An AI model for predicting pharmacokinetics that is incorporated into personalized dosage assessment for a patient falls within the definition of component. Article 8, paragraph 1, letter b), renders the manufacturer of the component (the supplier of the AI model) liable alongside the manufacturer of the finished product (the pharmaceutical company that commercializes the drug), and Article 12, paragraph 1, makes them jointly and severally liable. This provision imposes an integration of supply chains that traditionally operated in separate silos.

5.3.3 The Notion of Defectiveness and Continuous Learning Capability

Article 7 of Directive 2024/2853 defines a product as defective when it does not afford "the level of safety that a diligent person is entitled to expect." The evaluation criteria include the presentation of the product, the reasonably foreseeable use, the moment of distribution, and (crucial novelty) "the subsequent evolution" of the product itself.[21] Article 7, paragraph 2, letter c), adds an unprecedented element: "for products endowed with the capacity for continuous learning, the effect on the safety of the product of any capacity of the same to continue learning after being placed in service." This rule revolutionizes the framework of traditional civil liability.

---

[20] Art. 4(1), Directive (EU) 2024/2853 (definition of 'product', expressly including software); see also recital 13.

[21] Art. 7, Directive (EU) 2024/2853 (defectiveness); Art. 7(2)(c) makes relevant the effect on safety of a product's ability to continue to learn or to acquire new features after being placed on the market or put into service.

In the past, liability crystallized at the moment of commercialization; the product was evaluated for its conformity and safety at that precise instant, and the manufacturer did not respond for subsequent deterioration (save for abuse or consumer negligence). In the algoraceutical domain, this temporal frame becomes inadequate. A machine learning model can degrade over time (model drift) due to statistical changes in the data with which it is fed post-commercialization. A pharmacovigilance algorithm could lose predictive capacity as the epidemiological context evolves, with the consequence that a system safe at the moment of placing on the market may become unsafe over time.

Additional defectiveness criteria include, in Article 7, paragraph 2, letters f) and g), inadequate management of cybersecurity risks and failure to observe regulatory requirements. Article 7, paragraph 2, letter g), further renders relevant, for the assessment of defectiveness, any withdrawal of the product from the market for safety reasons ordered by a competent authority.

5.3.4 The Evidentiary Regime and Presumptions

Article 9 of Directive 2024/2853 imposes on the manufacturer a duty of disclosure, that is, to provide the injured party, on request of the authority, with information pertinent to the product, in compliance with data protection legislation.[22] Article 10 articulates the proof regime in three progressive steps.

In the first step, paragraph 2, the legislator establishes a presumption of defectiveness where the defendant fails to disclose the evidence required under Article 9, where the product does not comply with mandatory safety requirements intended to protect against the risk of the harm suffered, or where the harm results from an obvious malfunction of the product during reasonably foreseeable use. In the second degree, paragraph 3, it establishes a presumption of causality, such that where the product is established to be defective and the harm is of a kind typically consistent with the defect in question, the causal nexus is presumed, the defendant retaining in any event the right to rebut the presumption. In the third degree, paragraph 4, the new dimension: "save otherwise provided in this Article, where proof of defectiveness or causality is excessively difficult due to the technical complexity of the product and the technology used, the claimant may ask the court to reverse the burden of proof."[23]

This reversal of the burden of proof is the most important regulatory instrument for algoraceutical liability. The question motivating the norm is as follows: how can the claimant prove that the harm was caused by algorithmic opacity, when that very opacity makes proof impossible? A patient who contracts an unforeseen adverse

[22] Art. 9, Directive (EU) 2024/2853 (disclosure of evidence).

[23] Art. 10, Directive (EU) 2024/2853 (burden of proof): the presumption of defectiveness is in Art. 10(2), the presumption of a causal link in Art. 10(3), and the alleviation of proof where defectiveness or causation is excessively difficult to establish owing to technical or scientific complexity in Art. 10(4).

effect from a drug designed through opaque generative models cannot reasonably analyze the model to prove the causal nexus. Consider the GAN/RANC case described in Chap. 4, Sect. 4.2; in the causal chain leading from training data to toxic molecule, no link is reconstructible. The European legislator recognized this inequality and permitted the court to suspend the general rule of proof, reversing the balance; the manufacturer would then have to prove that the defect did not exist or did not cause the harm. Paragraph 4 of Article 10 is thus the norm that most directly addresses the problem of algorithmic opacity, transforming a technical limitation into a procedural advantage for the injured party.

5.3.5 The Development Risk Defense

Article 11 of Directive 2024/2853 maintains, but with significant limitations, the development risk defense. Paragraph 1, letter e), permits the manufacturer to escape liability where the claimant does not prove that "the state of scientific and technical knowledge at the moment of distribution of the product in question to the consumer did not enable the manufacturer to identify the existence of the defect."[24]

This formulation, consistent with Directive 85/374, poses a radically new question in the algoraceutical context. The state of scientific and technical knowledge (state of the art) is a concept that presupposes an epistemically aware subject, such that the industry, in the abstract, could or could not have known of a given defect at the date of commercialization. But where the manufacturer is an AI, this presupposition does not hold. A deep learning algorithm does not "have awareness" of the state of scientific knowledge; it does not possess declarative knowledge of the achievements of biomedical research. It simply manipulates data according to statistical functions. If a molecule generated by a GAN proved toxic in subsequent tests and the model could not identify this toxicity because the training data did not contain chemically similar molecules, can the manufacturer invoke the defense asserting that "the state of scientific knowledge at the time did not allow prediction"? Or does the algorithmic character of the manufacturer imply a form of more stringent liability?

The question requires a sharp distinction between two levels. At the level of the AI provider (pharmaceutical AI company), the state of scientific knowledge encompasses the achievements of machine learning research, computational chemistry, molecular biochemistry. If the provider was aware of cross-validation techniques that could have mitigated overfitting risk and did not implement them, it cannot invoke the defense. At the level of the AI model itself, the concept of "knowledge" of the state of the art becomes metaphorical. The European legislator provided no explicit answer, leaving this further ambiguity to jurisprudence. See Chap. 6, Sect. 6.3, for legal developments.

[24] Art. 11(1)(e), Directive (EU) 2024/2853 (exemption from liability; the development-risk defense).

Paragraph 2 of Article 11 severely limits the defense, in that where harm is caused by a defect deriving from modifications of the product made by third parties, or from the manufacturer's failure to update the product (where technically and economically feasible) to eliminate a known defect, the defense is not available.[25] For adaptive algorithms, this constraint is disruptive; the manufacturer cannot limit itself to providing the model and disavow itself of its subsequent evolution. If it discovers that the model is generating problematic molecules, it has the obligation to update the system and to withdraw, if necessary, molecules already generated. The cost of this continuous vigilance is significant.

5.3.6 Economic Operators and Chain of Responsibility

Article 8 of Directive 2024/2853 delineates the responsible subjects along the supply chain. The manufacturer is the principal subject. But the Directive widens this category, since a subject that modifies a product can become the manufacturer of the modified version. Article 8, paragraph 2, treats as a manufacturer any person who substantially modifies a product, the notion being defined in Article 4 as any modification of the design, manufacture, or composition of the product not intended or authorized by the original manufacturer that could affect safety.[26] In the context of AI, fine-tuning a model on new data, retraining on a different patient population, or integrating the model with new data sources could constitute substantial modification. If a small or medium enterprise uses the platform of a large AI company and personalizes it for its internal portfolio, it becomes responsible for the conformity of the modified version.

Article 12, paragraph 1, establishes joint and several liability when multiple economic operators have contributed to the harm. In the algoraceutical domain, this means that the injured party can take action against the supplier of the model, the supplier of the training dataset, or the pharmaceutical company that integrated the model into its drug discovery process, and each defendant remains jointly and severally liable for the full amount, even if it contributed only partially to the harm. This provision drives toward responsible integration of supply chains, such that no actor can operate in isolation.

---

[25] Art. 11(2), Directive (EU) 2024/2853, which precludes the development-risk defense where the defect is attributable to a component or related service within the manufacturer's control, or to the manufacturer's failure to provide safety-relevant updates or upgrades.

[26] Art. 8, Directive (EU) 2024/2853 (economic operators liable for defective products); a person who makes a substantial modification to a product, within the meaning of the Directive, is treated as a manufacturer (Art. 8(2), with the definition in Art. 4); joint and several liability of multiple operators is governed by Art. 12(1).

5.4 Withdrawal of the Artificial Intelligence Liability Directive

The Proposed Directive on civil liability related to artificial intelligence (COM(2022) 496) represented a parallel attempt to govern civil liability for AI systems without resorting to traditional notions of product defect or fault. The proposal provided, in Articles 3–4, a presumption of non-conformity where harm was caused by violation of one of the requirements of the AI Regulation or of technical standards correlating with it, and a consequent presumption of causality. The mechanism was elegant and targeted, since it directly aligned civil liability with regulatory compliance, creating compliance incentives.

The proposal was withdrawn in February 2025, with subsequent confirmation in the October 2025 European Council. The official reasons cited preferences for integrating the liability discipline in Directive 2024/2853. But reality is more nuanced. The withdrawal left a significant gap. Directive 2024/2853 disciplines harm from "defective product," a concept that presupposes a tangible good or, by extension, software supplied directly. But what happens with AI services? If a pharmaceutical company uses a Software-as-a-Service (SaaS) drug discovery service supplied by an external platform, without receiving the model itself, does Directive 2024/2853 still apply? Is the service supplier a "manufacturer" of a "product" in the sense of the Directive, or a service provider for whom other rules apply?

These questions remain open. In the Italian panorama, Article 2050 of the civil code (liability for hazardous activities) offers an alternative path, insofar as the provider of an AI service that causes harm to third parties can be held liable if the activity was conducted in a manner not conforming to principles of due diligence. Article 2050 is less specific than Directive 2024/2853 but could offer a subsidiary instrument where the Directive does not apply. For an in-depth examination of this interaction see Chap. 6.

5.5 The Machinery Regulation (Regulation (EU) 2023/1230)

The EU Machinery Regulation 2023/1230, applicable from January 20, 2027, completes the regulatory framework with specific disciplines for physical systems incorporating AI components. The Regulation defines "machinery" as a combination of interconnected parts, of which at least one is mobile, intended to perform a specific application.[27] In the pharmaceutical context, the definition acquires relevance for automated laboratories and robotic systems integrated with AI algorithms.

A concrete example illustrates the point. An automated laboratory for high-throughput screening combining robotic arms, sensors, fluidics systems, and an AI model for optimizing the next series of experiments constitutes a "machine" within

[27] Regulation (EU) 2023/1230 of the European Parliament and of the Council of 14 June 2023 on machinery, OJ L 165, 29 June 2023, applicable from 20 January 2027; see Art. 3(1) for the definition of 'machinery'.

the meaning of the Regulation. The AI software is considered a "component" of the machine, and if its malfunction poses risks to workers or to process continuity, it becomes a "safety component" subject to specific obligations of validation, certification and technical documentation. The Machinery Regulation does not derogate from the obligations of the AI Regulation but overlaps with it, creating a cumulative regulatory framework.

The practical relevance of the Machinery Regulation for algoraceutics is circumscribed but not negligible. Autonomous robotic laboratories described in Chap. 3, such as the University of Cambridge's EVE robot, integrate physical and algorithmic components in a closed loop in which AI does not limit itself to suggesting experiments but executes them. In this scenario, malfunction of the algorithm can translate into malfunction of the machine, with erroneous chemical synthesis, contamination, wrong dosage. The manufacturer of the safety component (in this case, the AI software supplier) is subject to the Regulation's obligations and is liable for harm deriving from malfunction according to the rules of Directive 2024/2853.

5.6 Classification of Pharmaceutical AI Within the European Regulatory Framework

On the basis of the regulations and directives examined, it is possible to delineate a functional classification of pharmaceutical AI in the three principal application pathways. The analysis is not purely theoretical and determines the compliance burden, responsibilities, and regulatory intervention lines.

The first category comprises algorithms for identification and characterization of biological targets, namely predictors of physicochemical properties (LogP, solubility, permeability), protein structure predictors (AlphaFold, RoseTTAFold), molecular docking models. These systems remain in a zone of regulatory marginality. They are not medical devices in the sense of Regulation 2017/745 because they are not directly interfaced with patients nor do they have direct implications for clinical safety. They do not explicitly fall within Annex III of the AI Regulation either. However, if integrated into automated laboratories, they could be subjected to the Machinery Regulation. The applicable regulatory regime remains the general one, with reduced documentation and tracking obligations.

The second category is de novo molecular design through generative models, namely generative adversarial networks (GANs), diffusion models, molecular scaffold generators that produce molecules not present in historical datasets. This is the space of the regulatory gray zone. The argument favoring classification as a high-risk system is that the model generates molecules without prior clinical history, whose safety remains speculative until experimentally validated. The argument against is that the model is not directly interfaced with patients and the pharmaceutical company remains responsible for biological validation before commencing clinical trials. The uncertainty has driven toward case-by-case classification; a generative model supplied as an autonomous tool could be classified as high-risk; the same model, if integrated into a commercial platform as a service, could be treated differently. This ambiguity is a source of friction between regulators and industry. The multilevel opacity of GANs, examined in Chap. 4 with the GAN/RANC case, aggravates the problem, in that for a doubly opaque system, the transparency requirements of Article 13 of the AI Regulation are virtually impossible to satisfy, which makes classification as a high-risk system simultaneously necessary (for the level of intrinsic risk) and problematic (for the impossibility of complying with requirements).

The third category, finally, is patient stratification and pharmacovigilance. Algorithms that identify patients eligible for clinical trials, or that detect adverse signals in post-commercialization databases, directly impact clinical safety and selection of subjects for therapeutic interventions. These systems are clearly classifiable as high-risk. The obligations are significant and include formal risk management, technical documentation, logging, human governance, transparency requirements. The provider's responsibility is full, both under the AI Regulation and under Directive 2024/2853.

The proposed classification does not exhaust empirical complexity. Many contemporary systems are hybrid; a diffusion model for generating candidate compounds is validated through predictive models of properties and the validated compound is then subjected to selection for patient stratification. The entire chain is algorithmically interconnected. The regulatory burden should flow to the riskiest element of the chain (patient stratification), but regulatory practice has not yet stabilized this rule. The result is that pharmaceutical companies investing in integrated AI platforms find themselves navigating a regulatory framework in which classification of the same system can vary depending on which point of the chain one considers, with direct consequences on determination of obligations and responsibilities.

5.7 Technical Standards and Good Practices

Parallel to binding legislation, an articulated system of technical standards and guidance provides tools for concretizing regulatory requirements. In 2023, ISO/IEC published two standards relevant to the pharmaceutical industry, namely ISO/IEC 42001:2023 (AI Management Systems) and ISO/IEC 23894:2023 (AI Risk Management).[28] Both provide PDCA (Plan-Do-Check-Act) frameworks for systematic implementation of AI risk management, with cross-cutting applicability to organizations that develop or use algorithmic systems. On the side of European harmonization, CEN/CENELEC has commenced work on harmonized standards for the AI Regulation. The first standard in public inquiry, prEN 18286 (Quality Management System for AI Act Regulatory Purposes), entered public consultation on October 30, 2025, and, once adopted, will allow presumption of conformity with

[28] ISO/IEC 42001:2023, *Information technology – Artificial intelligence – Management system*; ISO/IEC 23894:2023, *Information technology – Artificial intelligence – Guidance on risk management*.

Regulation requirements. Additional standards in development include prEN 18228 (AI risk management), prEN 18282 (cybersecurity for AI) and prEN 18284 (data quality and governance).

At the sector level, the EMA has published evolving guidance. The ICH Q14 guideline on analytical procedure development includes chapters on the application of AI throughout the drug product lifecycle, with distinction between minor risks (pre-clinical discovery) and maximum risks (patient enrollment and stratification). The EMA Reflection Paper on the Use of Artificial Intelligence (AI) in the Medicinal Product Lifecycle (final version, September 2024) anticipates the intention of more granular pharmaceutical regulation of AI compared to the generic European AI Regulation.[29] The FDA, for its part, published in December 2024 the final version of guidance on Predetermined Change Control Plans for AI-based devices, as well as in January 2025 a further Draft Guidance on the lifecycle of devices with AI-based software functions that provides criteria for distinguishing between minor updates (not requiring revalidation) and major updates (requiring revalidation).[30] These criteria are already flowing into the European panorama, also in light of the Guiding Principles of Good AI Practice in Drug Development published jointly by EMA and FDA on January 14, 2026, which mark a step toward transatlantic regulatory convergence.

On the pharmacovigilance front, the EMA guideline on the use of machine learning in pharmacovigilance (draft 2024) specifies that algorithms employed in the collection and analysis of adverse signals must be validated with historical data, tested on prospective data, and integrated into mandatory human review processes.[31] However, as discussed in Chap. 4, Sect. 4.5, the requirement for human oversight remains paradoxical, such that if the model is opaque, the human reviewer cannot verify its rationale and oversight becomes a legal fiction.

A cross-cutting element in all these standards is the concept of "state of scientific and technical knowledge." The notion recurs in the development risk defense (Directive 2024/2853, Article 11) and in Article 15 of the AI Regulation (accuracy "where technically feasible"). For pharmaceutical AI, the state of the art includes not only formal scientific literature but also the achievements of machine learning research and emerging capabilities of models in use. In the Italian context, the concept will be interpreted by judges on the basis of preexisting doctrine on product liability.[32] Extension to the algoraceutical domain remains charged with uncertainty,

---

[29] EMA, *Reflection paper on the use of artificial intelligence in the lifecycle of medicines*, EMA/CHMP/CVMP/83833/2023, final, September 2024, accessed 7 June 2026.

[30] FDA, *Marketing Submission Recommendations for a Predetermined Change Control Plan for Artificial Intelligence-Enabled Device Software Functions*, final guidance, December 2024; FDA, *Artificial Intelligence-Enabled Device Software Functions: Lifecycle Management and Marketing Submission Recommendations*, draft guidance, January 2025; EMA and FDA, *Guiding Principles of Good AI Practice in Drug Development*, 14 January 2026. Accessed 7 June 2026.

[31] On machine learning in pharmacovigilance, see EMA, draft guidance on the use of artificial intelligence and machine learning in pharmacovigilance (2024).

[32] On the 'state of scientific and technical knowledge', see Art. 11(1)(e), Directive (EU) 2024/2853, and Art. 15, Regulation (EU) 2024/1689 (accuracy 'where technically feasible').

in the sense that if the state of the art includes what an algorithm could have discovered, the defense narrows drastically; if it includes it only to the extent the manufacturer knew or should have known it, the problem shifts to the diligence of the manufacturer in updating and validating its models.

The European regulatory framework examined here is characterized by a stratification of normative acts which, applied to the algoraceutical fact pattern, produce a complex regime not without overlaps. The AI Regulation provides the general framework of obligations for high-risk systems; Directive 2024/2853 disciplines liability for harm produced by defective systems; the Machinery Regulation covers systems incorporated in physical devices. The absence of the Artificial Intelligence Liability Directive leaves a void for fact patterns that do not fall within the notion of defective product. The classification of algoraceutical applications remains uncertain for molecular design activities, which are situated in a gray zone between laboratory research and the medical device. This uncertainty is not immaterial, since it determines the burden of obligations, the liability regime, and, ultimately, the propensity of industry to invest in AI systems for drug discovery in the European market.

The following chapters will examine how this regulatory framework translates into concrete questions. Civil liability for the harm that the algorithm contributes to producing (Chap. 6), intellectual property for the invention that the algorithm contributes to generating (Chap. 7), competition for the market that the algorithm contributes to reshaping (Chap. 8), regulation for the ecosystem of rules that must govern a process in which human decision is progressively substituted by algorithmic decision (Chap. 9).

Civil Liability and the Algoraceutical Product

6

Abstract

This chapter analyses civil liability for harm caused by the algoraceutical drug, the medicinal product whose discovery or design depends on artificial intelligence. It situates the problem at the intersection of two Italian regimes, liability for dangerous activities under Article 2050 of the Civil Code and producer liability under the Consumer Code, and the reformed European framework of Directive (EU) 2024/2853. The analysis shows how the extended notion of product, the inclusion of continuous learning within the concept of defect, the presumptions that alleviate the claimant's burden of proof, and the restriction of the development-risk defense reshape the allocation of responsibility along the pharmaceutical supply chain. Particular attention is devoted to algorithmic opacity as the structural obstacle to proving causation, to the residual role of Article 2050 after the withdrawal of the proposed Artificial Intelligence Liability Directive, and to the use of the AI Act obligations as parameters of diligence. Five scenarios, from fully internal development to *in silico* clinical trials and explainability as evidence, test the framework against industrial practice. The chapter concludes that liability for the algoraceutical drug occupies an expanded zone in which product, presumption, and causation jointly redefine the producer's exposure.

6.1 Introduction: Artificial Intelligence as a Productive Technique and Its Impact on Liability

Artificial intelligence is not merely a computation tool, a sort of sophisticated calculator that reduces data processing times. It is a genuine productive technique that intervenes directly in the design and development of algoraceutical drugs, altering three fundamental pillars of civil liability: the burden of proof, the reconstruction of causation, and the applicability of the development risk defense. This chapter

G. Rotino, *Algoraceutics - Legal Perspectives on Artificial Intelligence in Drug Discovery and Development*, Law for Professionals,
https://doi.org/10.1007/978-3-032-38537-6_6

addresses the central question of civil liability in the algoraceutical context, bringing into dialogue the positive law in force with the theoretical problems underlying the use of AI systems in the critical phases of pharmaceutical discovery.

The algoraceutical drug represents a new category of dangerous product, namely an entity that is not a simple combination of drug and software, but a hybrid entity in which the therapeutic function is generated by the continuous interaction between the molecule and the algorithmic system that conceived it. This phenomenon introduces a notion hitherto absent from civil liability law, that of the "algoraceutical datum," meaning the therapeutically relevant information that the AI system extracts from the training data and that embodies the system's judgment concerning the toxicological, pharmacokinetic, and pharmacodynamic profile of a molecule. The present chapter…

The path we shall take is structured as follows. We shall first examine the regulatory framework in force regarding drug-related damage liability, both according to Article 2050 of the Italian Civil Code (art. 2050 c.c.) and according to the Italian Consumer Code (Codice del Consumo). We shall then advance toward Directive (EU) 2024/2853, which extends producer liability to defects that emerge post-distribution in a formulation revolutionary for the algoraceutical context. We shall then address the regulatory gap left by the withdrawal of the proposed AI Liability Directive (the so-called AILD), demonstrating how Article 2050 c.c. remains the cornerstone of protection, integrated by the principles of the AI Regulation. We shall then examine the problem of reconstructing causation in an opaque system, introducing Searle's "Chinese Room" argument as a theoretical foundation for justifying presumptions of liability. Finally, we shall analyze five concrete scenarios of liability allocation and two specific case studies (GAN/RANC and DeepTox) that illustrate how theory translates into forensic practice.

Before proceeding, it is worthwhile to recall some fundamental concepts developed in the previous chapters. Algorithmic opacity (Chap. 4) is the ontological prerequisite from which derives the impossibility of deterministically reconstructing causation.[1] The distinction between drug and medicinal product (Chap. 3) determines which liability regime is prevalent and what the "space of responsibility" is between regulatory certification and algorithmic integrity.[2] The autonomy of the algoraceutical system (Chap. 4) raises the central problem of who commands when the system makes decisions that are nominally human but factually elaborated by a synthetic neural network.

6.2 Drug-Related Civil Liability in Italian Law

6.2.1 Article 2050 of the Italian Civil Code and Dangerous Activity

Article 2050 of the Italian Civil Code (art. 2050 c.c.) constitutes the foundation of civil liability of pharmaceutical producers in Italian law. The provision establishes

[1] On algorithmic opacity as the epistemic premise of the causal problem, see Chap. 4.

[2] On the interaction between regulatory certification and civil liability, see also Chap. 5.

that one who causes damage to others by means of a dangerous activity, even if lawful, is liable for the damage unless he proves that he has adopted all measures suitable to prevent it.[3] The regime is singular with respect to common law, in the sense that it is not the injured party who must prove fault or negligence of the tortfeasor, but the latter who must prove the contrary, namely that he has employed all the diligence required. This is a form of presumptive liability that reverses the burden of proof once the dangerous activity and the damage deriving therefrom are established.

Pharmaceutical activity is undoubtedly dangerous. A drug, by its nature, contains pharmacologically active properties which, even when administered at therapeutic doses, can generate adverse effects that are often serious. The famous dictum of Paracelsus, according to which "all substances are poisonous; nothing is free from toxins. Only the dose makes the poison," expresses the concept that the drug is always, by its essence, a substance with both therapeutic and potentially harmful properties. This duality of the pharmakon, taken up from the Greek philosophical tradition,[4] is the legal prerequisite for the application of Article 2050 c.c.

The drug possesses an intrinsically dangerous nature. It is not an accidental danger due to a manufacturing defect or to producer negligence, but an ontological danger linked to its very therapeutic efficacy. Precisely because the drug acts on the human body by modifying its biological functions, it inescapably carries the risk of adverse effects. Jurisprudence has recognized this principle, establishing that Article 2050 c.c. applies fully to drugs and that the producer cannot invoke the lawfulness of his activity to escape civil liability. To the contrary, the lawfulness of drug commercialization is accompanied by a rigorous obligation of diligence.

Jurisprudence has confirmed that a drug manufacturer must prove that it has adopted all measures suitable to prevent damage, not only in the development and authorization phase, but also in formulation, communication of risks, and post-commercialization pharmacovigilance.[5] A report of great relevance prepared by the Ministry of Economic Development (MISE) in 2019[6] emphasized that the adoption of AI systems in pharmaceutical research must conform to the same principles of transparency, traceability, and human review that positive law imposes on traditional drugs. The concept of "all suitable measures" has progressively broadened to include obligations of knowledge of the state of the art, implementation of automated controls, continuous data monitoring, and updating of information systems where new toxicological evidence emerges.

[3] Art. 2050 of the Italian Civil Code: whoever causes damage to another in the performance of a dangerous activity, by its nature or by the nature of the means employed, is liable unless he proves that he adopted all suitable measures to avoid the damage.

[4] On the ambivalence of the *pharmakon* in the Greek tradition, see Plato, *Phaedrus*, 274e–275a.

[5] On the diachronic structure of pharmaceutical liability (development, authorization, formulation, risk communication, pharmacovigilance), see Chap. 9.

[6] Gruppo di esperti del MISE sull'intelligenza artificiale, *Proposte per una strategia italiana per l'intelligenza artificiale* (2019), which identified Art. 2050 of the Italian Civil Code as the reference rule for damage caused by AI. Accessed 7 June 2026.

In the context of the algoraceutical drug, the concept of "suitable measures" acquires an even more complex dimension. Suitable measures are not limited to preclinical and clinical validation of the molecule according to FDA or EMA standards. Suitable measures now also include validation of the algorithm that generated the molecule, documentation of the training data, analysis of the system's limits and biases, and implementation of post-commercialization surveillance mechanisms that monitor not only the clinical behavior of the molecule, but also the behavior of the algorithm in the context of new molecules generated subsequently. A producer who implements an algorithm for pharmaceutical discovery without this complex of measures has not satisfied the obligation under Article 2050 c.c., regardless of the regulatory compliance of each individual molecule generated.

Moreover, the concept of diligence in the algoraceutical context introduces a responsibility of "continuous learning" on the part of the producer. The moment a molecule generated by the algorithm causes an unexpected harm, the producer cannot simply assert that the risk was unknowable at the time of commercialization. The producer must interrogate its algorithm, asking itself whether the system could learn to avoid this specific harm on the basis of better data and whether it could learn to recognize this type of molecule as problematic. If the answer is yes, then the producer had the obligation to update the algorithm. This continuous responsibility contrasts sharply with the regime of Directive 85/374/EEC, where the development risk defense operates as a fixed temporal snapshot at the moment of putting into circulation.

6.2.2 Consumer Protection Rules and the Italian Consumer Code

The Italian Consumer Code (Codice del Consumo), which implements Directive 85/374/EEC on product liability, introduces a parallel regime and, in certain aspects, an alternative one with respect to Article 2050 c.c.[7] Articles 114–127 of Legislative Decree 206/2005 (d.lgs. 206/2005) govern producer liability for damages caused by product defects. Unlike Article 2050 c.c., which presumes liability on the basis of the dangerousness of the activity, the Consumer Code requires that the injured party prove three elements, namely the product defect, the damage, and the causal link. However, once these three elements are proved, the producer's liability is objective, independent of any fault.

A central element of consumer protection rules is the development risk defense, introduced in Article 118 of Legislative Decree 206/2005 (d.lgs. 206/2005).[8] According to this provision, the producer is not liable if he proves that the defect could not have been known on the basis of the scientific and technical knowledge available at the time of distribution. This defense has a subtle logical structure, as it does not ask whether the producer could have known, but whether the defect was

[7] Codice del consumo, d.lgs. 6 September 2005, n. 206, Arts. 114 ff. (transposing Directive 85/374/EEC), which establishes a regime parallel to Art. 2050 of the Italian Civil Code.

[8] Art. 118, d.lgs. 206/2005 (development-risk defense).

knowable in the abstract on the basis of the state of scientific art. This is a presumption of fact in favor of the producer, subject to a heavy burden of proof.

"Putting into circulation," namely the temporal moment at which the defect is evaluated, is that of the initial distribution of the product to the market.[9] At this temporal point defects crystallize. A defect that becomes knowable 3 years after commercialization will not necessarily render the producer liable, because it was unknowable at the time of distribution. This principle will have significant consequences when we examine Article 11(2) of Directive (EU) 2024/2853, which deviates from this scheme for AI systems.

However, there is a "perverse effect" in the consumer protection regime that deserves attention in the algoraceutical context. Regulatory compliance can transform itself into a ceiling of diligence, in the sense that a producer who has obtained Marketing Authorization (AIC) from the regulatory authority might feel legitimated to cease its monitoring and improvement efforts subsequently. In reality, regulatory certification does not exempt the producer from the obligations under Article 2050 c.c. The AIC license represents a judgment on safety at the moment of distribution, not a perpetual safe passage. In the context of the algoraceutical drug, this problem expands, since the algorithm continues to learn (if implemented with continuous updates) and therefore continues to evolve. The producer cannot invoke the initial certification of the model to justify the omission of subsequent updates that would have prevented the harm.

6.2.3 Interaction Between the Two Regimes

Article 127 of Legislative Decree 206/2005 (d.lgs. 206/2005) operates a conjunction between the Consumer Code and other rules on civil liability, including Article 2050 c.c.[10] According to this provision, the rules of the Consumer Code do not exclude recourse to other rules on civil liability, provided they are more favorable to the injured party. This means that the injured party can choose to act according to the Consumer Code or according to Article 2050 c.c., depending on which regime allows him to obtain a greater degree of protection.

In the context of the algoraceutical drug, recourse to Article 2050 c.c. appears prevalent. The reason is twofold. First, Article 2050 c.c. reverses the burden of proof in favor of the injured party the moment the dangerous activity and the damage deriving therefrom are established. Second, Article 2050 c.c. does not provide the development risk defense, except in the most restricted form of an outright denial of the dangerousness of the activity, something that can scarcely be sustained in the context of a molecule that produces adverse effects. Artificial intelligence, far from reducing recourse to Article 2050 c.c., reinforces its application, since the opacity

[9] Arts. 117 and 120, d.lgs. 206/2005 (defect assessed at the time the product is put into circulation).

[10] Art. 127, d.lgs. 206/2005, which preserves the application of other rules on civil liability, including Art. 2050 of the Italian Civil Code.

of the algorithmic system makes it even more difficult for the producer to prove that it has employed all suitable measures.

6.3 Producer Liability in Light of Directive (EU) 2024/2853

6.3.1 The Algoraceutical Drug as a "Product"

Directive (EU) 2024/2853 extends the notion of "product" to explicitly include software and artificial intelligence systems.[11] The extension is significant because for decades European jurisprudence has debated whether software, as an immaterial entity, could fall within the concept of "product" as originally intended by Directive 85/374/EEC. Directive (EU) 2024/2853 resolves the doubt by affirming that software is a product and that an AI system, whatever its degree of autonomy and complexity, is the responsibility of its producer.

Also decisive is the definition of "component."[12] A component is any article that forms an integral part of a product and whose removal prevents the product from functioning as intended. In the context of the algoraceutical drug, the algorithm for predicting toxicity or molecular structure is unquestionably a component. This means that the producer of the algorithm, even where it is not the final producer of the drug, remains liable for the quality and defects of the component that it has provided.

Article 8, paragraph 1, letter b) of the Directive expressly establishes that the producer of a component is liable even when the component is incorporated into a product by another producer.[13] This means that in the case of an algoraceutical drug, liability extends not only to the producer of the final medicinal product (the holder of Marketing Authorization), but also to the producer of the algorithm and, possibly, to the one who provided the training data used to train the AI system. A chain of liability is thus generated that, as we shall see, has profound implications for the attribution of damage.

6.3.2 The Concept of Defect: The Drug/Medicinal Product Distinction as an Interpretive Pivot

Directive (EU) 2024/2853 defines defect as "any lack of safety or any characteristic, including the behavior of the product, that a person is entitled to expect, taking into

[11] Art. 4(1), Directive (EU) 2024/2853 (definition of 'product', expressly including software).

[12] Art. 4(4), Directive (EU) 2024/2853 (definition of 'component').

[13] Art. 8, Directive (EU) 2024/2853 (liability of the manufacturer of a defective component incorporated into another product).

account all relevant factors."[14] In the context of the algoraceutical drug, this definition must be read in light of the distinction between drug and medicinal product taken up from Chap. 3.[15] The drug, as a substance with intrinsic therapeutic properties, is subject to rigid evaluation of efficacy and safety by the regulatory authorities. The medicinal product, as the authorized formulation of that drug, is the product that actually circulates on the market and on which the attention of liability law is focused.

In an algoraceutical drug, there is a "space of responsibility" that separates two zones: the zone of regulatory certification, within which the regulatory authorities have evaluated the drug on the basis of data presented by the producer, and the zone of algorithmic integrity, within which the AI system continues to operate post-authorization, possibly discovering risks that the pre-commercialization clinical trials had not detected. The notion of defect, in the algoraceutical context, embraces not only defects manifest at the moment of authorization, but also defects that emerge from the post-distribution evolution of the system.

6.3.3 Article 7, Paragraph 2, Letter c) and the Capacity for Continuous Learning

One of the most revolutionary provisions of Directive (EU) 2024/2853 is Article 7, paragraph 2, letter c), which extends the notion of defect to include not only what the product contains, but also what the product should have learned and did not learn.[16] In the context of an AI system capable of continuous learning, this means that the product can become defective over time, not due to an external change, but due to its own inertia in learning.

This formulation is particularly relevant for deep learning systems employed in pharmaceutical discovery. If an AI system for predicting toxicity is trained on a dataset that does not contain information on certain damage mechanisms (for example, epoxidation, as in the DeepTox case), the system will remain "blind" to this mechanism even after distribution. Article 7, paragraph 2, letter c) transforms this silence from an acceptable characteristic of the system into a defect, because the system could, in principle, acquire this knowledge from a more complete dataset or from an improved training methodology.

The direct consequence is that the producer of an AI system has the continuous obligation to evaluate whether the system is committing systematic errors and, if so, to update the model. This continuous obligation is cemented by Article 11(2),[17] which excludes the availability of the development risk defense precisely in the case

[14] Art. 7(1), Directive (EU) 2024/2853 (defectiveness).

[15] On the distinction between drug and medicinal product, see Chap. 3.

[16] Art. 7(2)(c), Directive (EU) 2024/2853.

[17] Art. 11(2), Directive (EU) 2024/2853 (obligation to provide safety-relevant updates; exclusion of the development-risk defense in case of omission).

where the defect consists in the omission of software updates that the producer was capable of providing.

6.3.4 Burden of Proof and Presumptions

Article 10 of Directive (EU) 2024/2853 governs the burden of proof in matters of liability for defective products. As a general rule,[18] the burden remains with the injured party, who must prove the defect, the damage, and the causal link. However, paragraph 4 of Article 10 introduces a presumption that favors the injured party where the technical complexity of the product makes direct proof excessively difficult.[19]

In the context of an AI system, technical complexity is notoriously maximal. A deep learning system with billions of parameters is not intrinsically transparent and even to its designers it is not always clear how the system arrives at a particular decision. Article 10(4) therefore allows the court to presume the fault of the producer in the case where the injured party proves the defect and the damage, without need to prove how the system arrived at producing that defect. This presumption is a procedural tool that compensates for the ontological opacity of the AI system.

In addition, Article 9 of the Directive permits disclosure orders,[20] a mechanism of administrative justice whereby the court can order the producer to disclose the technical information relevant to the case, provided that this does not violate intellectual property rights or trade secrets protected by Directive 2016/943.[21] An equilibrium is thus created between the need for adequate proof by the injured party and the protection of the producer's industrial secrets.

However, in an algoraceutical drug, the mechanism of disclosure orders presents additional peculiar complexities. An AI system trained on highly sensitive data (for example, confidential clinical data from previous patients) cannot be disclosed integrally without violating privacy rights. On the other hand, the search for equilibrium between protection of innovation and the claimant's right to defense creates concrete barriers for injured parties attempting to prove causation. The economic and temporal cost of an expert assessment to reconstruct the internal behavior of the system can prove prohibitive, effectively preventing access to justice. Article 10(4), with its presumption against the producer, thus proves to be a decisive tool for balancing this informational asymmetry.[22]

---

[18] Art. 10, Directive (EU) 2024/2853 (burden of proof).

[19] Art. 10(4), Directive (EU) 2024/2853 (alleviation of the burden of proof where defectiveness or causation is excessively difficult to prove owing to technical or scientific complexity).

[20] Art. 9, Directive (EU) 2024/2853 (disclosure of evidence).

[21] Directive (EU) 2016/943 on the protection of undisclosed know-how and business information (trade secrets); see Art. 9(4), Directive (EU) 2024/2853 on the proportionate protection of confidential information.

[22] Art. 10(4), Directive (EU) 2024/2853 (reversal of the burden of proof).

6.3.5 The Development Risk Defense in the Algorithmic Era

Article 11(1)(e) of Directive (EU) 2024/2853 maintains the availability of the development risk defense in the algoraceutical context, albeit with a slightly amended formulation, according to which the producer is not liable if it proves that the defect could not have been known on the basis of the scientific and technical knowledge available.[23] The central interpretive question consists in determining what "available" means in the context of an AI system.

On this point, we sustain an intermediate thesis.[24] On the one hand, a restrictive interpretation is not tenable, according to which the defect must be known at the moment of commercialization by all producers in the field, because this would lead to excluding the defense in nearly all cases where there is even a single voice in the scientific literature that mentions the risk. On the other hand, neither is a broad interpretation tenable, according to which the producer can invoke the defense where the risk was theoretically foreseeable but not known in practice, because this would empty the Directive of meaning, particularly in the algoraceutical context.

The intermediate thesis proposed is as follows. The development risk defense remains available even in the algoraceutical context, but must be interpreted in light of the best machine learning technology available at the moment of commercialization. If the best AI available on the market could have detected the defect through a standard training methodology, then the producer cannot invoke the defense. If, to the contrary, even the best available AI could not have detected the defect (for example, due to a gap in the sector's reference data), then the defense remains available. This approach maintains the defense but raises it to a more severe standard, consistent with the continuous obligation to update sanctioned by Article 11(2).

The proposed intermediate thesis reflects an attempt to balance two opposing needs. On the one hand, one cannot demand of the producer omniscient knowledge of all potentially possible toxicological risks; on the other hand, in the context of a machine learning system operating in a well-structured scientific domain (toxicology is a science with consolidated literature), it is reasonable to expect that the producer incorporate into its training set known and documented damage mechanisms. The producer who deliberately omits from the training set available toxicological information incurs a violation of diligence, regardless of whether the best contemporary techniques could have nonetheless failed to detect the specific mechanism of the molecule.

For a more detailed treatment of this thesis and its concrete implications, we refer to Chap. 4, Sect. 4.4, where the DeepTox case is analyzed as a practical application of this interpretive scheme.[25]

---

[23] Art. 11(1)(e), Directive (EU) 2024/2853 (development-risk defense).

[24] On the author's intermediate thesis on the development-risk defense, see Sect. 6.3.5 below.

[25] On the DeepTox case, see Chap. 4, Sect. 4.4.

6.4 The Regulatory Gap Following Withdrawal of the AI Liability Directive

6.4.1 Article 2050 c.c. as a Safeguard Clause

The European Commission had proposed in 2022 a specific Directive on AI liability (COM(2022) 496).[26] The text would have constituted the first systematic attempt to address the problem of civil and administrative liability in AI systems at the European level. However, the text was withdrawn in February 2025 due to pressure from the technology industry and disagreements among Member States over the definition of "artificial intelligence" and the scope of liability.

This withdrawal leaves a significant regulatory gap. There is currently no specific European Union legislation on AI liability. The framework in force remains fragmented, entrusted to sectoral rules (the Consumer Code, the Regulations on medicinal products, the AI Regulation) and common law rules (such as Article 2050 c.c.). In this context of regulatory uncertainty, Article 2050 c.c. assumes even greater relevance as a safeguard clause.[27]

The reason is structural. Article 2050 c.c. does not require identification of an "intention" of the actor, nor does it presuppose that the tortfeasor was perfectly aware of the risk that hung over his activity. It establishes that whoever exercises a dangerous activity is liable for damage deriving therefrom, unless he proves he has adopted all suitable measures to prevent it. In the context of an AI system, whose opacity is ontological and not merely epistemic, this scheme is particularly suited. The producer of an algoraceutical drug must prove not only that the system works well, but that he has adopted all reasonable measures to prevent harm. This proof, in the case of an AI system, is considerably difficult and justifiably so, because the risk is considerably elevated.

6.4.2 AI Regulation Requirements as Diligence Parameters

Although Regulation (EU) 2024/1689 is not directly applicable to civil liability (it is an administrative regulation of producer compliance), its requirements operate as diligence parameters in the context of Article 2050 c.c.[28] In other words, when a court evaluates whether the producer of an algoraceutical drug has adopted "all suitable measures," it can consult the positive obligations provided by the AI Regulation as concrete indices of diligence. These obligations, already analyzed in Chap. 5,[29] include the following.

---

[26] Proposal for a Directive on adapting non-contractual civil liability rules to artificial intelligence (AI Liability Directive), COM(2022) 496 final, 28 September 2022; withdrawn in 2025 (see Chap. 5, Sect. 5.4).

[27] Art. 2050 of the Italian Civil Code.

[28] On the use of the AI Act obligations as parameters of diligence, see Arts. 9–15, Regulation (EU) 2024/1689, and Chap. 5, Sects. 5.2.4–5.2.5.

[29] Arts. 9–15, Regulation (EU) 2024/1689 (requirements for high-risk systems).

(a) Article 9 of the AI Regulation Governs Risk Management A producer who does not implement any system for assessing and mitigating algorithmic risk has certainly not adopted the suitable measures according to Article 2050 c.c. Risk analysis must be documented, traceable, and subject to continuous review.

(b) Article 10 Governs Data Quality An AI system trained on poor quality data, not representative of the target population or affected by systematic bias, is not suitable. The producer must demonstrate that it has adopted measures to ensure data quality, their completeness, and their representativeness with respect to the phenomena that the system must predict.

(c) Article 13 Governs Transparency and Information The producer must provide clear information on the capabilities and limitations of the AI system. In the context of an algoraceutical drug, this means documenting which types of molecules the system was trained to evaluate and which damage mechanisms remain beyond its predictive capacity.

(d) Article 14 Governs Meaningful Human Oversight An AI system used in pharmaceutical discovery must not operate in a completely autonomous manner; it must be subject to human review by expert pharmacologists and chemists, who have authority for veto and override. Human oversight must be documented and must include a register of cases in which the supervisor disagreed with the algorithm's suggestion.

(e) Article 15 Governs Accuracy, Robustness, and Cybersecurity The system must be tested against adversarial examples (examples constructed to deceive the system) and must include mechanisms of protection against manipulation, data injection, and other cyber attacks.

This "*de facto* harmonization" between the administrative discipline of the AI Regulation and the civil discipline of Article 2050 c.c. creates a systematic coherence that, while not formally required by positive law, is solidly rooted in the logic of liability for dangerous activity.[30]

6.4.3 The Technological Unknown and the Fallacy of Algorithmic Neutrality. Refutation of the Thesis of Non-liability of AI Systems

The applicability of Article 2050 c.c. to artificial intelligence systems has recently been challenged with arguments that merit analytical confrontation. In an editorial

[30] On liability for dangerous activities, see Art. 2050 of the Italian Civil Code and the case law cited below.

appearing recently in an important journal,[31] it was argued that AI cannot be qualified as an intrinsically dangerous activity, nor as an entity endowed with illicit autonomy, rather appearing as a "functional amplifier" operating within the scope of human choices. Civil liability, according to this thesis, should rest exclusively on the user, the only subject capable of exercising an effective power of prevention.

The central argument of this thesis rests on what we can define as the fallacy of instrumental neutrality. According to this view, since the same machine can generate an innocent textual summary or contribute to a distorted business decision, what separates the lawful from the unlawful would be the conduct of the user, not an immanent risk to the activity. This argument, however, has been formulated and refuted many times in the history of science and technology, concerning substances and technologies that later proved to be intrinsically dangerous.

Asbestos, used for over a century as thermal insulation, was considered an inert and safe material; it could be used to build roofs, piping, gaskets, in a completely "harmless" manner. Its fibrous structure, however, generated an endogenous danger that transcended the specific use, namely the capacity to release carcinogenic microfibers upon inhalation. The causal relationship with mesothelioma was established only in 1964, after a century of exposure; Italy banned asbestos with Law No. 257 of 1992.[32] DDT, awarded the Nobel Prize in 1948 for its benefits in combating epidemics, was for over 20 years considered a safe product; its bioaccumulation in the food chain was a risk unknown to the state of knowledge of the era.[33] Thalidomide, marketed by Chemie Grünenthal as "the safest sedative on the market," was prescribed to pregnant women for morning sickness, causing approximately ten thousand cases of phocomelia; the teratogenicity studies of the era were unable to detect the mechanism endogenous to the molecule.[34] Diethylstilbestrol (DES), prescribed to over ten million women in pregnancy between 1940 and 1971, revealed its own carcinogenic effects only a generation later, in the daughters of treated women. Perfluoroalkyl substances (PFAS), used for decades as "inert" components in nonstick cookware and waterproof textiles, revealed chronic toxicity due to bioaccumulation in human tissues that the chemical knowledge of the era did not permit to foresee.[35]

The parallelism with artificial intelligence is structural. The algorithm, like asbestos or DDT, presents an endogenous danger that does not depend on specific use but on its own technical nature, a danger that we can designate as the technological unknown. This danger manifests itself in at least four forms. The first is structural opacity (black box), whereby machine learning models, and in particular deep neural networks, produce statistical correlations uninterpretable by the

[31] On the doctrinal critique of strict liability for AI systems, see the recent debate discussed in the text.

[32] Legge 27 March 1992, n. 257 (cessation of the use of asbestos). The causal link with mesothelioma was scientifically established only in 1964.

[33] On the delayed recognition of the toxicity of DDT, a further example of development risk.

[34] On the thalidomide tragedy and its role in the evolution of pharmaceutical liability, see Chap. 9.

[35] On per- and polyfluoroalkyl substances (PFAS) as a further example of development risk.

designer himself; this is not a correctable defect but a constitutive characteristic of the technology.[36] The second is the phenomenon of hallucinations, whereby generative models produce false but formally coherent content, whose erroneous character is not recognizable to the average user; this risk is intrinsic to the statistical functioning of the model, not to the application context. The third is the bias incorporated in the training data, in that the systematic prejudices present in the datasets translate into algorithmic discriminations that operate independently of the user's intention.[37] The fourth is the emergence of unexpected behaviors (emergent capabilities), whereby large models manifest capacities not programmed nor anticipated by designers, which constitute by definition an uncontrollable risk *ex ante*.

To assert that these dangers are not "intrinsic" to AI is like asserting that asbestos was not intrinsically dangerous because it could also be encapsulated without releasing fibers, or that thalidomide was not intrinsically dangerous because it caused harm only if taken during pregnancy. The danger ceases to be endogenous for the fact that it requires an application context to manifest itself. The analogy, moreover, can be pushed further. Chemical components for manufacturing explosives do not become "harmful" until combined with other elements; ammonium nitrate is a fertilizer until certain conditions trigger its detonation. Yet law qualifies it as a dangerous substance because its capacity to cause harm is intrinsic to its chemical structure. The algorithm is in the same position, given that its capacity to produce erroneous, discriminatory, or harmful output is intrinsic to its statistical architecture, independent of the user's intention.

Nor is it tenable the thesis that Article 2050 c.c. would presuppose a risk operating "independently" of use. The Court of Cassation has qualified as dangerous activity the production and distribution of electrical energy,[38] which produces damage only in case of contact or distribution defect. It has qualified as dangerous activity the production of toxic waste,[39] although waste becomes harmful only in certain environmental conditions. The argument that the risk does not lie in the algorithm but in the "combination of contextual decision and instrumental use" could be formulated identically for any dangerous activity; taken to its logical consequences, it would dissolve the entire field of application of Article 2050 c.c.

As for the thesis that responsibility should concentrate on the user as the only subject endowed with "factual proximity" and an effective power of prevention, it is vitiating by a relevant factual error. In the current state of technology, the user of an AI system does not have the power of prevention attributed to him, for at least three reasons. First, there is a radical informational asymmetry, in that the user, even if a qualified professional, does not have access to the model's parameters, training data, internal performance metrics; the opacity of the system is not a correctable

[36] On the constitutive, non-correctable character of algorithmic opacity, see Chap. 4.

[37] On bias in training data, see Chap. 4, Sect. 4.3, and Art. 10, Regulation (EU) 2024/1689.

[38] On the qualification of the production and distribution of electrical energy as a dangerous activity under Art. 2050 of the Italian Civil Code, see the consistent case law of the Corte di Cassazione.

[39] On the qualification of the production of toxic waste as a dangerous activity, see the case law of the Corte di Cassazione on Art. 2050 of the Italian Civil Code.

accident but a structural fact that renders illusory the power of prevention. Second, in many pharmaceutical contexts the output of the algorithm is not verifiable by the user through ordinary means. If a system suggests a candidate molecule or identifies a protein target, the researcher cannot verify the correctness of the prediction except through the experimentation itself, that is, after the risk has already materialized. Third, the producer and designer of the system have a significant power of prevention that cannot be underestimated, namely the selection and curation of training data, the choice of model architecture, the implementation of guardrails and safety filters, pre-release testing, and post-commercialization monitoring. These are obligations that the AI Regulation explicitly imposes on providers of high-risk systems,[40] confirming that the European legislator recognizes in the producer, not in the user, the subject with the greatest power of prevention.

For algoraceutics, these considerations take on even greater force. If pharmaceutical activity is dangerous activity ex Article 2050 c.c., as consolidated by the jurisprudence examined in Sect. 6.2.1, and if AI is employed as an essential tool of that same activity, algoraceutical activity necessarily inherits its qualification. The insertion of the algorithm into the pharmaceutical pipeline does not attenuate the dangerousness of the activity; it stratifies it, adding to the traditional pharmacological risk the endogenous algorithmic risk. Even if one were to admit, purely hypothetically and for the sake of argument, that AI as such does not constitute dangerous activity, its application to an activity already qualified as dangerous by jurisprudence accentuates, not reduces, its risk profile. A dangerous activity does not cease to be so because it is exercised with new tools; to the contrary, the introduction of tools that add opacity and unpredictability aggravates its dangerousness.

There remains to be refuted the residual argument that extending liability to the producer of the AI system would freeze innovation, generating a "technological desert." The chilling effect argument is historically refuted in every sector in which it has been invoked. Liability of the drug producer has not prevented the development of the pharmaceutical industry; liability of the vehicle producer has not prevented the automobile industry; liability for environmental harm has not prevented the chemical industry. In all these cases, liability has incentivized safer innovation, not the absence of innovation.[41] The argument, moreover, mirrors the historical defensive strategies of the asbestos and tobacco industries, which contended that regulation would destroy entire productive sectors. In both cases, the argument proved unfounded. The industries transformed themselves; they did not disappear.

Article 2050 c.c., therefore, remains not only applicable but necessary in the algoraceutical context. Its function as a safeguard clause, already highlighted in Sect. 6.4.1, is reinforced by the consideration that the endogenous danger of the algorithm presents the same structure as technological risks that the history of science has repeatedly demonstrated to be unknown at the time of technology introduction and recognizable only retrospectively. The absence in the Article 2050 c.c. regime of the development risk defense, available instead in Directive (EU)

[40] Arts. 9–16, Regulation (EU) 2024/1689 (obligations of providers of high-risk systems).

[41] On the relationship between liability and the incentive to safer innovation, see Chap. 5, Sect. 5.1.

2024/2853, makes this norm the most effective instrument to protect the injured party in the context of algoraceutics, where the technological unknown is not an exception but a structural fact.

6.5 Searle's "Chinese Room" and Causation

The argument of the "Chinese Room" formulated by John Searle in 1980,[42] already examined in Chap. 2,[43] constitutes the theoretical foundation for understanding why the reconstruction of causation in an AI system is ontologically impossible. The argument proceeds as follows. An individual located in a room and receiving input written in Chinese, without understanding Chinese, can consult a manual that teaches him how to manipulate Chinese symbols following mechanical rules. By applying these rules, the individual will produce output in Chinese that will be indistinguishable from those of a native Chinese speaker. However, although the individual can perfectly simulate understanding the language, he does not actually understand the meaning of the symbols, as he merely executes syntactic manipulations.

A deep learning system is analogous to this individual. The system receives input (for example, the molecular structure of a substance, encoded as a vector of chemical descriptors) and produces output (for example, a toxicity prediction) by applying a complex network of mathematical transformations. Externally, the system appears to understand toxicology; internally, it merely executes syntactic manipulations of numbers. This distinction has three direct consequences for liability law.

1. The system cannot anticipate risks that lie outside the space of data on which it was trained. If epoxidation is not represented in the molecular descriptors on which DeepTox was trained, then the system cannot even in principle "understand" this mechanism; it can only execute calculations on descriptors that do not capture the reality of the chemical reaction.
2. The reconstruction of causation within the system is ontologically impossible. There is no logical-semantic path that the system followed to reach a particular decision; there is only a cascade of mathematical transformations. Asking the system "why did you assign to this molecule a toxicity score of 0.15?" is like asking the individual in the Chinese Room "why does this Chinese character mean this thing?" The answer is that the system does not know; it only knows how to manipulate symbols according to the rules it has been taught.
3. The black box cannot be opened even by its designers. The authors of a complex AI system cannot, in general, explain exactly how the system reaches a particular decision in the specific case. They can explain the general architecture, the training algorithm, and the data used, but the specific decision is the result of billions of matrix multiplications that even the designers cannot compute by

[42] Searle (1980).

[43] Searle (1980); see also Chap. 2.

hand. This irreducible opacity is the foundation of the presumption of liability provided by Article 10(4) of Directive (EU) 2024/2853.

The presumptions of Article 10(4) of the Directive are not a matter of policy choice but of logical necessity. A system whose opacity is ontological cannot be subjected to a standard of proof that would require a causal-semantic reconstruction of the decision. The presumption is the legal device that operates where harm is caused by the system but the reconstruction of the mechanism is impossible, so the liability of the producer is presumed. It is a form of liability without knowledge, appropriate to a technology without transparency.

This theoretical transformation has a decisive practical implication, namely that the civil liability of the producer of an algoraceutical drug assumes the characteristics of strict liability in the narrow sense. Although formally remaining a presumptive liability (the producer can rebut by proving that the risk was unknowable), in practice the inverted burden of proof renders the regime indistinguishable from liability without fault. The producer can no longer demonstrate the absence of fault by operating at the level of intention or negligence; he must instead prove the ontological impossibility of the risk, something that in a dynamic field like pharmaceutical discovery becomes progressively more difficult. The algorithm is not an excuse, but the prerequisite for even more severe liability.

6.6 Five Scenarios of Liability for the Algoraceutical Drug

6.6.1 Case 1: Fully Internal Development

Let us consider the first scenario. Company Alpha develops an algoraceutical drug entirely internally, from the conception of the molecule to the design of the algorithm that generated it.

(a) Article 2050 c.c. applies fully. Alpha, as executor of a dangerous activity (the administration of a drug with therapeutic properties), must prove that it has adopted all suitable measures to prevent harm. This includes rigorous clinical trials, implementation of molecular quality control systems, documentation of the process by which the algorithm was generated, and validation of the model on independent datasets.

(b) Directive (EU) 2024/2853 designates Alpha as the "producer" in the strict sense. Alpha is liable for any defect of the molecule that its algorithm has generated. There is no intermediary; there is no external compartment to which to attribute responsibility for the molecule. The liability is integral.

(c) The presumption of opacity benefits the injured party. In the case where the injured party establishes that the molecule has caused unforeseen damage, the technical complexity of the design chain (from algorithm to molecule to toxicological properties) allows the court to presume, according to Article 10(4) of the Directive, that Alpha has not adopted all suitable measures. Alpha must therefore rebut by proving that the risk was unknowable even on the basis of the best available technology.

(d) The development risk defense remains available, but in a restricted form. Alpha can demonstrate that the defect could not have been known on the basis of the best machine learning techniques available at the moment of commercialization. If, however, the evidence shows that another company in the field has employed a superior methodology for predicting toxicity, then Alpha cannot invoke the defense; it should have adopted the same better methodology.

6.6.2 Case 2: AI Supplied by Third Parties (Externalization of the Algorithm)

Let us consider the second scenario. Company Alpha acquires the toxicity prediction algorithm from a third party, Beta. Beta is a company specialized in machine learning that has developed a generalist model for predicting toxicity across a wide range of molecules. Alpha integrates it into its pharmaceutical discovery process, generating a candidate molecule M on the basis of suggestions from Beta's algorithm. Molecule M causes unforeseen harm.

(a) Liability is joint but parameterized to the facts. Beta's contribution to algorithm design and model training determines its share of responsibility. If Beta provided the algorithm and Alpha provided the domain-specific training data for pharmaceuticals, then responsibility is divided between the two, in the sense that Beta is liable for defects inherent to the algorithm architecture, Alpha is liable for defects related to the adaptation of the model to domain data. Article 8, paragraph 1, letter b) of Directive (EU) 2024/2853 renders Beta liable as producer of the algorithmic component, even if incorporated in a final product of Alpha.

(b) Contractual allocation of responsibility between Alpha and Beta (for example, through indemnification or hold harmless clauses) has effect merely internal between the parties and does not bind the victim's rights. If the injured party sues Alpha, Alpha remains liable according to law. The circumstance that Alpha has negotiated with Beta a hold harmless clause does not reduce Alpha's liability toward the victim; simply, Alpha will be able to seek recourse against Beta subsequently. This principle is central to product liability law and is not altered by the intervention of AI.

(c) Alpha's due diligence in selecting and validating Beta constitutes a relevant element in the evaluation of liability. If Alpha has conducted independent validation studies on Beta's algorithm, has verified that the model was robust and accurate in the specific pharmaceutical context, and has implemented human oversight mechanisms, then Alpha has acted reasonably according to Article

2050 c.c. If, to the contrary, Alpha has employed Beta's algorithm without any specific validation, then Alpha has not adopted suitable measures.

In this scenario, the legal mechanism of "third-party notice" (or calling in a third party) becomes instrumental.[44] Alpha, sued by the victim, can invoke the right to call in Beta as liable for the algorithmic component that generated the defect. The advantages of this mechanism are twofold. On the one hand, it allows the victim to obtain judgment against Alpha (primary producer), which is more easily identifiable and has greater resources; on the other hand, it allows Alpha to seek recourse against Beta subsequently. However, the mechanism of third-party notice is not automatic, as Alpha must demonstrate the causal link between the defect and Beta's contribution. In the algoraceutical context, where causation is ontologically opaque, this demonstration can prove difficult. The presumption provided by Article 10(4) of Directive (EU) 2024/2853, however, favors the actor (in this case, Alpha against Beta), precisely because the technical complexity of the algorithm makes direct proof excessively difficult.

6.6.3 Case 3: The CDMO and Third-Party Development

Let us consider the third scenario. Alpha has conceived the molecule M and generated the algorithm that designed it, but entrusts production to a Contract Development and Manufacturing Organization (CDMO), Gamma. Gamma synthesizes the molecule and formulates it according to Alpha's specifications. The molecule causes harm.

(a) Alpha remains the primary producer and the holder of Marketing Authorization (AIC). Alpha is liable according to Article 2050 c.c. for the suitability of the molecule generated by its algorithm. The circumstance that Alpha has entrusted production to a third party does not exempt it from liability toward the injured party.
(b) Gamma is liable as producer of a component of the final product, according to Article 8, paragraph 1, letter b) of Directive (EU) 2024/2853. If the harm derives from non-compliance of production (for example, Gamma has synthesized the molecule with unforeseen impurities), then Gamma is liable pro rata for the portion of damage attributable to the production defect.
(c) Liability is joint and several according to Article 2055 c.c.,[45] which provides that where damage is caused by the concurrence of multiple persons, all are jointly and severally liable toward the injured party. The injured party can sue Alpha, Gamma, or both. Subsequently, Alpha and Gamma have reciprocal rights of recourse based on the facts of the harm and their actual liability.

[44] On the *chiamata in causa* of a third party, see Art. 106 of the Italian Code of Civil Procedure.
[45] Art. 2055 of the Italian Civil Code (joint and several liability of multiple tortfeasors).

The figure of the CDMO represents an intermediate category in the pharmaceutical supply chain that deserves special attention in the algoraceutical context.[46] A CDMO is an organization specialized in providing third-party pharmaceutical development and manufacturing services. In the case of an algoraceutical drug, the CDMO does not participate in the algorithmic design phase, but assumes responsibility for the quality of synthesis and formulation of the molecule generated by Alpha's algorithm. This operational model creates a situation of diffuse liability, since the CDMO cannot control the quality of the molecule in absolute sense (since that was determined by the algorithm), but can control the quality of its synthesis. If the CDMO discovers during synthesis that the molecule presents properties suggesting greater dangerousness than indicated by the risk score from Alpha's algorithm, the CDMO has the obligation to report it to Alpha and might have the right to refuse production. The omission of this report and of due diligence in process control can render the CDMO liable as a joint tortfeasor in the harm.

6.6.4 Case 4: Digital Twin and *In Silico* Clinical Trials

Let us consider the fourth scenario. Unlike the three preceding ones, in which artificial intelligence intervenes in the molecule discovery or production phase, Case 4 addresses the clinical trial phase, namely the moment when the algoraceutical drug must be validated on patients before Marketing Authorization. In this segment, the use of digital twins is profoundly modifying clinical trial methodology, to the point of necessitating an autonomous legal qualification. The clinical digital twin is a dynamic, individual computational replica of a patient, constructed from biometric, genomic, and clinical record data and updated in real time through the integration of heterogeneous sources. A single-patient digital twin serves to project, in the form of a counterfactual, how the patient would have fared in the absence of treatment, or under alternative treatments. A cohort of digital twins, conversely, serves to construct what the scientific literature designates as an external control arm synthetic, namely a virtual control arm that substitutes, in whole or in part, the real patients to whom placebo would have been administered.[47]

The distinction between the two applications is not merely technical but legally qualifying. In the first case, the digital twin operates as an individual diagnostic and prognostic tool; in the second, it operates as a methodological component of the experimental design and, simultaneously, as an evidentiary element of the registration dossier. In both configurations, the digital twin is generated by a machine learning system that inherits integrally the characteristics of opacity already examined in Chap. 4 and the logic of generative networks already discussed in Chap. 3 concerning Generative Adversarial Networks, from which many contemporary synthetic

[46] On contract development and manufacturing organizations (CDMOs) in the pharmaceutical supply chain, see Sect. 6.6.3.

[47] On synthetic (in silico) control arms, see Chap. 3 and Sect. 6.6.4 below.

cohort generation techniques derive directly.[48] Awareness of this lineage is essential, because it requires recognizing that the digital twin is not a simple "tabular datum" but an algorithmic product with all the degrees of freedom and therefore margins of error proper to deep models.

Let us imagine then the concrete case. Company Delta develops a new drug for a rare neurodegenerative disease and submits to the European regulatory authority a registration dossier that includes a Phase III trial with a hybrid design. The experimental arm has three hundred real patients, while the control arm comprises sixty real patients accompanied by an external control arm synthetic of a further one hundred eighty digital twins, generated from a historical cohort of over six thousand patients from previous trials, disease registries, and real-world databases. The prognostic model employed to construct the digital twins was trained and validated by a specialized technology provider, named Epsilon, and its method of adjustment for prognostic covariate was subject to qualification by the European Medicines Agency in the context of a qualification opinion procedure. Twenty-two months after authorization, a portion of the patients in the experimental arm develop a grave adverse effect, an irreversible peripheral neuropathy, whose frequency, measured on the real cohort, proves significantly higher than what the control arm digital twin had predicted as the expected difference from placebo. One of the patients sues Delta, arguing that the registration dossier would have underestimated the risk profile through the use of the synthetic control and requests to extend liability also to provider Epsilon. The legal question is twofold: which subjects are liable for the harm and according to which probative regime?

Before responding, it is worthwhile to reconstruct the regulatory perimeter within which the scenario falls. Unlike Cases 1, 2, and 3, Case 4 takes place in territory already supervised by a regulatory framework specifically directed at *in silico* models.[49] The Committee for Medicinal Products for Human Use of the European Medicines Agency adopted in September 2022 a favorable qualification opinion regarding the "PROCOVA" method, a method of adjustment for digital twin covariate and designed to increase the precision of effect estimates in trials controlled with continuous endpoints; this was the first time a regulatory authority formally recognized a machine learning methodology as a suitable tool to reduce the sample dimension of pivotal studies.[50] On the U.S. side, the Food and Drug Administration published in February 2023 the guidance "Considerations for the Design and Conduct of Externally Controlled Trials for Drug and Biological Products" and subsequently intervened with an additional document under consultation in December 2023, in implementation of Section 3629 of the Food and Drug Omnibus Reform Act of 2022, which requires the agency to update its discipline on the use of

[48] On Generative Adversarial Networks, see Chap. 3; Goodfellow et al. (2014).

[49] On the regulatory qualification of in silico methodologies, see Chap. 9.

[50] EMA, Committee for Medicinal Products for Human Use (CHMP), qualification opinion on the PROCOVA methodology (15 September 2022), the first qualification of a machine-learning methodology to reduce the sample size of pivotal trials.

real-world data and evidence for regulatory purposes.[51] Alongside these specific sources, international practice has consolidated a technical standard for verification and validation of computational models in medicine, "ASME V&V 40," which serves as a benchmark for methodological diligence and has provided, through the U.S. Medical Device Development Tools program, an autonomous qualification procedure for modeling tools supporting regulatory decisions.[52]

This network of instruments is not irrelevant to the civil discourse. Regulatory qualification of a method means that the authority recognizes use of that methodology as acceptable in a registration dossier; it does not mean that the authority certifies the correctness of each individual application, nor, least of all, that it assumes the civil consequences of a calibration error. For Delta, the qualification opinion of the PROCOVA method is worth what Marketing Authorization is worth for the traditional medicinal product, namely a condition of access to the market and not a safe passage with respect to Article 2050 of the civil code. The opposite thesis, according to which method qualification would transform diligence into a merely administrative attribute, would repose in algorithmic key that "ceiling of diligence" already refuted in Sect. 6.2.2. The existence of a specific regulatory framework, far from reducing the civil liability of the producer, strengthens it, because it provides the court with more concrete and rigorous diligence parameters than those available in the other three scenarios of Sect. 6.6.

The allocation of liability in Case 4 thus follows a four-step path. The first step consists in qualifying the digital twin as a "component" of the registration dossier according to Article 4, paragraph 4, of Directive (EU) 2024/2853. An algorithmic artifact that forms an integral part of the proof of efficacy and safety and whose removal would prevent the dossier from circulating as conceived by the holder responds without interpretive tension to the notion of component embraced by the new discipline. From this it follows, in application of Article 8, paragraph 1, letter b), that the technology provider Epsilon is liable as producer of a component even when it is incorporated into a final product of Delta, with full capacity to be a defendant against the injured party.[53]

The second step concerns Delta's position. The holder of AIC does not cease to be primary producer by having externalized prognostic modeling. Its diligence is measured, in Case 4, by criteria functionally analogous to those of Case 2, namely accurate selection of provider Epsilon, independent validation of the model on the specific domain, documentation of the hybrid design, calibration of the synthetic arm against the real population, post-commercialization surveillance mechanisms calibrated also to possible deviations between prognostic prediction and clinical

---

[51] Food and Drug Omnibus Reform Act of 2022 (FDORA), signed 29 December 2022 (Consolidated Appropriations Act, 2023); § 3629 on real-world data and evidence. See also FDA, *Considerations for the Design and Conduct of Externally Controlled Trials for Drug and Biological Products*, draft guidance, February 2023.

[52] On the U.S. FDA Medical Device Development Tools (MDDT) program and the ASME V&V 40-2018 standard, see FDA, *Qualification of Medical Device Development Tools*, guidance (2017).

[53] Art. 8, Directive (EU) 2024/2853 (liability of the manufacturer of a component).

observation. The regulatory framework described in the previous block now provides the court with objective indices with which to evaluate each of these profiles, so that the judgment of diligence under Article 2050 of the civil code is enriched with concrete technical standards and no longer merely aspirational ones.

The third step concerns the capacity for continuous learning. The prognostic model, exactly like a toxicity prediction system, is not a static object. Its parameters can and must be updated as new real cohorts become available, as new clinical endpoints are validated, and as new epidemiological evidence modifies the baseline distribution of the disease. In this dynamic dimension the direct application is found of Article 7, paragraph 2, letter c), and Article 11, paragraph 2, of Directive (EU) 2024/2853, whereby provider Epsilon is liable not only for the model as delivered, but for what the model should have learned and did not learn and cannot invoke the development risk defense when the defect consists in the omission of an update that would have been technically possible in light of the best available practice. The continuous obligation to update, already argued in Sect. 6.3.3 in general terms, finds here one of its most severe applications, since the prognostic model produces not laboratory predictions but evidence designed to support a marketing authorization.[54]

The fourth step concerns joint and several liability. Delta and Epsilon are jointly and severally liable toward the injured party under Article 2055 of the civil code, with faculty of reciprocal recourse according to the apportionment of factual fault. The mechanism of third-party notice, illustrated in Sect. 6.6.2, applies with the same logics and with the same probative limits. Should the digital twin have been trained on cohorts provided by additional subjects, for example disease registries or research consortia, liability extends also to the holders of that data as providers of components, with a potentially ramified chain that recalls, from a structural perspective, the multilevel opacity of the GAN/RANC Case of Sect. 6.7.

The peculiarity of Case 4 with respect to the other scenarios consists in the aggravation of algorithmic opacity. The algorithmic opacity that in Sect. 6.5 was analyzed through Searle's "Chinese Room" argument presents itself here in an aggravated form, because the digital twin does not predict an observable phenomenon but generates a magnitude structurally unobservable, namely the counterfactual. The real patient, once enrolled in the experimental arm, can never be observed in its hypothetical pathway of non-treatment; what the digital twin calculates is not comparable to a parallel reality and is, consequently, not directly falsifiable *ex post*. This circumstance imposes two consequences. The first is that direct proof of the defect, in the sense of Directive (EU) 2024/2853, becomes structurally impossible for the injured party, since there is no real datum against which to measure the error of the synthetic control, except at the cost of statistical reconstructions that are themselves opaque. The second is that the presumption of Article 10, paragraph 4, of the Directive finds in Case 4 its most fertile terrain, since the technical complexity of the product and the unobservability of the generated parameter make direct proof "excessively difficult" in a heightened sense compared to what was already

[54] Art. 13, Regulation (EU) 2024/1689 (transparency obligations for high-risk systems).

seen in Sects. 6.3.4 and 6.7.[55] In conceptual terms, if Searle's "Chinese Room" illustrates the opacity of one who manipulates symbols without understanding their meaning, the clinical digital twin adds a second room, placed in parallel to the first, wherein the object to be predicted has never entered and will never enter.

From this double opacity there descends a methodological consideration that opens the way to Sect. 6.6.5 and the sections dedicated to procedural explainability. If the presumption of Article 10, paragraph 4, favors the injured party, it does not exhaust the probative problem, as it leaves open the question of how to reconstruct, before the judge, the specific contribution of the digital twin to the genesis of the harm. Techniques of explainable artificial intelligence, and in particular Shapley value attributions and saliency maps, are assuming, in the practice of clinical trials with digital twins, a function that is no longer merely regulatory but also procedural, since they provide to the parties and the judge a local, replicable, and contestable representation of the weight of each prognostic variable in the individual prediction. This is a point to which we shall return in the next scenario, regarding the "Alpha SHAP" case, and more systematically in Chap. 4, where the procedural use of explainability will be reconstructed as a tertium genus between administrative compliance and free civil proof.[56] Chapter 9, for its part, analyzes how the regulatory governance of the external control arm must be coordinated with the needs for civil protection of the injured party.

In summary, Case 4 illustrates a hypothesis in which the civil liability of the producer is not measured on the quality of the molecule, but on the quality of a probabilistic proof that precedes the molecule itself. Delta and Epsilon are called to answer for a model that generated evidence destined for the regulatory authority and the civil judge finds itself evaluating, for the purposes of Article 2050 of the civil code, the diligence in the production of a counterfactual. The intermediate thesis on the development risk defense, elaborated in Sect. 6.3.5, bends coherently to Case 4, whereby Epsilon can invoke the defense only if it demonstrates that at the moment of submission of the dossier it adopted the best prognostic calibration methodology available according to state of the art and subsequently updated the model every time new evidence would have imposed its revision.[57] The framework that emerges is that of a regime of presumptive objective liability, harmonized with Regulation 2024/1689 and founded on external technical standards that, for the first time in Italian pharmaceutical liability law, enter directly into the evaluation of diligence.

6.6.5 Case 5: Alpha SHAP, Explainability as Evidence

Let us consider the fifth scenario. Company Alpha, already protagonist of Cases 1, 2, and 3, has obtained Marketing Authorization for molecule M, designed internally

---

[55] Art. 10(4), Directive (EU) 2024/2853; see Sects. 6.3.4 and 6.7.

[56] On the procedural use of explainability as a tertium genus probatorio, see Chap. 4, Sect. 4.6.

[57] Art. 11(2), Directive (EU) 2024/2853 (obligation to update; exclusion of the development-risk defense for omitted updates).

with a toxicity prediction model trained on a cohort of two hundred thousand compounds. Eighteen months after commercialization, a cluster of patients carrying a variant of the CYP2C9 polymorphism develops acute hepatotoxicity Grade 3 according to the "Common Terminology Criteria for Adverse Events" classification. Post-authorization pharmacovigilance traces the event to anomalous metabolism of an intermediate metabolite of molecule M in the genetic subgroup. One of the patients sues Alpha under Article 2050 of the civil code. The defendant's expert, proceeding from the technical dossier filed in disclosure pursuant to Article 10 of Directive (EU) 2024/2853, subjects Alpha's internal model to a local attribution procedure founded on Shapley additive explanations and demonstrates that the interaction variable between the intermediate metabolite and the CYP2C9 polymorphism had, at the moment of the model's decision, a relative weight approaching zero, despite being already known to the pharmacogenomics literature of 2024.[58] The legal question is twofold: namely, whether a SHAP attribution can constitute proof of the defect in civil judgment, and in what terms?

The answer requires an exercise of qualification of scientific evidence that our legal system, unlike the U.S. one, does not address with a preliminary admissibility test but with an evaluation of reliability entrusted to the prudent assessment of the judge under Article 116 of the Code of Civil Procedure. The experience gained across the ocean with the "Daubert" criteria nonetheless provides a useful decalogue of reliability, namely empirical verifiability of the technique, peer review, known error rate, application standards, and acceptance in the relevant scientific community. SHAP attributions, from this point of view, enjoy a robust theoretical foundation rooted in Shapley's cooperative game theory and assure their mathematical coherence, in the sense that the attribution of each variable respects the axioms of efficiency, symmetry, nullity, and additivity.[59] Their practical implementation has been validated by the machine learning community and systematically applied to pharmaceutical discovery in the last 5 years. There remain, however, two margins of fragility that the judge must consider, namely the dependence of the result on the reference distribution chosen for the calculation of the counterfactual, which renders the attribution sensitive to the choice of background dataset, and the conceptual difference between "interventionist" SHAP attribution and "observational" attribution, which can lead to significantly different rankings with the same model. To these limits are added the problem, common to every local explainability technique, of non-identity between the weight attributed to a variable and substantive causality, since a variable can prove relevant to the prediction without being causally determinant in the physical world.[60] Scientific proof, in Case 5, cannot therefore consist in the mere production of the SHAP map, but requires an articulated probative package: justified choice of background dataset, stability of attribution over random perturbations of the model, comparison with attributions obtained with alternative

[58] On SHAP attributions, see Lundberg and Lee (2017); Chap. 4, Sect. 4.6.2.

[59] On the axiomatic properties of Shapley values (efficiency, symmetry, nullity, additivity), see Lundberg and Lee (2017).

[60] On the distinction between predictive relevance and physical causation, see Chap. 4.

techniques (in particular local interpretable model-agnostic explanations), and, where available, correlations with biological evidence.

Satisfied these requirements, SHAP attribution fulfills a procedural function that the literature had not heretofore focused on with clarity. It constitutes the hinge that allows the injured party to reach the threshold of "sufficient allegation" required by Article 10, paragraph 4, of Directive (EU) 2024/2853 to trigger the presumption of defectiveness. In the original proof model, the injured party was asked to demonstrate that the product was objectively defective; in the new model, it suffices that he allege a "plausible" reconstruction of the defect and such reconstruction can take the forms of a SHAP map that locally identifies the variable undervalued by the model. The presumption thus shifts the burden onto the producer, who must demonstrate either that the SHAP attribution is methodologically flawed (for example due to inadequate choice of background dataset or instability of attributions), or that the identified variable, while having statistical weight, is not causally relevant to the harmful event. Article 10 of the Directive, for its part, assures the injured party access to the technical dossier necessary to materially execute the calculation of attributions and constitutes the operative prerequisite of this entire probative dialectic. In the Italian legal system, coordination with Article 210 of the Code of Civil Procedure on documentary production and with seizure under Article 670 offers the judge concrete tools to guarantee this disclosure even in cases where the producer opposes reasons of trade secret.[61]

In summary, Case 5 shows how explainability techniques are being transformed, before the attentive eyes of the jurist, from pure administrative compliance into a genuine civil evidence tool. Alpha, in the scenario considered, can both undergo the procedural production of a SHAP map in support of the claimant's claim and employ it defensively to demonstrate the robustness of its own model with respect to the contested variable. The symmetry of this use, typical of every "evidence" in the technical sense, is precisely what distinguishes procedural explainability from regulatory explainability. The former serves a contentious decision, the latter an administrative judgment *ex ante*. The systematic treatment of this distinction, with the framing of SHAP, LIME, and saliency maps as a tertium genus between administrative compliance and free civil proof, is developed in Chap. 4 in the section dedicated to procedural explainability, to which we refer entirely for the analysis of admissibility criteria, the relationship with Article 2697 of the civil code, and the deontological implications for the appointed technical expert.[62] What matters, in the economy of this chapter, is to grasp the systematic nexus with Sect. 6.5, in that if the "Chinese Room" expresses the impossibility, for the model, to understand the meaning of its own decisions, local explainability is the tool that permits the judge to reconstruct from outside, and in contestable form, which part of those decisions

[61] Art. 670 of the Italian Code of Civil Procedure (giudiziale sequestration), as an instrument to secure disclosure.

[62] Art. 2697 of the Italian Civil Code (burden of proof); on court-appointed expert evidence, see Chap. 4, Sect. 4.6.4.

is relevant to the dispute. Case 5 is, in this sense, the procedural response to the epistemological problem formulated in Sect. 6.5.

6.7 The GAN/RANC Case: Multilevel Opacity and Attribution of Causation

The case of molecule generation through Generative Adversarial Networks (GAN) architecture combined with a network additive for control of reactivity (RANC) represents a paradigm of multilevel opacity,[63] already examined in Chap. 4.[64] A generator (G) is trained to produce plausible molecular structures; a discriminator (D) is trained to distinguish molecules generated by G from molecules known in the literature. Through this adversarial game, G learns to generate ever more realistic molecules. Subsequently, a RANC network is superimposed to filter the generated molecules, excluding those that present undesirable chemical reactions.

The GAN architecture, introduced by Goodfellow et al.[65] in 2014, functions as an antagonistic game between the generator and the discriminator. In the training phase, G produces synthetic molecules based on random vectors, while D learns to distinguish synthetic molecules from "real" ones (namely, taken from the chemical literature). As D becomes better at discriminating, G must become more sophisticated to fool D. This iterative process causes the emergence of a distribution of generated molecules that increasingly resembles the distribution of real molecules. However, the process is intrinsically unstable, so it is possible that G "collapses" and generates only a handful of diverse molecules; it is possible that D diverges and becomes unable to discriminate; it is possible that the process converges toward a state where G generates molecules that are statistically identical to real molecules but behave completely differently in the human body.

The opacity is not monolevel but composite. Generator G is opaque about molecule formation; discriminator D equally about selection criteria; network RANC about determination of undesirable reactions; the joint training process adds a further layer; and the data themselves can contain distortions or gaps. When these levels interact recursively, opacity does not sum linearly but compounds, producing a hermeneutic complexity that vanquishes any attempt at sequential tracing of the decision.

At the moment when a molecule generated by this system causes unforeseen harm, the court must determine where the defect lies. Is it in the generator? The discriminator? The RANC network? The data? Or in the combination of these elements? Multilevel opacity makes this exercise literally impossible. The court cannot, even in principle, isolate the point of origin of the defect. Article 10(4) of Directive (EU) 2024/2853 therefore permits the court to presume the fault of the producer without necessity of proving which component of the architecture is

[63] On the GAN/RANC case, see Chap. 4, Sect. 4.2.

[64] See Chap. 4, Sect. 4.2.

[65] Goodfellow et al. (2014).

responsible. This approach is consistent with the theoretical conclusion of Chap. 6, namely the impossibility of causal reconstruction becomes the prerequisite for the presumption.

Article 8, paragraph 1, letter b) of the Directive furthermore extends liability to each producer of a component. If the producer of G is company Beta, the producer of D is company Gamma, and the producer of RANC is company Delta, all are liable as producers of components toward the victim, regardless of who has assembled the final system.

Article 9 of the Directive finally permits disclosure orders, whereby the court can order the producers to disclose how the system was trained, what data were used, and what quality control methodologies were employed, in order to verify whether the producers adopted all suitable measures under Article 2050 c.c.

The theory of liability in the GAN/RANC context can be summarized in four procedural phases. First phase: the injured party demonstrates that the molecule generated by the GAN/RANC system has caused harm. Second phase: the court presumes the defect of the molecule, since multilevel opacity makes positive proof of the defect exceptionally difficult. Third phase: the producers must rebut the presumption by proving that they have adopted all suitable measures. Fourth phase: the court determines the apportionment of liability among the various component producers according to the gravity of their respective contributions.

The GAN/RANC case illustrates an interpretive paradigm of primary theoretical significance, namely the shift from deterministic causation to probabilistic causation in civil liability law. In traditional law, causation is conceived as a binary relation, in the sense that given an antecedent X, necessarily follows a consequence Y. A molecule produced according to a specific synthetic scheme will have a specific structure and that structure will have specific toxicological properties. In the context of AI systems, causation becomes probabilistic. Given an input (a desired molecule), the GAN system produces not a single molecule with a single structure, but a family of plausible molecules, each with a different probability of being "good" according to selection criteria. The RANC filters this family, but the filter itself is probabilistic (it is based on a neural network that assigns plausibility scores, not a deterministic algorithm that generates absolute yes/no decisions).

This probabilistic paradigm has direct implications for civil liability. In the deterministic model, the producer can theoretically prevent all harm by identifying the cause and eliminating it. In the probabilistic model, the producer can only reduce the probability of harm, but cannot eliminate it completely. The consequence is that the liability of the producer in a probabilistic system cannot be founded on fault or subjective negligence, since the producer has adopted "all suitable measures" but harm occurs anyway. Liability must necessarily be founded on an objective scheme, where the sole fact that harm derives from a dangerous activity imposes liability, independent of the individual conduct of the producer. This is precisely what Article 10(4) of Directive (EU) 2024/2853 sustains in the algorithmic context.

6.8 The DeepTox Case: Risk Score and Development Risk Defense

DeepTox is a deep learning model trained to assign toxicity scores to molecules on the basis of chemical descriptors.[66] The concrete case that we shall examine is as follows. A molecule M receives from DeepTox a risk score of 0.15 (low risk), suggesting that the molecule is safe. However, M contains an epoxidation mechanism that DeepTox is unable to detect, since the descriptors on which the model was trained do not capture this type of reaction. Consequently, M causes harm. Who is liable?

According to the intermediate thesis on the development risk defense developed in Sect. 6.3.5,[67] the answer depends on a counterfactual analysis. If the producer of DeepTox had access to data on epoxidation (or should have had access on the basis of the best available AI), then the defect was knowable and the producer is liable. If, by contrast, even the best available AI could not have detected the epoxidation mechanism, then the producer is not liable.

In the concrete case of DeepTox, experts in toxicology have known for decades that epoxidation is an important mechanism of hepatic damage.[68] However, it is possible that in the dataset on which DeepTox was trained, this mechanism was not adequately represented or that the available molecular descriptors did not capture the phenomenon. The legal question is whether the producer should have included this data in the training data? And should have developed better descriptors?[69]

According to the thesis of the author, the answer is yes. The producer of DeepTox should have adopted measures to include in the training data relevant information on epoxidation and should have developed or adopted molecular descriptors that captured this phenomenon. If it omitted to do so, then the defect cannot invoke the development risk defense. If, to the contrary, the producer attempted to include this data and descriptors but the model failed to learn the mechanism (a plausible possibility given the infinite number of possible chemical phenomena), then the defense remains available, since the risk could not have been known even by one who had access to the correct data.

This approach maintains the development risk defense in the algoraceutical context, but raises the standard of proof for invoking it, requiring that the producer demonstrate it made a genuine effort to include in the training set all toxicologically relevant information according to state of the art at the moment.[70] Moreover, Article 11(2) of Directive (EU) 2024/2853 excludes the defense in the case where the defect

---

[66] Mayr et al. (2016); see Chap. 4, Sect. 4.4.

[67] See Sect. 6.3.5 above.

[68] On the state of the art and the development-risk defense, see Art. 11(1)(e), Directive (EU) 2024/2853.

[69] On the diligence required in the constitution of training datasets, see Art. 10, Regulation (EU) 2024/1689.

[70] Art. 11(1)(e), Directive (EU) 2024/2853 (the development-risk defense is assessed against the state of scientific and technical knowledge).

consists in the omission of subsequent software updates.[71] If, after commercialization, new data on epoxidation become available in the literature, the producer of DeepTox has the obligation to update the model; the omission to do so cannot be justified by the development risk defense.

6.9 Human Oversight Between Formal Obligation and Substantive Impossibility

Article 14 of the AI Regulation establishes that high-risk AI systems must be subject to meaningful human oversight.[72] For an algoraceutical drug, this means that algorithmic decisions in discovery and development must be subject to review by competent human experts. However, Chap. 4 has illustrated how AI systems distribute themselves over a spectrum of autonomy ranging from tool (low autonomy, high interpretability) to assistant (medium autonomy, medium interpretability) to agent (high autonomy, low interpretability).[73]

As the system moves toward the agent extremity, two phenomena manifest themselves simultaneously. On one hand, (1) the system becomes more sophisticated, more accurate in predictions, and more autonomous in decisions; (2) the human supervisor becomes progressively less capable of understanding the system's decisions and therefore less capable of exercising substantive control. This paradox constitutes the heart of the question regarding human oversight in the algoraceutical context.

A differentiated analysis by autonomy levels emerges as necessary. At the first level (AI as tool), the system functions as a sophisticated calculator that suggests options to the human researcher, who remains responsible for the final decision. In this case, human oversight is substantive since the researcher fully understands how the system arrived at the recommendation and can validate or reject the proposal knowingly. For example, an AI system that calculates physicochemical properties of a molecule and presents them to a human chemist, who decides whether to proceed with synthesis on the basis of his understanding of the problem.

At the second level (AI as assistant), the system not only suggests options, but integrates recommendations based on the researcher's past behavior, creating a sort of "intelligent copilot" that knows the operator's preferences and adapts recommendations in real time. In this case, human oversight becomes more fragile, as the researcher might find himself in a state of excessive trust (automation bias),[74] accepting the system's recommendations without adequate critical review. For example, a system that suggests synthesis sequences based on the history of

[71] Art. 11(2), Directive (EU) 2024/2853 (exclusion of the development-risk defense for failure to provide subsequent updates).

[72] Art. 14, Regulation (EU) 2024/1689 (human oversight).

[73] On the taxonomy of autonomy (tool, assistant, agent), see Chap. 4, Sect. 4.5.

[74] On automation bias and the fragility of human oversight, see Chap. 4, Sect. 4.5.

previously successfully synthesized molecules, progressively learning from the operator's choices.

At the third level (AI as autonomous agent), the system operates with minimal human interference, making decisions autonomously and implementing them directly (for example, in a roboticized laboratory). Human oversight becomes almost illusory, since the human operator cannot hope to understand the system's behavior in real time and can only intervene retrospectively should the system behave drastically anomalously. This is the state of autonomous laboratories, where the supervisor intervenes principally to reload reagents or address mechanical errors, not to validate algorithmic decisions.[75]

Autonomous laboratories ("self-driving laboratories") represent the extremity of this spectrum,[76] already examined in Chap. 3.[77] In these laboratories, AI systems entirely manage the design-synthesis-test cycle of new molecules, with reduction of human supervision to sporadic interventions in cases of evident anomaly. In theory, the laboratory remains subject to human oversight; in practice, the supervisor does not fully understand how the system generated a particular molecular synthesis sequence and therefore cannot exercise true control.

The legal consequence is that human oversight, when insufficiently solid, becomes an aggravating element of civil liability, not a mitigating factor.[78] If the producer, aware of the system's opacity, implements human oversight that is merely formal (namely, superficial, not competent, not documented, not actually exercised), then this circumstance demonstrates that the producer was aware of the risk and omitted to take adequate measures. A court could conclude that the producer violated Article 2050 c.c. precisely by having, knowingly, implemented insufficient oversight.

To the contrary, robust human oversight, exercised by domain experts with decision authority and with meticulous documentation of override decisions, constitutes a positive element in the evaluation of the producer's diligence under Article 2050 c.c.

6.10 Concluding Remarks

Civil liability for the algoraceutical drug rests on three fundamental pillars. The first pillar is the burden of proof. Directive (EU) 2024/2853, integrated by Article 10(4), introduces presumptions that invert the burden of proof at the moment when the injured party proves the defect and the damage, transforming a regime of proved fault into a regime of presumptive liability. The second pillar is causation. The ontological impossibility of deterministically reconstructing the internal decision

[75] On self-driving laboratories, see Chap. 3.

[76] On autonomous (self-driving) laboratories, see Chap. 3.

[77] See Chap. 3.

[78] On the paradox of formal human oversight, see Art. 14, Regulation (EU) 2024/1689, and Chap. 4, Sect. 4.5.

path[79] of an AI system legitimates this presumption, as it requires the producer to prove, conversely, that the system was suitable. The third pillar is the development risk defense. The intermediate thesis proposed raises the standard of this defense in the algoraceutical context, requiring that the producer demonstrate it included in the training set all toxicologically relevant information accessible at the moment, according to state of the art.

These three pillars create an "expanded zone of liability"[80] in which the producer of the algoraceutical drug is liable not only for proved fault, not only for violation of contractual standards, but for any defect that emerges post-distribution and which the system could have learned to prevent on the basis of the data and methodologies available. Article 2050 c.c. and Regulation (EU) 2024/1689 operate in synergy to extend liability, compensating for the regulatory gap left by the withdrawal of the proposed AI Liability Directive.

The five scenarios analyzed (internal development, algorithm externalization, CDMO, digital twin, procedural explainability) show how liability distributes among the different actors in the algoraceutical supply chain. None of these actors can escape liability simply by subdividing the chain of command. Article 12, paragraph 1, of the Directive and Article 2055 c.c. on joint and several liability assure that the victim can seek recourse against any link in the chain and that liability remains integral regardless of organizational fragmentation.

The case studies of GAN/RANC and DeepTox illustrate how these principles operate in practice. The multilevel opacity of the GAN and the incompleteness of DeepTox's training set are not legal excuses; they are prerequisites for the application of presumptions of liability. Human oversight remains a legal obligation, but only if exercised substantively, not merely formally.

The path that civil liability law must follow in the coming years is that of coherent integration between the three pillars: Article 2050 c.c. as primary safeguard, Directive (EU) 2024/2853 as modern implementation of sectoral discipline, and the AI Regulation as a parameter of administrative diligence. This integration will transform the paradigm of liability from a scheme founded on individually proved fault to a scheme founded on presumptive objective liability, more coherent with the opaque and uncontrollable nature of the algoraceutical system.

The following chapters develop this analysis according to three complementary vectors. Chapter 7 examines how the new allocation of civil liability interacts with intellectual property rights.[81] Chapter 8 addresses the competition implications and the position of training data suppliers.[82] Chapter 9 finally addresses regulatory surveillance questions and the implications of public policy.[83]

---

[79] On the presumptions of defectiveness and causation, see Art. 10, Directive (EU) 2024/2853.

[80] On the cumulative effect of the three pillars (extended notion of product, presumptive regime, expanded causation), see Sects. 6.3–6.9 above.

[81] See Chap. 7.

[82] See Chap. 8.

[83] See Chap. 9.

References

Goodfellow IJ, Pouget-Abadie J, Mirza M, Xu B, Warde-Farley D, Ozair S, Courville A, Bengio Y (2014) Generative adversarial nets. In: Advances in neural information processing systems 27. Curran Associates, Red Hook, pp 2672–2680

Lundberg SM, Lee S-I (2017) A unified approach to interpreting model predictions. In: Advances in neural information processing systems 30. Curran Associates, Red Hook, pp 4765–4774

Mayr A, Klambauer G, Unterthiner T, Hochreiter S (2016) DeepTox: toxicity prediction using deep learning. Front Environ Sci 3:80

Searle JR (1980) Minds, brains, and programs. Behav Brain Sci 3(3):417–457

Intellectual Property and Algoraceutical Invention

7

Abstract

This chapter examines how intellectual property law applies to the algoraceutical invention, the molecule or therapy whose conception depends on artificial intelligence. It proceeds in two movements. The first concerns the input, the data on which pharmaceutical models are trained, analysed through the database right (Directive 96/9/EC) and trade secret protection (Directive (EU) 2016/943), and through the tension between proprietary control and access. The second concerns the output, the patentability of AI-generated inventions, addressed through the requirements of disclosure, novelty and inventive step, and above all through the inventor problem. The chapter reconstructs the DABUS and Thaler litigation across five jurisdictions, the EPO, the United Kingdom, Germany, Japan and Switzerland, and the shift marked by the United States Patent and Trademark Office Revised Guidance of November 2025, which treats AI as a laboratory tool rather than an inventor. The Chematica/Synthia system serves as a paradigmatic case of computer-assisted synthetic planning. The chapter concludes by proposing a regime for algoraceutical invention that locates the human inventive contribution in problem formulation, dataset curation and recognition of the inventive output, anticipating the competition concerns analysed in the following chapter.

7.1 Introduction: The Creative Contribution of the Algorithm

The preceding chapters have traced the legal pathway of pharmaceutical artificial intelligence, from its position within the European regulatory context, to consideration of the mechanisms of opacity and civil liability, through to questions of governance and transparency. A complementary question now merits full attention: can the algorithm create patentable value? Can the AI system, as a complex technical

G. Rotino, *Algoraceutics - Legal Perspectives on Artificial Intelligence in Drug Discovery and Development*, Law for Professionals,
https://doi.org/10.1007/978-3-032-38537-6_7

system, be a legitimate source of intellectual innovation to which the law recognizes proprietary protection?

The initial response is unequivocally affirmative. Over the past 5 years, the process of discovery and development of new drugs has progressively transformed into a diffuse and structurally embedded algorithmic process. This is no longer marginal automation of repetitive tasks; it is a profound penetration of artificial intelligence into the creative core of pharmaceutical research. Machine learning algorithms today contribute to every stage of the pharmaceutical chain, from the identification of biological targets[1] that underpin every new therapeutic program, to the rational design of molecules[2] according to multidimensional optimization criteria, from automated planning of organic syntheses[3] to the selection and stratification of patients[4] in clinical trials.

In many of these tasks, the algorithm's contribution is not merely auxiliary, not a simple acceleration of what humans would do anyway. It is genuinely creative, in the sense that the algorithm generates original solutions that were not predictable from human ingenuity and that often surprise the researchers themselves who created the system.

In Chap. 4, we articulated the autonomy problem across three levels of increasing sophistication. The first level is that of AI as a tool, a kind of sophisticated but still passive calculator, fully controlled by the human; the second level is that of AI as an assistant, a system that proposes, suggests, facilitates, but remains always subordinate to human decision; the third level is that of AI as an agent, a system that possesses a certain decision-making autonomy, that can explore spaces of possibility independently of direct human control.[5] This distinction is absolutely central to understanding the legal implications of intellectual property applied to algoraceutical invention.

When AI operates at the first level (as a pure tool) the question of patentability and inventorship finds a simple and intuitive answer; the inventor is naturally the person using the tool, just as the inventor using an optical microscope is nonetheless the human inventor who conceived the experiment and interpreted the results. When AI operates at the third level (as an autonomous agent that generates output with absent or so marginally human contribution as to be evanescent) the question becomes vertiginous. Who is the inventor? To whom should the intellectual property in the patent be attributed? How should the entire legal ecosystem be recalibrated around this radically different reality?

But pharmaceutical AI in 2026 does not inhabit these conceptual extremes; rather it inhabits an intermediate, articulated, and nuanced space, that of the aware assistant and at times partially self-directed. It is a space of legal ambiguity, where

[1] On AI applications across the pharmaceutical chain, see Chap. 3.

[2] On the rational design of molecules, see Chap. 3.

[3] On automated synthetic planning, see Sect. 7.5 below.

[4] On patient selection and stratification, see Chap. 3 and Chap. 5, Sect. 5.2.3.

[5] On the taxonomy tool/assistant/agent, see Chap. 4, Sect. 4.5.

the traditional categories of intellectual property law enter into tension with the operational reality of contemporary research.

This chapter addresses three deeply interconnected questions. The first concerns the legal protection of input data. Who owns the training data used by the algorithm? Under what legal conditions can they be used, reused, or transferred? How is the exclusive right of access distributed? The second concerns patent protection of outputs. Is an invention generated by an algorithm patentable under current regulations? What are the patentability requirements that the output must satisfy and how are these requirements applied in the context of algorithmic opacity? The third, the most insidious and complex, concerns the inventor. When an algorithm generates a pharmaceutical invention, which legal subject should the patent be attributed to? Who is responsible for that intellectual creation?

In Chap. 3, we introduced the concept of "digital space," the virtual and topological space in which the algorithm generates, evaluates, and recombines molecular structures according to mathematical logics, according to sets of data that continuously feed it, according to scoring functions that guide exploration. It is in this digital space, more than in the physical laboratory, that the patent question arises in all its urgency and complexity, because the invention forms not in the mind of the researcher, nor in the wet laboratory where molecules are synthesized and tested, but in the computational graph, in the vector "embeddings," in the scoring functions that the algorithm navigates autonomously. Who invented, therefore? Who merits legal recognition and the economic reward of intellectual property?

Let us suppose a realistic scenario already verified in contemporary practice: a molecular design algorithm, trained on millions of biologically active and inactive compounds, on millions of test results, on annotated chemical and biophysical properties, generates a new molecule, never before synthesized, that shows extraordinary affinity[6] for a protein target just identified as critical in small-cell lung cancer. Is the molecule original from a chemical point of view? Could it be patented according to current norms? Has the system that generated it accomplished an invention in the legal sense of the term?

7.2 Input Data: What Protection

7.2.1 Training Data Between Ownership and Access

The first crucial element in the algoraceutical chain is the curation and critical selection of input data. A machine learning algorithm is only as good as the data it was trained on. If the dataset contains bias, systematic omissions, or incomplete information, then the resulting model will inherit these defects.

---

[6] On de novo molecular generation, see Chap. 3.

In the pharmaceutical context, input data comes from a variety of public and private sources. The most important public databases include PubChem[7] (National Library of Medicine), ChEMBL[8] (European Bioinformatics Institute), and DrugBank.[9] These resources contain information on millions of chemical compounds, their physicochemical properties, results of biological tests, and annotations on toxicology. The dimensions are impressive; PubChem contains over 150 million compounds,[10] ChEMBL 2 million biologically active compounds,[11] DrugBank catalogs 13,000+ approved and experimental substances.[12]

The first legal problem is that of ownership. Who is the title holder of rights in the training data? If a pharmaceutical company downloads data from PubChem and uses it to train its algorithm, does the company's proprietary system create ownership of the dataset itself? Or do the rights remain with the custodian of the public database?

The answer depends on the legal regime of databases in European law. However, a further complication emerges when one considers proprietary training data, constituted by datasets formed internally by pharmaceutical companies on the basis of their own private biological tests and their own intellectual property. These data can be considered "industrial secrets" in the sense of Directive 2016/943[13] on the protection of trade secrets. In the algoraceutical context, the value of the proprietary dataset can exceed the value of the algorithm itself, because the dataset incorporates decades of research and biological testing.

Moreover, there are datasets derived from clinical trials, which contain information on drug efficacy in real patients, on therapeutic responses, on adverse effects, on predictive markers. These data have enormous (perhaps incommensurable) value for training machine learning models predictive of clinical efficacy and safety. But ownership of this data is profoundly contested. Does it belong to the subjects who participated as patients in the trial? To the pharmaceutical company that conducted the clinical study? To the entities and research centers that administered the drug? To the public, insofar as data produced by publicly funded research constitute a common good?

The underlying question is thus radical and disruptive. Is the algoraceutical datum a commodity? Is it a right? Is it an essential condition of competition, an essential infrastructure in antitrust language? The contemporary answer in

[7] On the principal public and private chemical databases, see the sources cited below (PubChem, ChEMBL, DrugBank).

[8] PubChem is maintained by the US National Library of Medicine (National Center for Biotechnology Information); ChEMBL by the European Bioinformatics Institute (EMBL-EBI).

[9] DrugBank (2024).

[10] PubChem (2024).

[11] ChEMBL (2024).

[12] DrugBank (2024).

[13] Directive (EU) 2016/943 of the European Parliament and of the Council of 8 June 2016 on the protection of undisclosed know-how and business information (trade secrets), OJ L 157, 15 June 2016.

international and European law is multiple, contradictory, and evolving. In European Union law, data are initially and formally qualified as common goods, in the sense that the Data Governance Regulation, Regulation (EU) 2022/868, qualifies data as European public goods. However, the same legal system simultaneously recognizes the full capacity of the private party to appropriate data through the database regime, whereby whoever has substantially invested in the collection, verification, or presentation of contents receives an exclusive right over those data.

A company that has invested billions of euros in the collection of chemical and biological data, in their validation, in their structuring in databases, can prohibit others from reusing those data for research purposes, for commercial purposes, for training competing AI models. This exclusion, if practicable and applied, creates a barrier to entry; only whoever possesses the original databases can train really competitive AI models. In Chap. 8 we will address in depth the theme of the "algoraceutical datum" as "essential infrastructure" in the pharmaceutical market and the implications for competition and antitrust law; here it suffices to note that the first link in the chain of intellectual property in algorithmic invention is precisely control of ownership of input data.

The problem of "backward opacity" emerges here; a researcher observing an algorithm with good performance will sometimes be able to infer which training data have been used and therefore what is the structure of the underlying intellectual property. This reversal of opacity (data reverse engineering) represents a significant threat for holders of proprietary datasets.

7.2.2 The Database Regime (Dir. 96/9/EC)

Directive 96/9/EC on the legal protection of databases[14] protects two distinct rights: copyright in the selection and arrangement of contents and the *sui generis* database right, which protects substantial investments in data collection and verification. This second form of protection is particular to European law and has no equivalent in the United States.

According to Directive 96/9/EC, a "database" is defined as a collection of works, data or other independent contents, systematically organized and individually accessible by means of electronic means or otherwise. The database receives legal protection through the *sui generis* right if, in its constitution, verification or presentation of content, a substantial investment has been made. The substantial investment does not concern the intellectual creation of the data themselves, but rather the investment in the process of collection, verification, annotation, validation, and organization.

The application of this directive to pharmaceutical machine learning datasets is, however, profoundly problematic and unresolved. A pharmaceutical dataset (composed of chemical structures, biological activity data, physicochemical properties,

[14] Directive 96/9/EC of the European Parliament and of the Council of 11 March 1996 on the legal protection of databases, OJ L 77, 27 March 1996.

experimental results) is undoubtedly a "collection of data" in the sense of the directive. Its creation has undoubtedly required substantial investment; the cost of a biological activity test on a single compound can be hundreds of euros; the cumulative cost for a database of millions of compounds is astronomical.

But here the first crucial regulatory conflict arises. Directive 96/9/EC in Article 7 prohibits the database right holder from prohibiting extraction and reuse of the database. Article 9, paragraph 1, letter a, furthermore, permits limitations on the exclusive right when there is a "legitimate use" of the database in the context of scientific research. The question then becomes the following. When an AI pharmaceutical company extracts data from a proprietary database of a major pharmaceutical company to train a machine learning model, does it violate the exclusive right in the database? Does training an AI model constitute a form of "extraction" and "reuse" in the terms of the directive, or is it a legitimate use for scientific research?

The European Commission has not yet provided a definitive and binding interpretation, although consultations are underway with experts. Some patent attorneys and legal scholars argue that machine learning training clearly constitutes a form of database extraction and reuse in the terms of Article 7 and therefore is prohibited absent authorization from the right holder. The logical basis is strong, because the training process extracts millions of records from the database, stores them in the form of weights and parameters of the neural network, and uses them continuously in the operation of the model. This is, by definition, "reuse" in the sense of the directive.

Other experts argue that machine learning training for purposes of scientific research falls within the "legitimate use" exception in Article 9 and therefore does not violate the rights of the database holder. The logical basis lies in that the ultimate purpose is research, not direct commercial exploitation of the database itself.

In the meantime, while this question remains suspended, industrial practice gravitates toward a *de facto* nationalization of scientific data; only whoever owns the original databases can train really competitive AI models without exposing themselves to legal risks of violation of the database right. This creates a structural and growing competitive asymmetry. Pharmaceutical giants and technology giants that own vast proprietary databases can create proprietary AI models and keep them confidential as industrial secrets. Smaller innovators, startups, university research groups are structurally excluded, or must negotiate data access at significant royalties.

As for public databases such as PubChem and ChEMBL, these are products of public investment and academic research and their data are generally available under open license (often Creative Commons Zero). However, as for training data proprietary built by private pharmaceutical companies, the situation is different. The company has invested in expensive biological experiments. This investment is protected by the database regime of Directive 96/9/EC.

A second layer of protection for proprietary training data derives from the regime of trade secrets and industrial secrets, examined in the following section.

7.2.3 Trade Secret and Industrial Secret (Dir. 2016/943)

Directive (EU) 2016/943[15] on the protection of know-how and confidential business information against unlawful acquisition, use and disclosure creates a stronger and more modern protection regime than Directive 96/9/EC. An industrial secret (trade secret) according to Directive 2016/943 is information that presents three characteristics. First, it is not generally known; second, it has commercial value because it is secret; and third, it is the subject of reasonable protective measures.

A proprietary training dataset easily satisfies these three criteria. It is not generally known (the owner keeps it confidential), has significant commercial value (because it incorporates high experimental costs), and is protected by physical, digital, and organizational measures (limited access, encryption, nondisclosure agreements). For this reason, the regime of Directive 2016/943 offers more robust protection than the database right of Directive 96/9/EC.

However, a fundamental tension emerges between protection of trade secrets and the obligation of disclosure arising from civil liability. As will be examined in Chap. 6, a manufacturer of algoraceutical drug that is sued for damages can be obligated to disclose information about the structure of the training dataset, data selection, and methodology of construction. This legal coercion can effectively transform a trade secret into public information.

Directive 2016/943 permits exceptions to disclosure when protection of the trade secret outweighs the public interest in transparency. However, in the context of civil liability for personal injury, courts are generally reluctant to grant absolute protection to trade secrets.

7.3 Output Data and Patent Protection

7.3.1 Patentability Requirements and Algorithmic Invention

The European Patent Convention (EPC),[16] signed in Munich in 1973 and today subscribed to by 38 states, in Article 52, paragraph 1, prescribes the fundamental requirements that a patent must satisfy for to be granted: inventions that are novel (objective novelty), that involve an inventive step (non-obviousness), and that are susceptible of industrial application (capacity to be produced or used in any kind of industry).

Article 52, paragraph 2, of the EPC excludes from patentability a series of categories of "non-inventions." These include discoveries, scientific theories, abstract mathematical methods, presentations of information, abstract creations of a purely intellectual or aesthetic character, and, a crucial element for our purposes,

[15] On trade secrets, see Directive (EU) 2016/943, cited above.

[16] Convention on the Grant of European Patents (European Patent Convention), Munich, 5 October 1973, as subsequently amended.

"computer programs as such."[17] This exclusion has constituted for decades a formal obstacle to patentability of inventions generated by computer and algorithms.

However, from the 2000s onward, the case law of the EPO (European Patent Office) developed a doctrine that permits the patentability of "computer-implemented inventions"[18] when the algorithm produces a "further technical effect"[19] that goes beyond the mere execution of abstract mathematical calculations. A "further technical effect" means that the result of the algorithm has an impact on physical reality, on the internal structure of the system, or on the behavior of the system itself in a non-obvious manner.

In the pharmaceutical context, when an algorithm generates a new molecule with predicted properties (superior binding affinity,[20] lower toxicology, improved bioavailability), the molecule is patentable because it has a "further technical effect," in the sense that it is a real chemical structure, with concrete physical and biological properties, not a simple mathematical abstraction.

However, the underlying question remains. If the algorithm has autonomously generated this molecule through deep learning processes, by what right can a human claim to be its inventor? Or, alternatively, is the inventor truly the algorithm itself and the human merely the owner of the tool?

7.3.2 Sufficiency of Disclosure of the Invention. The "Black Box" Problem

A fundamental requirement for patentability of every invention is "sufficiency of disclosure." Article 83 of the EPC prescribes that "the application must contain a description of the invention sufficiently clear and complete to allow a person skilled in the art to put it into practice."[21] This principle is known as the enablement principle.

Article 83 of the European Patent Convention requires that the patent application describe the invention in a sufficiently clear and complete manner to allow a "person skilled in the art" to realize it on the basis of that description. This is the rule of "sufficiency of disclosure," in the sense that it is a fundamental element of the social contract inscribed in patent law. The inventor obtains a temporal monopoly (20 years from filing date), but in exchange reveals his secret, his know-how, allowing others

[17] Art. 52(2), European Patent Convention, excluding 'programs for computers as such' from patentable inventions.

[18] On computer-implemented inventions in EPO practice, see EPO, Guidelines for Examination, Part G-II, 3.3 (2024 edn).

[19] EPO, Guidelines for Examination, Part G-II, 3.3.1 (2024 edn), on the 'further technical effect' required for the patentability of computer-implemented inventions.

[20] On binding affinity as a parameter of pharmacological optimization, see Chap. 3.

[21] Art. 83, European Patent Convention: the European patent application must disclose the invention in a manner sufficiently clear and complete for it to be carried out by a person skilled in the art.

(once the patent has expired) to reproduce the invention on the basis of the description provided.

For a molecule generated by an AI algorithm, what does it mean to "describe" the invention sufficiently? The patent owner could provide multiple forms of description. These include the precise chemical structure of the molecule, easily describable in SMILES notation[22] or as a molecular graph, the methods of organic synthesis to reproduce the molecule in the wet laboratory, data of affinity and biological activity measured experimentally, and the biological mode of action, if known. All these elements are describable in a rigorous and verifiable manner.

But there is a crucial and controversial point. Can the patent applicant explain (and must he do so to satisfy Article 83?) how the algorithm arrived at conceiving this particular molecule, rather than others? If the algorithm is a "black box" in the sense discussed in Chap. 4, the answer is in most cases no, he cannot, at least not in a complete and causal manner. The algorithm has processed billions, sometimes trillions, of parameters and operations, has navigated a chemical space of astronomical dimensionality, has evaluated the molecule according to scoring functions whose decisions are in detail opaque, non-linear, dependent on complex interactions. Not even the creator of the model, the researcher who developed the algorithm, can say with certainty and completeness why the algorithm chose that specific molecular structure.

The inventor might describe the algorithmic process in the following terms. "A machine learning model, composed of a convolutional neural network with N layers, trained on a dataset of X compounds and Y chemical properties, was used to generate molecular candidates. The model was trained according to the following hyperparameters: Learning rate = [...], batch size = [...], optimizer = [...]...." But this description, however scrupulous, does not explain the "why" in a causal and mechanistic sense and does not illuminate the internal mechanism by which the molecule was identified as preferable compared to others.

It explains the procedure, the process of work, the workflow. But it does not explain the underlying causality, does not illuminate the conceptual structure. One might object that we know how the candidate was generated, but not why it is better. A person skilled in the art might not understand whether the molecule was selected for a profound conceptual reason, or for a fortunate coincidence, or for bias in the training dataset, or for a spurious feature captured by the neural network.

The legal question is therefore the following. Is this procedural description sufficient under Article 83 of the EPC? A person skilled in the art (an expert pharmaceutical chemist familiar with machine learning, who has the same algorithms and the same training data available) could reproduce the result? Formally and literally, yes, he would have the same model, the same input data, and could rerun the algorithm. If the algorithm is deterministic, rerunning would lead to the same result. If the algorithm contains stochastic elements,[23] slightly different results might emerge, but statistically equivalent.

[22] Weininger (1988).

[23] Srivastava et al. (2014).

However, a person skilled in the art might not truly "understand" why that molecule is preferable compared to thousands of others that the algorithm might have proposed, what its conceptual contribution to the field of chemotherapy is, what its deeper scientific significance is. Is it possible to reproduce an invention without understanding why?

The author's thesis is that Article 83 EPC must be reinterpreted in the context of modern generative AI, in order to make it compatible with the epistemic reality of algorithmic opacity. The requirement of "sufficiency of disclosure" should gradually shift from the focus on "mechanistic and causal understanding" of the discovery to the focus on "practical reproducibility" of the output. If a person skilled in the art, using the same algorithm and the same training data, could reasonably reproduce the same result (or results equivalent from the biological and chemical standpoint), then the requirement of sufficiency is satisfied. The structural opacity of the algorithm should not invalidate the patent; it should rather direct the patent applicant toward a description that emphasizes practical reproducibility rather than theoretical and mechanistic understanding.

This parallels exactly the opacity problem discussed in Chap. 4, Sect. 4.2, where it was argued that opacity is endemic to modern artificial intelligence, especially in deep neural networks, and that the legal system must adapt to this structural reality, not pretend to eliminate it with requirements that have become anachronistic.

Applied to algoraceutical inventions, the requirement of sufficiency of disclosure creates a paradoxical tension. If the algorithm is a deep neural network with millions of parameters, by what method can the patent owner "describe" this architecture sufficiently completely so that another researcher can "put it into practice"? The developers of the algorithm themselves often cannot explain how millions of parameters produce a particular prediction (the phenomenon of the "black box").

An important EPO case is "Case T 1017/19"[24] on "sufficiency of disclosure" for inventions generated by AI. The patent office recognized that for inventions generated by deep learning algorithms, the description of "how the model was trained" can substitute for the mechanistic description of "how the model works internally." Thus, discoverability can consist of three elements: (1) the architecture of the model (number of layers, type of layers, activation functions), (2) the training dataset (where it was obtained, how it was normalized), (3) training methods (learning rate, batch size, number of epochs), and (4) evaluation metrics (accuracy, precision, recall).

This thesis of "reproducibility substitutes for mechanistic understanding"[25] is a pragmatic solution to the black box problem, but raises a deeper philosophical

---

[24] On sufficiency of disclosure for inventions generated by machine-learning systems, EPO practice has developed from decision T 161/18 (Technical Board of Appeal 3.5.05, 12 May 2020), concerning an artificial neural network for determining blood pressure, and the subsequent decisions T 1191/19 and T 1539/20: the description must allow reproduction of the trained model, including characterization of the dataset and training parameters, without requiring full disclosure of the proprietary dataset. See EPO, Guidelines for Examination, Part G-II, 3.3.1 (2024 edn).

[25] The thesis advanced here, namely that sufficient reproducibility can substitute for the traditional requirement of mechanical understanding in inventions generated by AI systems.

question. If the system can be reproduced by rerunning training on an identical dataset, in what sense does the system remain an "invention" in the traditional legal meaning, where the invention is understood and controlled by its creator?

7.3.3 Novelty and Inventive Step. Is AI-Generated Output Patentable?

Even if the problems of discoverability were resolved, the fundamental question remains. Is the molecule generated by the algorithm truly "novel" in the sense of patentability? The novelty of an invention, according to Article 54 of the European Patent Convention, is evaluated on the basis of the "state of the art" (prior art), that is, the totality of all teachings made accessible to the public before the filing date of the patent application. A molecule never before synthesized, never described in world scientific literature, never patented by anyone, is by definition novel from the standpoint of the state of the art.

In the chemical context, novelty means that the molecule must not have been synthesized, described, or patented before. If an algorithm generates a molecule that already exists in the state of the art (perhaps deposited in a database of synthesized compounds) but had not been physically synthesized, the question becomes whether the molecule is patentable. Here the algorithm has a notable advantage from the standpoint of novelty; it can generate molecules in regions of chemical space never explored by humanity, it can combine structures and functionalities in ways no human chemist would have tried, it can navigate spaces of such high dimensionality that manual human research would be practically impracticable. A molecule generated by a well-trained algorithm on high-quality data is very likely to be novel in a formal and objective sense.

The question of inventive step (non-obviousness) is even more delicate. Under the classical definition, an invention shows inventive step if "it would not have been obvious to a person skilled in the art in light of the state of the art." In the algoraceutical context, the question becomes the following. If a machine learning algorithm generates a molecule optimized according to known parameters, is this generation obvious or inventive?

The answer depends on counterfactual analysis. If a person skilled in the art, having access to the same algorithm and the same training data, would reasonably have been able to arrive at the same result, then the generation is obvious and the patent should not be granted. If, instead, the result is surprising even to an expert in the field, then there may be inventive step.

Consider the concrete case of AlphaFold,[26] the neural network model developed by DeepMind for prediction of the three-dimensional structure of proteins on the basis of amino acid sequence. Many expert patent attorneys would persuasively argue that the answer is no. The reason is that a person skilled in the art in the field of structural biology (a molecular biologist familiar with AlphaFold) would have

[26] Jumper et al. (2021).

been able and indeed should have, used the same system to generate the same prediction. There is no inventive step in pressing the button of a public tool. The inventor did not devise a new strategy, an unprecedented approach, an original vision on how to predict protein structure; he simply operated a standard tool.

However, the situation changes radically if the researcher has trained a customized model, specifically calibrated on proprietary data, or has developed a new prediction algorithm not previously known, or has identified a neural network architecture never attempted before. In these cases, the algorithm itself can be the subject of a patent as a computer-implemented invention and the results it produces will have a significantly greater probability of receiving patent protection, because the "person skilled in the art" could not easily replicate that result without having the same algorithmic innovation.

In practice, patent offices (both the EPO and the USPTO) have granted patents on molecules generated by machine learning algorithms, recognizing that even if the algorithm is known, the result often exceeds expectations and demonstrates non-obvious inventive step.

7.4 The Inventor Problem

7.4.1 The Regulatory Framework: EPC, 35 U.S.C. §§100–103, Italian Patent Law

If a molecule generated by an algorithm is patentable, the next question is crucial from a legal standpoint. Who is the inventor? In whose name must the patent be filed?

The regulatory framework is traditionally anthropocentric. The European Patent Convention, United States patent law (United States Code, Title 35),[27] and the Italian Industrial Property Code[28] all presuppose that the inventor is a natural person. There is no legal category, in any of these regimes, of "non-human" inventor or "algorithm" inventor.

In Italian law, Article 58 of the Patent Law prescribes that "the right to a patent belongs to the inventor or to those to whom the right has been transferred." The inventor is always presumed to be a natural person unless proven otherwise.

When, therefore, an algorithm autonomously generates a molecule, the legal regime enters a regulatory vacuum. Technically, the algorithm cannot be the legal inventor, because the algorithm is not a natural person. Consequently, the current practice of patent offices is to list as inventor the natural person who programmed

---

[27] 35 U.S.C. § 103: a patent may not be obtained if the differences between the claimed invention and the prior art are such that the claimed invention as a whole would have been obvious, before the effective filing date, to a person having ordinary skill in the art.

[28] D.lgs. 10 February 2005, n. 30 (Codice della proprietà industriale), Gazzetta Ufficiale, serie generale, n. 52, 4 March 2005.

or supervised the algorithm, even if that person might not have fully understood how the system generated the result.

7.4.2 The DABUS Saga. Five Jurisdictions and an Emerging Consensus

The debate over the role of AI as inventor reached a turning point with the "DABUS" case (Device for the Autonomous Bootstrapping of Unified Sentience). Stephen Thaler, an American inventor working on artificial intelligence, filed patent applications in multiple jurisdictions for two inventions autonomously generated by DABUS. These are a beverage container with non-obvious ergonomic design and a food jar with superior thermal properties. The crucial particularity is that Thaler designated DABUS itself as the inventor in the patent application form.

Patent offices, in five different jurisdictions, faced an unprecedented legal dilemma. Thaler argued that DABUS, being an autonomous system that had genuinely created the inventions without direct human intervention, should be recognized as inventor. Patent offices, by contrast, argued that patent law does not permit recognition of non-human inventors.

The DABUS saga proceeded through courts in five major jurisdictions.

1. In the European legal system, the European Patent Office rejected Thaler's application holding that the inventor designated in the application must be a natural person. The matter was resolved by the Legal Board of Appeal in joined cases J 8/20 and J 9/20,[29] decided at hearing on December 21, 2021 with written reasons filed July 6, 2022. The Legal Board of Appeal established that, under Article 81 EPC and Rule 19 of the Implementing Regulations, the designation of inventor must refer to a person having legal capacity. No ruling of the Enlarged Board of Appeal intervened on the point and the question of non-human inventorship remains committed to legislative intervention by the European legislator.
2. In Germany, the Bundesgerichtshof,[30] with judgment X ZB 5/22 of June 11, 2024, confirmed the impossibility of designating an artificial intelligence system as inventor under German patent law, given that patent law presupposes qualification as a natural person. The German judgment introduces, however, a significant clarification vis-à-vis the European line, in that it clarifies that the human contribution need not be inventive or substantial, but it is sufficient that it be present, as in the selection of the problem or the formulation of the query posed

[29] European Patent Office, Legal Board of Appeal, decision of 21 December 2021 in joined cases J 8/20 and J 9/20 (reasons filed 6 July 2022), OJ EPO 2022, A58. On the substantive aspects, see Shemtov (2019); in Italian doctrine, Ricolfi (2022).

[30] Bundesgerichtshof, decision X ZB 5/22 of 11 June 2024, GRUR 2024, 1234, with note by Haedicke: the human contribution required by German patent law (PatG), while not needing to be inventive, requires at least the formulation of the problem or the choice to employ the system.

to the system. The BGH position is thus placed in an intermediate zone between the rigidity of the EPO and more flexible approaches of other jurisdictions.

3. In Japan, the Intellectual Property High Court[31] ruled on January 30, 2025 in the proceeding Thaler v. Commissioner of the Japan Patent Office, confirming the decision of the Tokyo District Court of May 16, 2024. The IPHC established that the inventor under Japanese patent law is limited to natural persons and rejected the request to recognize DABUS as inventor. While adhering to the anthropocentric principle, the court invited Japanese legislators to systematic reflection on algorithmic inventorship, a prompt subsequently taken up by the Cabinet Office which in 2025 published the Intellectual Property Strategic Program 2025, devoted also to inventive authorship in AI-assisted inventions.
4. In Switzerland, the Federal Administrative Court (Bundesverwaltungsgericht),[32] with judgment B-2532/2024 of June 26, 2025, confirmed that only natural persons can be designated as inventors, given that inventorship implies an act of intellectual creation that an AI system is not capable of accomplishing autonomously. The judgment presents, however, a notable peculiarity, in that the Court rejected the request to appoint DABUS as inventor but contemporaneously recognized that Thaler, having provided the data, trained the system, and evaluated the output as a patentable invention, can be designated himself as inventor. The Court annulled the denial of the Swiss intellectual property office and ordered the continuation of examination with the indication of Thaler as inventor. The Swiss approach, while confirming the exclusion of DABUS, offers a pragmatic solution that attributes inventorship to the natural person who consciously controlled the algorithmic process.
5. In the United Kingdom, the Supreme Court,[33] with judgment of December 20, 2023 in Thaler v. Comptroller-General of Patents, Designs and Trade Marks, definitively established that the Patents Act 1977 presupposes a human inventor and that DABUS cannot be recognized as inventor under British law. The judgment closes the internal jurisdictional path and refers any further evolution to the legislator.

[31] Intellectual Property High Court of Japan, judgment of 30 January 2025, Thaler v Commissioner of the Japan Patent Office, confirming the Tokyo District Court decision of 16 May 2024. On subsequent policy, see Cabinet Office of Japan, Intellectual Property Strategic Program 2025 (Tokyo, 2025).

[32] Bundesverwaltungsgericht (Swiss Federal Administrative Court), judgment of 26 June 2025, case B-2532/2024, Stephen L. Thaler v Eidgenössisches Institut für Geistiges Eigentum: while reaffirming that only natural persons can be inventors, the Court annulled the refusal of the Swiss Federal Institute of Intellectual Property and ordered examination to continue with Thaler designated as inventor, as a substantial contributor to data provision, system training and recognition of the output as an invention.

[33] United Kingdom Supreme Court, Thaler v Comptroller-General of Patents, Designs and Trade Marks, judgment of 20 December 2023, [2023] UKSC 49, confirming the Court of Appeal ([2021] EWCA Civ 1374) and the High Court ([2020] EWHC 2412 (Pat)): the Patents Act 1977 requires an inventor to be a natural person.

Although the five jurisdictions reached substantially convergent outcomes in refusing recognition of DABUS as inventor, a nuanced picture emerges, because the reasoning and application formulas diverge significantly. The EPO adopts a formal approach centered on Article 81 EPC, the BGH admits a minimum threshold of non-inventive human contribution, the Japanese IPHC invokes legislative intervention, the Swiss federal administrative court recovers Thaler as inventor on the basis of his actual role in the creation chain, and the UK Supreme Court adheres to a strictly textual reading. Current law presupposes a human inventor, but the heterogeneity of the concrete solutions signals that the long-term answer must be legislative, not judicial.

7.4.3 The Revised Guidance USPTO (November 2025): AI as Laboratory Tool

On February 13, 2024, in an attempt to provide operational guidance to patent attorneys and inventors, the United States Patent and Trademark Office issued an initial Inventorship Guidance for AI-Assisted Inventions.[34] The 2024 Guidance required significant human contribution for each claim using artificial intelligence technologies, applying by analogy the so-called Pannu factors,[35] consolidated in United States patent law for evaluating joint inventorship in inventions conceived by research teams. The approach was restrictive and cautious, imposing a relevant evidentiary burden on whoever intended to patent an AI-assisted invention. It was necessary to demonstrate, through claim-by-claim specific analysis, that the human contribution was not merely procedural. The practical result was a gray zone as to the patent status of many pharmaceutical inventions developed with the support of artificial intelligence systems.

On November 28, 2025, the USPTO published in the Federal Register the Revised Inventorship Guidance for AI-Assisted Inventions,[36] which completely rescinds the February 2024 Guidance and represents a methodological turning point in United States administrative law on inventive authorship.

The Revised Guidance establishes that there is no separate standard for AI-assisted inventions and that the same rules on inventorship apply to all

[34] United States Patent and Trademark Office, Inventorship Guidance for AI-Assisted Inventions, 89 Fed. Reg. 10043, 13 February 2024, subsequently rescinded by the Revised Guidance of 28 November 2025.

[35] The 'Pannu factors', from Pannu v Iolab Corp., 155 F.3d 1344 (Fed. Cir. 1998), are the established test for joint inventorship in US patent law: each co-inventor must have contributed significantly to the conception of the invention, contributed in a non-negligible way to the claimed subject matter, and done more than merely explain the state of the art.

[36] United States Patent and Trademark Office, Revised Inventorship Guidance for AI-Assisted Inventions, 90 Fed. Reg. 54636, 28 November 2025 (PTO-P-2025-0014): there is no separate standard for AI-assisted inventions; the Guidance of 13 February 2024 is rescinded; the Pannu factors are relevant only where multiple natural persons are potential joint inventors. The revision implements Executive Order 14179 of 23 January 2025.

inventions, regardless of the use of artificial intelligence systems in the inventive process. From the substantive perspective, the Office withdrew the analogical application of Pannu factors to the AI context and clarified that the Pannu test is relevant only when multiple natural persons are involved as potential joint inventors, given that an artificial intelligence system is not a person and cannot qualify as joint inventor. Consequently, rejection under §§ 101 and 115 of Title 35 U.S.C. strikes any application that designates an artificial intelligence system as inventor or as joint inventor.

On the operational front, AI is assigned the role of laboratory tool, assimilable to any sophisticated tool employed in experimental research, such as a scanning electron microscope, a mass spectrometer, a genomic sequencer, or an automated bioreactor. The person operating the system, selecting the training data, defining the biological problem, directing the exploration phases, and evaluating the output for the purpose of selecting the candidate to pursue, is inventor under Title 35. No longer is a claim-by-claim demonstration of human contribution required, provided that such contribution has directed the overall innovation process.

This revision represents a notable point of rupture in the evolution of United States patent law. The 2024 Guidance shifted the burden of proof onto the patent applicant, who had to demonstrate significant contribution. The Revised Guidance massively shifts the burden to the opponent, who must prove that the designated person is a mere puppet of the algorithm, without real directive and supervisory contribution.

For the pharmaceutical industry, this revision of the USPTO Guidance of November 2025 has enormous and immediate practical implications. It permits patenting of AI-generated inventions without the significant risk of invalidation for "lack of identifiable human inventor." The patent can be assigned to the principal researcher of the laboratory, to the head of the research department, to the director of pharmaceutical research, and, more generally, to whoever has guided the algorithmic process in a competent manner.

However, a critical and constructive evaluation of the Revised Guidance of the USPTO of November 2025 suggests that it significantly underestimates and undervalues the actual creative contribution, sometimes preponderant, of modern artificial intelligence. Treating the algorithm as an ordinary "laboratory tool," equivalent to a microscope or mass spectrometer, is a choice that is normatively questionable and perhaps inadequate to operational reality. The mass spectrometer reveals the structure of a molecule already existing in the physical world; the molecular design algorithm creates new molecules that do not exist in nature, that exist only in digital space until they are synthesized. The equivalence is legally convenient from an administrative and practical standpoint, but is intellectually and conceptually problematic.

On the plane of practice, the Revised Guidance distinguishes three operational scenarios, in which the AI system operates respectively as laboratory tool, as intelligent assistant that suggests research directions while remaining under human control, and as autonomous agent capable of independent decisions independent of human supervision.

In the first scenario, the natural person using the system is inventor, even in the absence of complete understanding of internal operation, just as the researcher employing a microscope remains inventor of what he observes under the microscope. In the second scenario, inventorship remains with the human researcher who guided the relevant decisions and validated the results. In the third scenario, that of the autonomous agent, the qualification becomes a gray zone in which the Guidance remits evaluation to a judgment of fact on the concrete modalities of employment of the system.

The classification as laboratory tool is therefore a question of fact, calibrated on how the system was actually used in the invention process. If the researcher formulated a defined technical problem, guided the algorithm toward the pertinent solution space, and critically validated the result, he can be recognized as inventor. If instead the researcher merely started the system without substantial supervision, the recognition of inventorship becomes fragile and contestable.

7.4.4 The EPO Position and European Case Law

The European Patent Office, while having explicitly rejected the designation of AI as inventor (DABUS decision, December 2021),[37] did not adopt the pragmatic and minimalist approach of the American USPTO. The Guidelines for Examination at the EPO, Part G-II, Section 3.3.1 ("Inventions Realized by Means of Computer"),[38] require a more profound and articulated analysis of the inventorship question in the context of AI.

The EPO requires that the "inventive concept" of the invention be clearly identified (the part that constitutes the true creative step, non-obvious, worthy of protection) and that this inventive concept be unequivocally attributable to a natural person. If the AI system has generated the molecular output, but the researcher has defined the chemical problem, has selected the training data, has critically evaluated the result on the basis of personal vision and competence, then the researcher might qualify as inventor of the "concept" even if he is not the one who materially generated the candidate.

Some studies and proposals from European legal doctrine, in particular work from German and Swiss universities, have suggested an approach of "transparent AI marking." The human inventor should be designated as is currently practiced, but the patent application should explicitly indicate the AI system used (with version, training date, training dataset, hyperparameters). This transparency would greatly facilitate subsequent evaluation of novelty, inventive step, reproducibility, and would create a useful register for purposes of civil liability.

The EPO position is thus median, balanced, between the minimalist approach of the USPTO (AI as mere ordinary tool) and a more rigorous hypothesis that would

---

[37] See the EPO Legal Board of Appeal decision cited above (joined cases J 8/20 and J 9/20).

[38] EPO, Guidelines for Examination, Part G-II, 3.3.1 (Computer-implemented inventions, 2024 edn).

require true and profound cognitive and creative interpenetration between human and machine. The EPO insists with awareness on the necessity that there be a "true contribution" from the human inventor, not purely procedural, but conceptually significant.

No referral on non-human inventorship has reached the Enlarged Board of Appeal, and the Legal Board in cases J 8/20 and J 9/20 framed the question as one lying beyond the interpretation of the present Convention. A possible evolution of the framework is therefore committed to legislative rather than judicial means.

This opening to legislative solutions represents a possible entry point for normative reform. Several European states have begun to consider modifications to their national patent law to recognize alternative forms of inventorship in the context of AI.

7.4.5 The Human Author as Supervisor: Human Contribution in Algoraceutical Invention

In the absence of legal recognition of AI as inventor, contemporary practice in algoraceutical patents is based on a legal fiction. The natural person who programmed, supervised, or controlled the algorithm is designated as inventor, even if he might not have intuitively generated the specific result of the invention.

However, this pragmatic solution conceals a profound philosophical and legal question. In what sense can a person be considered "inventor" of something he did not create and does not fully understand? What is the minimal contribution that a human must provide to be recognized as inventor of an AI output?

Returning to the real concrete process of pharmaceutical discovery through AI systems in the contemporary laboratory, what constitutes "human contribution" in the legal sense of inventorship? What are the concrete actions, choices, and orientations through which a researcher imprints his creative vision on an algorithm?

There emerge from contemporary practice three critical dimensions of human contribution. The first is "definition of the biological problem," the second is "curation and selection of training data," the third is "critical evaluation and selection of output."

First, definition of the biological problem. A researcher who directs the AI system to find a compound capable of inhibiting protein X with affinity below 1 nanomolar, of crossing the blood-brain barrier to reach the brain, of not activating serotonin receptor Y so as to avoid cardiac adverse effects, of presenting oral bioavailability above 50%, and of being synthesizable in fewer than 10 steps from common precursors, is providing the system with an extremely specific and sophisticated problem, which drastically restricts the search space. This is a first-order creative choice, because selection of the problem is a form of creative direction.

Second, curation and selection of training data. Whoever selects the training data, whoever cleans it of experimental error, whoever annotates it semantically, whoever creates the validation and test datasets, whoever chooses which distributions of molecules to include and which to exclude, is providing the algorithm the "sense organs" through which the system sees and interprets the chemical and biological world. A poor training dataset, contaminated by errors, imbalanced, leads to a poor AI model with bias and artifacts. A high-quality dataset, carefully annotated, balanced, leads to an excellent model. This is a highly significant contribution, often underestimated, to the quality of research.

Third, critical evaluation and selection of output. After the algorithm has generated thousands, sometimes tens of thousands, of molecular candidates, the human researcher must evaluate them according to criteria of chemical-biological intelligence, select a subset worthy of synthesis and experimentation, decide which trade-offs between different chemical properties are acceptable. If the compound has very high affinity but is poorly soluble, is it worth synthesizing? If it has good biological profile but is difficult to synthesize, is it practical? This critical evaluation is a form of supervision exercised by the human, of artistic direction, of curation.

The author's thesis, matured after analysis of the preceding chapters, is that human contribution in contemporary algorithmic invention is increasingly one of supervision, direction, and selection, not of conception in the traditional sense. In a completely automated automobile assembly line, the human worker does not personally conceive each automobile that comes out of the factory; he supervises the process, intervenes when something does not work, sets the operating parameters. Similarly, the researcher employing modern AI is not personally conceiving each molecule proposed by the algorithm; he is supervising the generation process, directing it toward certain biological objectives, filtering the results according to his experience.

But here emerges a central and profound tension with the traditional concept of patentability and inventorship in intellectual property law. Patent law has been historically constructed around the figure of the inventor as "conceptor," as one who generates the idea from the mind, who has a "vision" of something new, who gives form to something that previously did not exist. Patent law requires "invention" (inventive step), that is, real, non-trivial, non-obvious inventive activity. If human activity is primarily supervisory, is it still "inventive" in the traditional sense? In what sense is a person who supervises an automatic process an "inventor"?

The analogy with artistic direction in cinema is illuminating, because a film producer who directs the realization of a film provides creative direction, artistic supervision, selection of talents and solutions. But no one would say that the producer is the true artist, the intellectual creator of the film. The art director, the director, the actors are the artists. The producer is the supervisor, the curator. But patent law does not have the conceptual structure to recognize "curation" as a form of inventorship; it has a structure focused on direct intellectual "conception." This is a growing gap between law and reality.

As Chap. 6 demonstrated, when AI causes civil damages, civil and criminal liability must ascend to the ultimate responsible person, that is, to whoever chose the algorithm, whoever chose the data, whoever chose the output criteria, and whoever supervised the process. The attribution of responsibility follows the chain of causality and control. Similarly, when AI creates value (a patent), intellectual property law should recognize as inventor the person who exercised conscious and responsible supervision over the algorithmic process. Current global practice gradually moves toward this conclusion. Invention is attributed to the human supervisor, with awareness that this is not a "conception" in the traditional sense, but a modern form of generation mediated by tools.

According to this interpretation, the role of the human is that of a "supervisor" of the algorithm, in that he provides direction, approves important decisions, and validates results. This model is consistent with the Revised Guidance of the USPTO that classifies the algorithm as a "laboratory tool."

However, a critical tension emerges in the context of autonomous laboratories, where human supervision is reduced to occasional interventions to reload reagents or address mechanical errors. In these cases, human contribution becomes increasingly marginal and the inventorship question becomes even more acute.

7.5 Chematica/Synthia and Navigation of the Chemical Graph: A Paradigmatic Case

In Chap. 3 we alluded to the Chematica system, developed by Bartosz Grzybowski and his group at the Institute of Organic Chemistry of the Polish Academy of Sciences in Warsaw in the course of the 2010s, with seminal works dating to 2005 and progressive validations of the system between 2012 and 2016.[39] The Grzybowski Scientific Inventions company, which owned Chematica, was acquired in 2017 by Merck KGaA of Darmstadt and the system was relaunched commercially under the name Synthia® on the occasion of the American Chemical Society congress in 2018. We return to this case here because it embodies in crystalline form the tension described in the preceding paragraphs, given that the conflict between the operational reality of algorithmic invention and the regulatory framework of intellectual property manifests itself exemplarily therein.

Chematica is an artificial intelligence system that represents the knowledge of organic synthetic chemistry as an enormously complex and multidimensional graph, where the nodes are chemical molecules and the arcs are chemical transformations (organic reactions).[40] The system is not a simple database of reactions; it is a system with capacities for autonomous exploration and reasoning. The system navigates this graph of astronomical complexity to identify synthesis pathways for biologically significant target molecules. It does not limit itself to suggesting syntheses already known in world chemical literature; it discovers alternative, creative synthesis routes, not previously considered by the chemical community, sometimes skillfully sidestepping existing patents on synthesis processes.

In a seminal 2012 article, the Chematica system was used to propose an alternative synthesis of a molecule of commercial and biological importance, a cancer drug

[39] On the genesis of Chematica, see Kowalik et al. (2012) and Grzybowski et al. (2018). In 2017 Merck KGaA (Darmstadt) acquired Grzybowski Scientific Inventions, holder of the system, subsequently marketed as Synthia® from 2018.

[40] Szymkuć et al. (2016).

already patented decades earlier. The synthesis proposed by Chematica was radically different from that known in the literature, used different reagents, different retrosynthetic pathways, a different number of steps. The target molecule was already patented (the original patent was still in force), but the new synthesis route was not covered by the existing patent, which had protected only the original synthesis process. Chematica had "invented" a new way to reach the same destination.

This case is crucial to our theme not only for its factuality, but for what it means conceptually. It is not a matter of Chematica as a "tool that accelerates and facilitates what humans would do anyway." It is irrefutable evidence of AI that genuinely conceives, that navigates a space of possibilities so vast as to find original solutions that human ingenuity had not previously identified, not even in decades of intensive research. In Chap. 4, Sect. 4.5, we classified this level of performance as "agent," as AI that possesses genuine autonomy. Chematica truly behaves as an autonomous agent in this sense.

But under current patent law, who is the inventor of the new synthesis route discovered by Chematica? According to the Revised Guidance of the USPTO of November 2025, it is the researcher, the laboratory director, or the employee who formulated the chemical problem and critically evaluated the proposed result. It is not Chematica itself, obviously. According to the EPO approach, the question is more open, because it is necessary to verify whether the human researcher contributed to the "inventive concept" of the alternative synthesis. In no case, under contemporary law, is Chematica the inventor.

And here the legal tension is greatest and most visible. The creative work is clearly, honestly, that of the algorithm. The human performs primarily a facilitating function (he provided the software, the set of reaction data), a problem formulator (what to search for), and a validator (is this a good result?). But patent law assigns all intellectual property to the human. It is a necessary legal fiction for the practical functioning of the system, but it is a fiction, a divergence from reality.

A concrete illustration of these abstract principles emerges from the case of Chematica, subsequently renamed Synthia, a synthesis planning system developed at the Institute of Organic Chemistry of the Polish Academy of Sciences in Warsaw and commercialized by Merck KGaA.

Chematica/Synthia uses machine learning and neural networks to navigate an enormous space of possible chemical reactions. The system addresses the "synthetic planning" problem.[41] Given a molecular target, that is, a molecule the researcher wants to synthesize, the system calculates possible efficient synthetic routes, taking into account constraints such as chemical reactivity, availability of precursors, and synthesis costs.

The number of possible synthesis routes for a complex molecule is astronomical. The theoretical chemical space contains approximately 10^{60} possible molecules[42] and the number of possible synthetic pathways is even vaster. No human chemist, working with paper and pencil, could explore this space. Chematica/Synthia uses a

[41] Coley et al. (2018) and Segler et al. (2018).

[42] The theoretical chemical space is estimated at approximately 10^{60} possible molecules.

machine learning model trained on millions of reactions published in the literature to learn reactivity patterns and then uses graph search to navigate the space of possible synthetic pathways.

From the standpoint of patent invention, Chematica/Synthia has generated several relevant situations. First, the discovery of new synthesis routes for known molecules; second, the discovery of new chemical transformations that had not been published in the literature; third, the identification of innovative synthetic intermediates that reduce the number of steps or improve overall yield.

If a researcher uses Chematica to generate a new synthesis route for a target molecule, who can claim the invention of the route? The researcher formulated the problem (the desired target molecule), but the algorithm autonomously generated the route. According to the classification of the Revised Guidance of the USPTO, if the researcher chose to use Chematica and validated the proposed route, the researcher can be designated as inventor. If instead the system operated completely autonomously, the question remains open.

7.6 The Tension Between Operational Reality and Regulatory Framework

The gap and tension between the actual and contemporary functioning of pharmaceutical AI and the traditional regulatory framework of intellectual property is not merely theoretical or academic. It has three significant practical consequences that directly influence industry, research, and the competitive structure of the market.

The first consequence is attributive uncertainty. When an algorithm generates a valuable pharmaceutical invention in the context of a complex research team (as often happens in pharmaceutical companies), who exactly must be formally designated as inventor? If ten researchers have contributed in various ways (who selected the biological target, who prepared and curated data, who launched the algorithm, who evaluated the result, who coordinated the process) are they all joint inventors? And if so, what is the relative weight of their contribution? The law provides no clear and applicable criteria. This generates legal uncertainty, internal litigation, risks of patent invalidation for omission of inventors or incorrect inclusion. A company that files a patent does not know whether the designation of inventor will be accepted or contested.

The second consequence is systematic undervaluation of the creative contribution of the algorithm. By treating AI as a "mere ordinary tool," equivalent to a pipette or an incubator, contemporary law (especially the Revised Guidance of the USPTO) tends to minimize the real profoundly creative nature of the system. In the patent evaluation process (both in examination at the patent office and in any invalidation litigation), this systematic undervaluation can lead to a series of negative consequences for those holding the patent: narrower and less protective claims, greater difficulty in demonstrating inventive step before the examiner, greater risk of oppositions grounded in the alleged "obviousness" of the molecule generated by a public algorithm.

The third consequence is misalignment and distortion of incentives for innovation in the algorithms themselves. Currently, the patent for a discovery made with AI goes to the human operator of the AI, to the researcher, to the laboratory head. It does not go to the entity that has invested billions of euros in the development of the algorithm itself, that is, to the AI "startup," to the technology research unit, to the team of data scientists who created the model. If a startup like QuantumChemistry.AI invests 2 billion euros in the development of a superior molecular design algorithm, but every discovery made with that system is patented in the name of the employee researcher who found it, the incentives for the startup to invest massively in algorithm development are seriously altered and reduced. The startup does not capture the full value of its technological innovation.

Consider the paradigmatic example of DeepMind, which developed AlphaFold with an investment of hundreds of millions of dollars, with years of work by highest-level researchers. The system is made public and free. A researcher in any university anywhere in the world uses AlphaFold to predict the structure of a protein never before characterized, a protein of biological importance for a rare disease. This prediction leads to scientific discoveries.

In the actual contemporary operational reality, AI algorithms are not mere "sophisticated calculators," but autonomous systems that can generate surprising and original results. However, the regulatory framework continues to presume that the inventor is a natural person who understands and controls his own inventive process. This disparity creates a legal fiction in which a person is designated as inventor of a work he might not have intuitively created.

Furthermore, the inventorship question becomes even more acute in the context of civil liability. If a drug generated by an algorithm causes harm, who is responsible? The nominal "owner" of the invention, designated as inventor in the patent? Or the true creator, the algorithm itself (represented by its developer)? This ambiguity creates a zone of blurred responsibility where nobody can be held fully accountable.

A further tension emerges from the question of "algorithmic transparency" discussed in Chap. 5. If the algorithm operates as a "black box,"[43] how can the person designated as inventor justify a claim of inventorship that involves insufficient understanding of the underlying process? The opaque nature of the algorithm contradicts the regulatory presupposition that the inventor "understands" the invention.

7.7 Toward a Regime for Algoraceutical Invention

The contemporary solutions adopted by various legal systems (pragmatic from a practical standpoint but conceptually and theoretically unsatisfactory) are positioned along a spectrum of options. Three regulatory directions appear practicable and worthy of consideration.

The first direction is that of "persistent legal fiction." One maintains and accepts the fiction that the human is the inventor, one recognizes openly that this fiction is

[43] On the intrinsic opacity of deep neural networks, see Chap. 4, Sect. 4.2.

increasingly a convenience administrative and practical rather than an acceptable description of reality, and one proceeds anyway. It is the approach of the Revised Guidance of the USPTO of November 2025. It is pragmatic in its application. It permits patents to be filed, granted, exploited commercially, while maintaining continuity with the traditional patent system. But it is intellectually and philosophically dishonest. It forces the legal system to transfigure operational reality to adapt it to a normative model that has been superseded by technology.

The second direction is that of "extended authorship" or "transparent authorship." One designates the human inventor as is currently practiced in existing patent systems, but one adds a requirement of mandatory and structured transparency, in the sense that the patent application must explicitly disclose that the invention was conceived with the assistance of AI, must indicate the AI system used (with name, version, training date), the training dataset (or at least its aggregated characteristics and source), the evaluation and selection criteria of output. This approach, already discussed in European and Swiss academic and professional circles, maintains the current system of human inventor (providing continuity), but "marks" it permanently to trace the AI contribution.

The third direction is that of a new *sui generis* intellectual property category. One could create an exclusive right specifically and only for inventions conceived through artificial intelligence, distinct from traditional patent right. This *sui generis* right could have a duration shorter than that of the classical patent (for example, 10–15 years instead of 20), a different scope and breadth of protection, a structure of distribution and sharing of the right between the algorithm owner and the human operator. This approach would, however, require significant international legislative agreement and would be complex to implement coordinately between different jurisdictions. It has, however, the intrinsic merit of addressing the problem directly and honestly, rather than sidestepping it with legal fictions.

The author's evaluation, based on the analysis conducted in the preceding chapters, is that the second direction, that of extended authorship with requirements of mandatory and structured transparency, proves the most practicable and desirable in the medium term. It does not dismantle the existing patent system, which is well rooted in institutions, courts, and commercial practice worldwide; it modifies it gradually with acceptable increments.

Transparency regarding AI systems used in pharmaceutical discovery has multiple benefits: (1) it informs the public and the scientific community about the dynamics of contemporary innovation in drugs; (2) it significantly facilitates subsequent evaluation of novelty and inventive step in the patent process; (3) it creates a permanent and accessible register for purposes of civil and criminal liability (enabling the complainant to ascertain which algorithm contributed to the suffered damage); (4) it begins to systematically trace the economic value and innovation created by algorithms, which can then inform future policies of different, more equitable compensation and incentive.

The pharmaceutical sector demands structural regulatory clarity. Clinical trials last 5–10 years from first human test to regulatory approval; investment in a new drug averages $2.6 billion according to PhRMA's 2024 calculation.[44] Without clear protection of intellectual property in the algorithmic context, incentives for innovation are seriously compromised and distorted. A transition toward extended authorship with transparency provides this necessary clarity, in the sense that the patent is legally valid, is granted to the human operator of the AI, commercial value is protected, but simultaneously all stakeholders know it was generated with the assistance of AI. They know which AI, which data, which criteria. This transparency feeds both accountability and responsible innovation.

How should law evolve to reflect the contemporary reality of pharmaceutical AI?

A possible solution is the introduction of a new legal category. This would be the patent for "algorithmic invention," distinct from the traditional patent for "human invention." This new regime would have the following content.

(1) Designation of the Inventor For algoraceutical patents, both the AI and the natural person who supervised it could be codesignated as "inventors." This reflects the reality that both the machine and the human contributed to the result. Alternatively, a new concept of "AI system owner" could be introduced, distinct from the traditional concept of "inventor."

(2) The Transparency Requirement For patents on algoraceutical inventions, a specific requirement could require the owner to provide an "explicable description of the algorithm." This does not mean a complete mechanistic description (which might be impossible for "deep learning" algorithms),[45] but a description of the general principles of the system, the training data used, and the validation methods.

(3) Post-patent Obligations Algoraceutical patents could entail specific post-patent obligations. These would be the obligation to maintain and update the system over time, the obligation to subject the system to significant human control, consistent with the AI Regulation,[46] and the obligation of disclosure in case of litigation on liability.

(4) Duration of Protection Patent protection for algoraceutical inventions could be limited to a shorter period than traditional patents (for example, 15 years instead of 20), reflecting the fact that AI systems evolve rapidly and the value of protection decreases more quickly.

(5) The Right to Copy the AI as "Essential Infrastructure" Given the concentration of training datasets and AI systems in the hands of a few major pharmaceutical players, an obligatory licensing right in algoraceutical AI systems could be introduced, treating them as "essential facilities"[47] in the antitrust sense.

---

[44] PhRMA (2024).

[45] On opacity and explainability of the pharmaceutical algorithm, see Chap. 4, Sect. 4.2.

[46] Regulation (EU) 2024/1689 (Artificial Intelligence Act), OJ L, 2024/1689, 12 July 2024.

[47] See Chap. 8, on algoraceutical data as an essential facility.

This innovative regime would recognize the technical reality of algorithmic invention while maintaining safeguards against excessive concentration of economic power and scientific knowledge.

7.8 Concluding Observations

The question of intellectual property in the context of pharmaceutical algorithmic invention has no simple solution, because the phenomenon of creative AI challenges the fundamental presuppositions of traditional intellectual property law.

In conclusion, this chapter on intellectual property and algoraceutical invention closes with three synthetic and interconnected theses that summarize our analysis and provide a forward-oriented perspective.

The first thesis is that of established patentability and pragmatically resolved inventorship. There is no contemporary legal doubt that pharmaceutical inventions conceived through artificial intelligence are patentable under existing national and international laws. Contemporary patent law, after the conclusion of the DABUS saga (2024–2025) and after the Revised Guidance of the USPTO (November 2025), has established how to pragmatically resolve the inventor question, proposing to designate as inventor the human researcher who operated the algorithm, who supervised the process, who evaluated the output. This pragmatic solution is not a conceptually perfect solution from a philosophical and theoretical standpoint, but is practicable from an administrative and legal standpoint and permits industry to function, to invest, to innovate.

The second thesis concerns reinterpretation of sufficiency of disclosure. The requirement of "sufficiency of disclosure" of Article 83 of the European Patent Convention must be reinterpreted in the context of inventions generated by opaque AI systems ("black box"). The focus should not remain on mechanistic and causal understanding (the "why") of the invention (which is often impossible for deep neural networks), but rather on practical reproducibility (the "how"). If a person skilled in the art, with access to the same algorithm and the same training data, could reasonably reproduce the result or equivalent results, the requirement of sufficiency is satisfied. Algorithmic opacity is a structural fact, not an exception, and law must adapt.

The third thesis is that of structural tension between protection of trade secrets and transparency requirements. Contemporary law protects and incentivizes maintenance of industrial secrets (trade secret) and simultaneously requires transparency in high-risk AI systems (AI Regulation, art. 13, note).[48] In the specific context of algoraceutical invention, this tension is endemic, not accidental, and cannot be resolved through ordinary interpretation. It will be necessary to address and resolve it legislatively, with a solution that permits "limited transparency" in patent proceedings and civil liability litigation, while maintaining protection of industrial secrets in the ordinary forms of commercial competition.

[48] Art. 13, Regulation (EU) 2024/1689 (transparency obligations for high-risk AI systems).

A concluding reference to Chap. 8, because the input data used by the AI, the exclusive ownership of proprietary databases, the control and access to training datasets, will emerge as central legal questions not only for patent intellectual property, but for competitive structure and market power in the global pharmaceutical sector. A company that owns exclusive proprietary high-quality databases can train superior AI models and therefore obtain stronger patents more suitable to protect significant innovations. This creates barriers to market entry and concentrations of economic power that merit and require serious attention from the standpoint of antitrust law and competition regulation.

In the short term, law remains anchored to an anthropocentric conception of inventorship. Inventions generated by AI remain patentable, but the designation of inventor remains a natural person, probably the programmer or supervisor of the system. This solution is pragmatic but unsatisfactory from a conceptual standpoint.

In the medium term, there will probably be fragmentation of law. Some countries (such as Switzerland and potentially the United States) may evolve toward explicit recognition of AI as inventor or coinventor. Other countries (such as the European Union) may maintain the presumption that the inventor is human, but allowing more flexible designation of who the responsible human is.

In the long term, the patent regime for algoraceutical drugs will converge toward a solution that recognizes the hybrid nature of algorithmic invention, which is neither purely human nor purely mechanical, but rather a co-creation of human and artificial intelligence. This new regime would entail significant legislative modifications and a new way of thinking about intellectual property in the context of advanced research.

The following chapter develops the implications of this evolution in competition law (Chap. 8)[49] and in subsequent regulatory governance.

References

ChEMBL (2024). https://www.ebi.ac.uk/chembl/. Accessed 7 June 2026

Coley CW, Green WH, Jensen KF (2018) Machine learning in computer-aided synthesis planning. Acc Chem Res 51:1281–1289

DrugBank (2024). https://go.drugbank.com/. Accessed 7 June 2026

Grzybowski BA, Szymkuć S, Gajewska E, Molga K, Dittwald P, Wołos A, Klucznik T (2018) Chematica: a story of computer code that started to think like a chemist. Chem 4:390–398

Jumper J, Evans R, Pritzel A, Green T, Figurnov M, Ronneberger O, Tunyasuvunakool K, Bates R, Žídek A, Potapenko A, Bridgland A, Meyer C, Kohl SAA, Ballard AJ, Cowie A, Romera-Paredes B, Nikolov S, Jain R, Adler J, Back T, Petersen S, Reiman D, Clancy E, Zielinski M, Steinegger M, Pacholska M, Berghammer T, Bodenstein S, Silver D, Vinyals O, Senior AW, Kavukcuoglu K, Kohli P, Hassabis D (2021) Highly accurate protein structure prediction with AlphaFold. Nature 596:583–589

[49] See Chap. 8, where the qualification of algoraceutical data as an essential facility and its effects on competition are analysed, in continuity with the concentration of training-data banks observed here.

Kowalik M, Gothard CM, Drews AM, Gothard NA, Weckiewicz A, Fuller E, Grzybowski BA, Bishop KJM (2012) Parallel optimization of synthetic pathways within the network of organic chemistry. Angew Chem Int Ed 51:7928–7932

PhRMA (2024) Biopharmaceutical research industry profile. PhRMA, Washington

PubChem (2024). https://pubchem.ncbi.nlm.nih.gov/. Accessed 7 June 2026

Ricolfi M (2022) Artificial intelligence and patent law: notes on the DABUS saga. Il Diritto industriale 5:425 ff.

Segler MHS, Preuss M, Waller MP (2018) Planning chemical syntheses with deep neural networks and symbolic AI. Nature 555:604–610

Shemtov N (2019) A study on inventorship in inventions involving AI activity. Study commissioned by the European Patent Office, Munich

Srivastava N, Hinton G, Krizhevsky A, Sutskever I, Salakhutdinov R (2014) Dropout: a simple way to prevent neural networks from overfitting. J Mach Learn Res 15:1929–1958

Szymkuć S, Gajewska E, Klucznik T, Molga K, Dittwald P, Startek M, Bajczyk M, Grzybowski BA (2016) Computer-assisted synthetic planning: the end of the beginning. Angew Chem Int Ed 55:5904–5937

Weininger D (1988) SMILES, a chemical language and information system. 1. Introduction to methodology and encoding rules. J Chem Inf Comput Sci 28:31–36

Competition, Data, and the Algoraceutical Market

8

Abstract

This chapter analyses the algoraceutical market through the lens of competition law and data regulation. It asks whether pharmaceutical training data, the algoraceutical data, can be qualified as an essential facility under Article 102 TFEU, and how the concentration of data among Big Pharma and Big Tech reshapes barriers to entry and the risk of abuse of dominance. The analysis surveys the European framework that now governs data and digital markets, the Digital Markets Act, the Digital Services Act, the Data Act, the Data Governance Act and the European Health Data Space, and situates the pharmaceutical digital space as a relevant market. It then examines the processing of personal data in algorithmic clinical trials under the GDPR, including the conditions for scientific research and the debate opened by the Digital Omnibus package. Two competition problems specific to algoraceutics are addressed, algorithmic collusion in pricing and algorithmic discrimination in access to medicines, against the background of the Meta v Bundeskartellamt and Illumina/Grail judgments. The chapter concludes that the concentration of training data, more than any single conduct, is the structural variable that competition policy must learn to govern.

8.1 Introduction: Delimiting the Inquiry

The intersection between competition law and personal data protection represents one of the most critical frontiers of contemporary European regulation, particularly in industries characterized by data-intensive processing. In the pharmaceutical sector, this tension assumes even more pronounced contours, since computational research for drug discovery requires the accumulation, integration, and processing of large volumes of heterogeneous data, while at the same time the same algoraceutical innovation feeds phenomena of economic concentration and informational

G. Rotino, *Algoraceutics - Legal Perspectives on Artificial Intelligence in Drug Discovery and Development*, Law for Professionals,
https://doi.org/10.1007/978-3-032-38537-6_8

asymmetries among market operators.[1] We believe that an adequate understanding of these phenomena requires an integrated analysis that does not artificially separate the two orders of questions, but rather recognizes their profound interconnection.

The crucial question can be formulated in the following terms. Does data, in its algoraceutical sense, constitute an essential resource for competition in the market for drug discovery and pharmaceutical innovation? And if so, what degree of antitrust regulation should apply to enterprises that control access to this resource? These questions, which will emerge in the paragraphs below of this analysis, require particular attention to the way in which the European legislator has progressively constructed an integrated regulatory framework, combining tools for personal data protection with competition law rules and obligations for equitable access to digital infrastructure.

Another fundamental aspect concerns the way in which computational pharmaceutical research structurally modifies power relationships in the sector. Traditionally, competitive advantage in the pharmaceutical sector was founded on the intellectual property of research results, protected through patents. In the algoraceutical context, competitive advantage is increasingly founded on the control of data and computational infrastructure necessary to process it. This shift carries profound implications for the definition of the relevant market itself and for the modalities of application of antitrust law.

The present analysis proceeds through a series of logical steps. First, we address the definitional question concerning the notion of "algoraceutical data" and its legal characterization. Subsequently, we examine concentration phenomena in the pharmaceutical research market and the relative barriers to entry. Next, we analyze the recent European regulatory framework, with particular attention to the DMA, DSA, Data Act, and EHDS regulations. We then address specific issues relating to the processing of personal data in clinical experimentation. Finally, we examine competition law issues specific to matters such as algorithmic collusion and algorithmic discrimination in the pharmaceutical context.

8.2 Data as Good and Resource: The "Algoraceutical Data"

8.2.1 Definition and Legal Nature

The first step is to clarify the notion of "data" and, more specifically, "algoraceutical data." In European law, the notion of data has been progressively constructed through a multiplicity of regulations and directives, beginning with the definition in the Data Governance Act,[2] which qualifies it as "any digital representation of acts,

[1] Ottolia (2017), passim; for a general framework, see Libertini (2014).

[2] Regulation (EU) 2022/868 (Data Governance Act), Art. 2(1), defining data as 'any digital representation of acts, facts or information and any compilation of such acts, facts or information, including in the form of sound, visual or audiovisual recording'; the definition appeared, in similar terms, in the Proposal COM(2020) 767 final of 25 November 2020.

facts, or information." However, this definition remains insufficient to understand the complex reality of data in the pharmaceutical context, where data is not merely information, but rather an integrative complex of clinical, biological, genomic, and behavioral information, collected and aggregated over time.

A fundamental distinction is that between personal data and non-personal data. Personal data is governed by the GDPR,[3] while non-personal data is governed by Regulation (EU) 2018/1807.[4] In the algoraceutical context, however, most data is of hybrid or mixed nature, in the sense that it contains both elements of personal data and elements of non-personal data. Legal theory has highlighted that the legal discipline of immaterial goods is generally constructed on characteristics and interests pertaining to particular legal interests,[5] which requires preliminarily a careful definitional operation in order to determine which normative regime to apply.

The qualification of data as a legal good has been the subject of in-depth studies.[6] We believe that algoraceutical data does indeed constitute a complex legal good, characterized simultaneously by a dimension of protection of individual personality (where the data contains sensitive information relating to the subject), by an economic dimension (where the data has market value as an input to computational research), and by an ordinal dimension (where access to data represents a condition for participation in the market). The multidimensional nature of algoraceutical data thus requires an integrated approach to regulation.

8.2.2 Sources of Algoraceutical Data

In the context of computational pharmaceutical research, algoraceutical data comes from multiple diverse sources. One source consists of clinical databases, that is, collections of clinical information derived from controlled pharmaceutical studies (randomized controlled trials), which represent a traditional source of medical information with high levels of standardization. A second source is genomic, derived from DNA sequencing and analysis of genetic variants associated with disease susceptibility. A third source comes from neuroimaging (MRI, PET, EEG), tissue analysis, and quantifiable biomarkers.

A fourth source is that of electronic health systems, that is, data contained in electronic medical records, hospital information systems, disease-specific registries,[7]

---

[3] Regulation (EU) 2016/679 (GDPR), Arts. 4 and 9.

[4] Regulation (EU) 2018/1807 on a framework for the free flow of non-personal data in the European Union.

[5] Ottolia (2017), p. 16, cautioning that the legal discipline of the immaterial is generally built on the characteristics and interests of particular legal goods, and stressing the need for a preliminary definitional exercise before the legal qualification of data.

[6] On the qualification of data as a legal good, see Angiolini (2020).

[7] On 'mixed data', see European Commission, Guidance on the Regulation on a framework for the free flow of non-personal data in the European Union, COM(2019) 250 final, 29 May 2019, point 2.2, qualifying mixed data as aggregates of personal and non-personal data, 'the vast majority of data sets used in the data economy'.

and electronic health records.[8] These data are characterized by high temporal granularity, as they record practically every contact between the patient and the healthcare system. Their integration into a single repository represents a source of extraordinarily rich information.

A fifth source, growing in importance, is that of Real World Data (RWD), that is, data collected in contexts of ordinary drug use outside of controlled clinical trials. The European Medicines Agency increasingly recognizes the scientific and regulatory value of RWD, which allow for the generation of Real World Evidence (RWE) regarding the actual efficacy and safety of drugs in heterogeneous populations.[9] These data come from wearable devices, e-health apps, telemedicine systems, and represent a particularly rich source of information for computational research.

A sixth source is that of social media and digital platforms, where patients spontaneously document their own symptoms, therapeutic experiences, and side effects of drugs. Although this source is not traditionally considered in the context of formal clinical research, it acquires ever greater importance in computational research, as it provides signals of adverse effects and drug efficacy in real time.

This multiplicity of sources generates what Ottolia has effectively described as a "deposit" of heterogeneous data accumulated over time.[10] The deposit is characterized by increasing scale, by the difficulty of extraction and refinement, by the heterogeneity of origins, and by the need for massive investment of human and technological capital in order to be effectively exploited. This metaphor allows us to understand how Big Data in the algoraceutical context constitutes a genuine strategic resource, in the sense attributed by business economics literature,[11] that is, a factor of production not easily replicable that provides its possessor with a durable competitive advantage.

The strategic importance of the data deposit in the algoraceutical sector cannot be overemphasized. While in the traditional economy competitive advantage derived from the ownership of patents and the capacity for chemical synthesis, in the algoraceutical context competitive advantage derives from access to data that permit training of more accurate machine learning models. A larger, more granular, and temporally persistent data deposit enables training of models with greater accuracy, which translates directly into greater drug discovery capacity. Consequently, control of the data deposit confers a durable competitive advantage to whoever controls it.

The metaphor of the deposit has profound implications also from the perspective of competition and innovation. In the mining sector, the deposit is a finite resource

---

[8] Art. 9(1), GDPR: the processing of special categories of personal data (health, genetic, biometric data) is in principle prohibited, save the exceptions in Art. 9(2).

[9] On Real-World Data and Real-World Evidence, see FDA, Framework for FDA's Real-World Evidence Program, December 2018; in the EU, EMA, Reflection paper on the use of real-world data in non-interventional studies to generate real-world evidence, September 2024.

[10] Ottolia (2017), pp. 51 ff., using the metaphor of a 'deposit' to describe the progressive accumulation of heterogeneous data from diverse sources.

[11] The resource-based theory of competitive advantage originates with Wernerfelt (1984); see also Prahalad and Hamel (1990) and Barney (1991).

that is exhausted over time through extraction. In the context of data, by contrast, the deposit is a resource that self-perpetuates and grows over time, especially when managed by an operator that has data integration capacity and that continuously incentivizes the contribution of new data. This process of self-perpetuation of the deposit creates network effects and lock-in effects that limit the possibility for other operators to accumulate comparable deposits.

8.2.3 Algoraceutical Data as an "Essential Facility"

If algoraceutical data does indeed constitute a strategic resource, then the question arises whether it can be qualified as an "essential facility" within the meaning of Article 102 TFEU. The economic theory of the essential facility traces back to Palmer, who identified the concept to describe an infrastructure good whose control by a dominant operator could constitute a barrier to entry for competitors. In the digital context, this category has acquired increasing relevance.[12]

The question is posed in these terms. In the algoraceutical context, access to massive, granular, and temporally persistent data has become an essential condition for computational research. An operator that controls access to such data and that refuses to make it available to competitors on reasonable terms could effectively exercise a veto power over the innovation capacity of competitors. This configuration could constitute the constitutive elements of abuse of dominant position for unjustified refusal to access an essential resource.

The jurisprudence of the Court of Justice has already recognized that refusal to access essential information can constitute abuse where certain conditions are met.[13] Specifically, in the IMS Health case,[14] the Court clarified that refusal to grant a license on an essential resource constitutes abuse of dominant position when three conditions are satisfied jointly. First, the refusal prevents the emergence of an actually potential demand in downstream markets; second, the refusal is not justified by objective reasons; third, the refusal creates harm to consumers. In the algoraceutical context, these conditions could indeed be satisfied where a dominant operator refuses to make data necessary for pharmaceutical research available.

An important aspect concerns the way in which the definition of the relevant market intersects with the concept of essential facility.[15] In the algoraceutical context, the relevant market is not simply that of data supply, but rather that of supply

---

[12] European Parliament Think Tank, Is data the new oil? Competition issues in the digital economy (2020).

[13] Art. 102 TFEU. On the essential-facility notion in European case law, see Court of Justice, judgment of 26 November 1998, Case C-7/97, Oscar Bronner; judgment of 29 April 2004, Case C-418/01, IMS Health; General Court, judgment of 17 September 2007, Case T-201/04, Microsoft.

[14] Court of Justice, judgment of 29 April 2004, Case C-418/01, IMS Health, para. 38: a refusal to license may constitute an abuse of dominant position where the resource is indispensable for operating in a downstream market.

[15] On the relevant market in the data economy, see European Commission, Notice on the definition of the relevant market for the purposes of Union competition law, C/2024/4339 (2024).

of computational research capacity for drug discovery. If data constitutes a sine qua non condition for accessing this market, then control of data confers dominant position in the market itself.

8.3 Concentration and Relevant Market

8.3.1 Big Pharma-Big Tech Alliances

The last 10 years have registered a significant structural change in the pharmaceutical sector, characterized by strategic alliances between large traditional pharmaceutical groups (Roche, Merck, Johnson & Johnson, AstraZeneca, Pfizer) and large technology platforms (Google, Amazon, Microsoft, Apple). These alliances manifest themselves through partnership agreements, venture capital investments, and creation of joint ventures dedicated to computational research for drug discovery. This phenomenon represents one of the most significant structural changes in the history of the modern pharmaceutical industry.

A significant example is represented by the partnership between Roche and Google Cloud, aimed at developing machine learning capacity for large-scale analysis of genomic data. Another example is the collaboration between Merck and Amazon Web Services for the management of big data in the context of clinical research. Again, the partnership between Pfizer and Microsoft is dedicated to the application of artificial intelligence to the discovery of molecular targets for new therapies. These alliances do not represent merely commercial agreements, but rather configure a genuine strategic convergence between two industries historically separate.

These agreements testify to a structural transformation of the pharmaceutical market, in which the control of computational infrastructure, access to data centers, and ownership or control of data repositories assumes strategic relevance comparable to that of traditional chemical and biological competencies. Such transformation has a scope that merits being qualified as a shift in the competitive paradigm of the sector. The implications of this shift are profound both from an economic point of view and from the perspective of competition law regulation.

The convergence between Big Pharma and Big Tech also creates a series of network effects and positive externalities that further strengthen the dominant position of operators that already have combined access to data and computational infrastructure. An enterprise that controls both data and research infrastructure has access to an innovation ecosystem that is functionally superior to that available to operators that control only one of the two elements.

A further qualitative leap occurred in the 2025–2026 biennium with the shift from the partnership model to direct vertical integration. In February 2025, Isomorphic Labs, a subsidiary of Alphabet, announced the expansion of collaboration with Novartis and the achievement of contract milestones valued at over one-and-a-half billion dollars with Eli Lilly, transforming what had begun as an internal research platform into a systemic provider of algorithmic discovery capacity for the pharmaceutical industry. In March–April 2026, Anthropic, one of the leading foundation model laboratories, acquired Coefficient Bio, a stealth startup founded by former leaders of Prescient Design (the AI-biology research division of Roche/Genentech), in an operation valued at approximately four hundred million dollars paid predominantly in stock, integrating the team into the newly formed Anthropic Health Care and Life Sciences Group led by Eric Kauderer-Abrams.[16] The operation was expressly presented as instrumental to Anthropic's positioning on a significant percentage of overall work in the life sciences and accompanies the launch of Claude for Life Sciences, an integrated vertical solution with laboratory tools and electronic lab notebook platforms. These operations confirm that the algoraceutical market is traversing a phase of vertical integration in which AI laboratories no longer limit themselves to providing infrastructure or tools to pharmaceutical enterprises, but rather directly internalize the biopharmaceutical competencies that until a few years ago constituted the exclusive province of sector companies. From an antitrust point of view, the phenomenon is significant because it shifts the center of innovation from the traditional supply chain to a restricted number of operators that simultaneously control data, models, and a growing portion of the human competencies necessary to use them.[17]

8.3.2 Barriers to Entry and Natural Oligopoly

The notion of natural monopoly applies when the technical characteristics of production entail that average production cost decreases as production scale increases. In the context of cloud infrastructure, this characteristic is manifest. Amazon Web Services, Microsoft Azure, and Google Cloud represent infrastructure whose cost of replication would be prohibitive for a new competitor. Moreover, competition economists have documented that barriers to entry in one part of the supply chain could at least partially be overcome in another part of the chain.[18] In other words, in the context of pharmaceutical algorithmics, access to the data repository could compensate for the lack of proprietary computational infrastructure.

The analysis of barriers to entry in the algoraceutical market reveals further that they are not merely technological, but also economic and informational. Economic barriers derive from the cost of data accumulation over time, which requires massive and persistent investments over several years. Informational barriers derive

[16] On this development, see The Information, 'Anthropic acquires startup Coefficient Bio for about $400 million', 3 April 2026; PYMNTS, 3 April 2026; BioBuzz, 4 April 2026. Anthropic PBC (San Francisco), among the leading developers of foundation models, acquired Coefficient Bio Inc., a start-up founded by former researchers of Prescient Design (the AI-biology division of Genentech/Roche), predominantly in shares, integrating the team into its life-sciences group.

[17] On the expansion of the Isomorphic Labs-Novartis collaboration, see the joint press release of 28 February 2025, documenting the extension of the 2024 agreement and a parallel agreement with Eli Lilly whose total value, including milestones, exceeds USD 1.7 billion.

[18] Rubinfeld and Gal (2017), observing that 'high entry barriers in one part of the chain might at least be partly overcome by another part of the chain'.

from the fact that the utility of data depends on the specialized knowledge of the scientific community that knows how to actually use it. The vicious circle that emerges can be described in these terms. Operators that already have data progressively acquire more data, since their possession enables the generation of insight that in turn attracts further data sources and further research capital.

Barriers to entry also include reputational and brand loyalty aspects. A new operator that attempted to enter the market could not easily attract the necessary data, since data sources (hospitals, clinics, patients) would prefer to share data with already established and reputable operators. This phenomenon creates a feedback circle that perpetuates the dominant position of incumbents.

The picture that emerges is thus that of a market characterized by natural oligopoly, in which the number of viable operators is structurally limited by the need to have simultaneously data, computational infrastructure, and highly specialized competencies and reputation. In this condition, barriers to entry do not result as a transitory dysfunction of competitive dynamics, but rather as a structural characteristic of the market itself.

8.3.3 The Risk of Abuse of Dominant Position

Abuse of dominant position is prohibited, in the European legal order, by virtue of Article 102 TFEU and, in the domestic legal order, by virtue of Article 3 of Law 10 October 1990, no. 287, in line with the broader framework of antitrust prohibitions of which Article 101 TFEU and Article 2 of the same law apply.[19] The risk of abuse in the algoraceutical context manifests itself in multiple forms. In the first place, there is the risk of refusal to grant access to data,[20] that is, the practice by means of which an operator that controls a data deposit refuses to make it available to competitors, even in the face of a reasonable commercial request. This behavior limits the innovation capacity of competitors and perpetuates the oligopolistic configuration of the market.

In the second place, there is the risk of the practice known as leveraging,[21] that is, the use of dominant power in one market (that of data and computational infrastructure) to extend the same power toward downstream markets (that of drug discovery and commercialization). This phenomenon has been extensively documented in the context of digital platforms and represents a concrete risk also in the pharmaceutical context, in which operators controlling both data and research platforms could discriminate against competitors that do not use such platforms.

[19] Lycett (2013).

[20] Libertini (2014), illustrating the three cardinal principles of EU competition law: the prohibition of anticompetitive agreements (Art. 101 TFEU), the prohibition of abuse of dominant position (Art. 102 TFEU), and merger control (Regulation (EC) 139/2004).

[21] On non-rivalrous data as an argument against entry barriers, see Sokol and Comerford (2016); critically, Rubinfeld and Gal (2017).

In the third place, there is the risk of discrimination in the setting of prices for access to data, as well as the risk of the practice known as tying, by means of which the dominant operator binds access to data with access to complementary services, thus forcing the customer to purchase an integrated package of services. These practices have the effect of extending dominant power from one market to related markets.

A fourth risk concerns the practice of exclusion through preclosure of access. An operator that contemporaneously controls both data and the research platform could configure its platforms in such a way that they are more compatible with its own data input than with data input from competitors, thereby generating an informational asymmetry that favors its own research at the expense of that of competitors.

8.4 The European Regulatory Framework on Data and Digital Markets

8.4.1 The Digital Markets Act (Regulation (EU) 2022/1925)

The Digital Markets Act (DMA)[22] represents the first European legislative intervention that directly addresses the problem of digital markets characterized by structural asymmetries of economic power. Although the DMA is not specifically calibrated for the pharmaceutical sector, its principles apply with force to the algoraceutical context. The principal provisions of the DMA were introduced in antitrust jurisprudence with the aim of addressing the conduct of "gatekeepers," that is, digital platforms that function as critical intermediaries in digital markets.

A question that was not adequately addressed by traditional antitrust law is that of collusion phenomena facilitated by the availability of real-time market data.[23] In the pre-digital context, tacit collusion required a certain degree of transparency of prices practiced by competitors. In the digital context, this transparency is growing and can be exploited by algorithms to implicitly coordinate behavior. The DMA introduces transparency obligations aimed at limiting this possibility.

A second relevant aspect of the DMA is the recognition that gatekeeping power is not a necessary characteristic of digital markets, but rather a dysfunction that can be corrected through regulatory intervention.[24] The DMA introduces a list of positive obligations that rest upon gatekeepers, with the intent of reducing the veto power that they exercise over other operators in the value chain. These obligations include the prohibition of self-preferencing, the obligation of transparency, the obligation of interoperability.

The DMA approach differs significantly from the traditional approach of antitrust law. While traditional antitrust law intervenes *ex post*, once abuse of dominant

[22] Regulation (EU) 2022/1925 (Digital Markets Act).

[23] On algorithmic collusion, see Ezrachi and Stucke (2016) and OECD (2017).

[24] Regulation (EU) 2022/1925 (Digital Markets Act).

position has been committed, the DMA intervenes *ex ante*, imposing positive obligations on gatekeepers independently of whether they have committed a specific abuse. This preventive approach is particularly relevant in the algoraceutical context, where damage deriving from control of data could be difficult to reverse once committed.

In the specific context of pharmaceutical research, the application of the DMA could extend to cloud providers and data aggregators that control deposits of data essential for research. If one of these operators meets the criteria for qualification as a gatekeeper (significant economic impact, dominant position, consolidated access to end users), it would be subject to the obligations of the DMA, including the obligation to allow access to data on fair and non-discriminatory terms.

The notion of gatekeeper is defined by the DMA on the basis of three criteria.[25] First, significant economic impact on the supply chains of digital services. Second, dominant position in relevant markets. Third, consolidated access to end users. Once designated as a gatekeeper, a platform is subject to a series of positive obligations, aimed at guaranteeing interoperability, transparency, and equitable access to data.[26] In the algoraceutical context, cloud providers that control both data and infrastructure could well qualify as gatekeepers.

A significant interpretative question concerns the application of the notion of gatekeeper in the pharmaceutical context. An operator that contemporaneously controls a repository of genomic data and a computational research platform could qualify as a gatekeeper on the basis of the criterion of significant economic impact on pharmaceutical research supply chains. If so, such operator would be subject to the obligations provided by the DMA.

The evolution of the application of the DMA in the 2024–2025 biennium confirms the relevance of this interpretative hypothesis. On November 18, 2025, the European Commission opened a market investigation pursuant to Article 17 DMA to assess whether Amazon Web Services and Microsoft Azure should be designated as gatekeepers for cloud computing services, even though they do not reach the presumptive quantitative thresholds of Article 3. Concurrently, in the course of 2025 the Commission adopted the first non-compliance decisions under the DMA against Apple, for anti-steering practices, and against Meta, for the "pay or consent" model; the Commission has also opened proceedings on self-preferencing practices involving integrated search services and marketplaces.[27] For the purposes of the present analysis, the investigation into cloud providers is of particular importance because it expressly recognizes, for the first time, that cloud computing infrastructure can configure a gatekeeping position over operators that use it and that, in the absence

---

[25] For commentary on the DMA, see Colangelo (2023).

[26] Art. 5, DMA: the obligations on gatekeepers include the prohibition on combining personal data collected through different platform services without the user's consent.

[27] European Commission, market investigations into the cloud computing services of Amazon and Microsoft under the DMA, 18 November 2025; Commission decision of 23 April 2025 finding Apple in breach of the DMA anti-steering rules; Commission decision of 23 April 2025 finding Meta in breach over the 'pay or consent' model.

of presumptive designation, the Commission is nonetheless empowered to intervene *ex officio* where market conditions justify it. Extended to the algoraceutical context, this approach enables us to hypothesize that suppliers of cloud infrastructure and foundation models employed in pharmaceutical research could be subjected to analogous obligations, in particular regarding interoperability and non-discriminatory access to data.

8.4.2 The Digital Services Act (Regulation (EU) 2022/2065)

The Digital Services Act (DSA),[28] by contrast, addresses questions of platform responsibility and user rights. Although the DSA is primarily oriented toward questions of content moderation and protection of fundamental rights online, it exercises an indirect impact on the algoraceutical sector in so far as it introduces transparency obligations regarding the recommendation algorithms that platforms use.

In the specific context of pharmaceutical research, the DSA is particularly relevant insofar as it concerns the question of the transparency of algorithms used for selection of clinical trials and for identification of cohorts of patients candidates for research. These questions acquire significant ethical and legal significance, in so far as the opacity of selection algorithms could generate systematic distortions in research cohorts, with the result that certain demographic groups would be systematically excluded from research.

8.4.3 The Data Act (Regulation (EU) 2023/2854)

The Data Act[29] represents a legislative intervention of particular significance for the pharmaceutical context. This regulation establishes obligations to make data available to third parties on the basis of criteria of fairness and transparency. The Data Act governs the conditions of access to data generated by the use of connected products and related services[30] and establishes obligations of availability that operate both vertically and horizontally.

In the context of pharmaceutical research, the Data Act assumes crucial importance in that it imposes access obligations to data even when they have not been generated through active participation of data subjects, but rather through ordinary use of services. The application of this principle to the pharmaceutical sector entails the affirmation of a right of alternative innovators to access data generated through the use of research platforms controlled by dominant operators.

---

[28] Regulation (EU) 2022/2065 (Digital Services Act).

[29] Regulation (EU) 2023/2854 (Data Act); for commentary, see De Franceschi and Schulze (2024).

[30] The Data Act governs access to data generated by the use of connected products and related services (Arts. 3–7) and the obligations to make data available to third parties (Art. 5).

An important interpretative question concerns the application of the principle of fairness in the setting of prices for access to data in the algorithmic context. The regulation provides that access must be furnished on fair, transparent, and non-discriminatory terms. In the algoraceutical context, this principle entails that an operator that controls data essential for pharmaceutical research cannot fix prohibitive prices, but rather must fix prices that actually allow competitors to access the data.

8.4.4 The European Health Data Space (Regulation (EU) 2025/327)

The Regulation establishing the European Health Data Space (EHDS)[31] represents a legislative intervention of great importance for the pharmaceutical sector. The EHDS introduces an articulated framework for governance of health data at the European level, with the objective of promoting the reuse of health data for purposes of research, innovation, and definition of public policy.

It must be clarified immediately that the effectiveness of the Regulation is staggered over time. Reg. (EU) 2025/327 was adopted on February 26, 2025, and entered into force on March 26, 2025, but the substantive provisions on primary use and secondary use of health data become applicable gradually beginning March 26, 2029, while the interoperability of electronic health record systems and the procedures for access through the health data access bodies will become fully operational by March 26, 2031.[32] In the transitional period, member states are called upon to designate the competent national bodies, to establish the contact points for access to data, and to prepare the technical infrastructure for interoperability. Consequently, the following considerations concern a legal framework that, although already binding, will produce its full effects on the algoraceutical ecosystem in the second quinquennium of the current decade, which makes even more urgent the need to address from now the interpretative questions relating to the articulation between EHDS, GDPR, and competition law discipline.

The EHDS distinguishes between primary use of health data, relating to the patient's access to their own data and to their rights of correction and deletion,[33] and secondary use of health data, relating to reuse for purposes of research and innovation. In the context of algoraceutics, secondary use assumes particular significance, in so far as it creates the legal prerequisite for access to health data by researchers and pharmaceutical enterprises. The EHDS Regulation explicitly enumerates among

[31] Regulation (EU) 2025/327 of 11 February 2025 establishing the European Health Data Space.

[32] Regulation (EU) 2025/327, Arts. 103 (entry into force) and 104 (application). On implementation, see European Commission, The European Health Data Space Regulation: implementation roadmap, March 2025.

[33] The EHDS distinguishes primary use of health data (Arts. 3–12, patient access to their own data) from secondary use (Arts. 33–49, reuse for research, innovation and health-policy purposes).

the purposes of secondary use the "research and development of medicinal products or medical devices."[34]

A significant innovation of the EHDS is the introduction of governance structures for the sharing of health data at the national and European level. These structures, denominated "healthcare data altruism organizations" and "data intermediaries," are aimed at facilitating access to data by researchers and innovative enterprises, even outside of large dominant operators. This mechanism represents an attempt by the European legislator to limit the gatekeeping power of dominant operators in the health sector.

The creation of healthcare data altruism organizations represents an implicit acknowledgment by the European legislator that the market does not permit equitable access to health data when such data are controlled by private operators for profit purposes. The concept of "data altruism" presupposes that patients are willing to share their data for purposes of research that benefit society as a whole, even without direct economic compensation. However, for data altruism to actually function, it is necessary that an institutional mechanism (the healthcare data altruism organization) exist that actually manages the data and that guarantees that they are used in conformity with the declared research commitments.

A critical aspect of the EHDS concerns the determination of which subject is authorized to request access to secondary data. The EHDS provides that access can be requested by "public bodies, healthcare providers, researchers, and entities involved in the development of medicines or medical devices." This enumeration is sufficiently broad to include pharmaceutical enterprises, but raises the problem of how to determine whether an enterprise is genuinely engaged in the development of medicines or medical devices, or is simply attempting to exploit the data for marketing or pricing purposes.

8.5 The Pharmaceutical "Digital Space" as Relevant Market

8.5.1 Data Governance in the Digital Space

The concept of the pharmaceutical "digital space" was introduced in preceding chapters in relation to the notion of "chemical space," "biological space," and "digital space."[35] In this context, this concept is analyzed as a relevant market within the meaning of Article 102 TFEU. The definition of the relevant market is a critical phase of antitrust analysis, since upon the definition of the market depend both the identification of dominant position and the assessment of the conduct of the dominant enterprise.

[34] Art. 34(1)(e), Regulation (EU) 2025/327, listing among the purposes of secondary use 'research and development of medicinal products or medical devices'.

[35] On the pharmaceutical 'digital space', see Chap. 3, Sect. 3.2; here it is analysed as a relevant market within the meaning of Art. 102 TFEU.

The market of the pharmaceutical "digital space" can be defined as the market for services of computational data processing, storage, integration, and advanced analysis (through machine learning and artificial intelligence) of pharmaceutical data for purposes of clinical research and discovery of new drugs. This market includes both cloud infrastructure services and data analytics services and specialized consulting.

Data governance in the digital space is characterized by complex stratification of roles and responsibilities. There are operators that collect data (hospitals, clinics, patients), operators that aggregate data (data intermediaries, health structures), operators that provide infrastructure (cloud providers such as AWS, Azure, Google Cloud), operators that provide analytics services (data analytics firms), and finally operators that integrate all these elements for purposes of pharmaceutical research. Each level of the value chain introduces specific questions of access, control, and allocation of rights and obligations.

The Communication of the Commission on data governance in the digital space[36] has underlined that interoperability is an essential condition for competition. Without interoperability, operators that control data repositories have veto power over other operators in the value chain, since the cost of data migration to alternative platforms is prohibitive. This phenomenon is particularly critical in the algoraceutical context, where loss of continuity in chronological data can entail the loss of significant scientific information.

8.5.2 Interoperability and Data Access. Conditions for Competition

Interoperability, in the algoraceutical context, means two distinct things. First, the technical capacity to transfer data from one platform to another without loss of quality and semantic meaning, maintaining referential integrity and completeness. Second, the legal capacity to access data without being subject to contractual constraints that make migration economically prohibitive.

Interoperability as a condition for competition in digital markets has been explicitly affirmed by the European legislator in the DMA.[37] Article 30 of the Data Act introduces interoperability obligations that rest upon suppliers of data analytics services, providing for the obligation to furnish access to data in a machine-readable format and in a non-discriminatory manner.

In the context of computational pharmaceutical research, the absence of interoperability creates a situation of lock-in, in which pharmaceutical enterprises that have massively invested in a specific platform (for example, Google Cloud or Amazon Web Services) cannot easily migrate to alternative platforms even when the

[36] On data governance, see Regulation (EU) 2022/868 (Data Governance Act), establishing a framework for voluntary data sharing and data-intermediation services (Arts. 10–15).

[37] Interoperability as a condition of competition is affirmed by recital 67 of the DMA and Art. 30 of the Data Act.

economic conditions or technical capacities of the alternative platform would prove superior. This lock-in perpetuates the oligopolistic configuration of the market and discourages innovation. Interoperability thus represents not only a technical question, but rather a strategic question of fundamental importance for competition.

8.6 The Processing of Personal Data in Algorithmic Clinical Trials

8.6.1 GDPR and Health Data

The GDPR introduces rigorous discipline for the processing of particular categories of personal data, which require a particularly high level of protection. Among the particular categories are health data, genetic data, and biometric data. The processing of these categories of data is generally prohibited, except in the occurrence of specific exceptions. The discipline on particular categories represents one of the pillars of the protection offered by the GDPR.

The GDPR permits the processing of particular personal data for purposes of scientific research,[38] on condition that the processing is subject to adequate guarantees in order to guarantee the respect of the rights and freedoms of the interested parties.[39] Among the guarantees are the adoption of technical and organizational measures aimed at guaranteeing respect of the principle of data minimization, the principle according to which the processing of data must be limited to the necessary relative to the specified purposes.

The question of the practical application of these guarantees in the context of computational research is particularly complex. In February 2019, the European Data Protection Board published specific guidance on scientific research,[40] addressing questions such as the balancing of research and privacy protection, the pseudonymization of data, and appropriate security measures. However, the rapid evolution of technology has created situations that are not completely covered by these guidelines, requiring adaptive interpretations by regulators.

A critical aspect concerns the processing of pseudonymized data. In the context of computational research with machine learning, the risk of re-identification through linkage techniques is significant. If pseudonymized data can be easily re-identified, then the legal regime should treat them as personal data even if formally pseudonymized.

In the context of algorithmic clinical trials, this discipline assumes particular contours. Computational research for drug discovery typically requires massive

[38] Art. 9(2)(j), GDPR, permitting the processing of special categories of personal data where necessary for scientific research, in compliance with Art. 89(1).

[39] Art. 89(1), GDPR: processing for scientific research is subject to appropriate safeguards, in particular the principle of data minimization.

[40] Garante per la protezione dei dati personali, Prescrizioni relative al trattamento di categorie particolari di dati, provvedimento n. 146 of 5 June 2019, point 5.

volumes of heterogeneous data, and the principle of minimization can enter into tension with the requirement to have granular and temporally persistent data. Moreover, the use of machine learning algorithms entails the risk that data will be used for purposes not originally declared, in so far as an algorithm trained on a dataset can generate correlations and patterns not originally foreseen.

A central question concerns the compatibility between the GDPR and the processing of data necessary for computational research. In the traditional context of medical research, informed consent was sufficiently specific because the researcher knew *ex ante* what the research hypotheses would be. In the context of computational research, however, the algorithm can discover patterns and associations not initially foreseen, which makes problematic the acquisition of truly informed consent.

This knot has been partially addressed by the European legislator with the Digital Omnibus Package presented by the Commission on November 19, 2025, which proposes to simplify in a significant way the European digital acquis intervening on the GDPR, the Data Act, the AI Regulation, and the eIDAS. The most relevant proposals for the purposes of the present analysis concern, in the first place, the introduction of dedicated discipline on the modalities of reuse of personal data for purposes of scientific research, with the explicit recognition that processing for scientific research can be founded on legal bases different from consent (in particular the legitimate interest of which Article 6, paragraph 1, letter f) GDPR and the public interest of which letter e) of the same article apply), provided accompanied by adequate technical and organizational guarantees. In the second place, the package clarifies the perimeter of the concept of secondary use with respect to the purpose limitation principle of Article 5, paragraph 1, letter b) GDPR, allowing within certain limits the reuse of data collected for different purposes, if instrumental to research of general interest. These proposals have been received with significant reservations by the European Data Protection Board and some national authorities, which have signaled the risk that excessive attenuation of the principle of consent ends up weakening the protection of data subjects and amplifying asymmetries already denounced by doctrine. Pending the outcome of the ordinary legislative procedure, the current framework requires recourse to intermediate solutions, such as consent for categories of research (broad consent) and strengthened pseudonymization accompanied by impact assessments on data protection.[41]

8.6.2 Informed Consent in AI-Driven Experimentation

In the context of traditional clinical trials (based on randomized controlled studies), informed consent is governed rigorously by national and international rules and the

[41] European Commission, Digital Omnibus Package to simplify digital rules and boost competitiveness, proposal of 19 November 2025; European Data Protection Board, Statement on the Digital Omnibus Package, 9 December 2025, with reservations on the attenuation of the consent principle for scientific research. In doctrine, see Malgieri and Comandè (2017).

process of consent acquisition is relatively standardized. However, in the context of computational pharmaceutical research, new and significant questions emerge relating to consent.

A first question concerns the level of specificity of consent. The GDPR requires that consent be specific, that is, referred to determined purposes. In the context of computational research, however, the researcher often does not know *ex ante* what patterns and correlations will emerge from data analysis. Consequently, the request for specific consent can result in being impossible to satisfy completely.

A second question concerns the right of the interested party to revoke consent. In the context of computational research, once the data has been integrated into a broader dataset and subjected to processing through machine learning algorithms, it can result technically difficult or impossible to remove the specific contribution of that single datum. This characteristic contrasts with the right of cancellation affirmed by the GDPR.

A third question concerns the possibility of secondary uses, in other words the use of data collected for purposes different from those originally declared. In the context of pharmaceutical algorithmics, this practice is frequent and represents an important source of added value of research. However, it entails the risk that the interested parties are not actually informed regarding the modalities and purposes of use of their data.

The emergent orientation of jurisprudence and doctrine suggests that in the context of computational research it is appropriate to adopt a model of "elastic consent," in which the initial consent is sufficient to authorize the use of data for scientific research in general, but a process of monitoring and progressive information is required as specific purposes of research emerge. This model represents an attempt to balance the requirement of protection of personal data with the requirement of scientific research.

8.6.3 The Feedback Loop and Algorithm-Based Evidence Medicine

A characteristic aspect of computational research in the pharmaceutical sector is the feedback loop that is established between the use of the algorithm in the clinical context and the training of the algorithm through clinical data. This loop creates a situation in which data is not merely an input to research, but simultaneously an output of clinical practice that uses the algorithm.

The feedback loop entails a series of consequences on the ethical, legal, and epistemological plane. From an epistemological point of view, the feedback loop introduces the risk that the algorithm will generate systematic bias in clinical practice, amplifying it progressively over time. From an ethical point of view, the loop entails that the patient undergoing care through algorithm contributes simultaneously (often unknowingly) to the training of the algorithm itself and thus to the evolution of medicine for future patients.

From a legal point of view, the feedback loop raises questions of responsibility, informed consent, and protection of data. The practice that emerges from this literature is that of "algorithm-based evidence medicine," that is, the affirmation that clinical decisions must be guided by evidence generated through computational analysis of large datasets. This practice has profound implications for the governance of clinical data and for the responsibilities of the subjects involved in the feedback loop.

A crucial question concerns responsibility for errors committed by the algorithm. In the traditional context of medical research, responsibility was clearly attributed, since the physician was responsible for clinical decisions. In the context of medicine based on algorithms, responsibility becomes diffuse among the creator of the algorithm, the supplier of the platform, the physician who uses the algorithm, and the operators who trained the algorithm with previous data. This distribution of responsibility creates significant problems for the protection of patients.

8.7 Competition Law Issues Specific to Algoraceutics

8.7.1 Algorithmic Collusion in Pharmaceutical Pricing

A competition law issue particularly relevant in the algoraceutical context is that of algorithmic collusion in pharmaceutical pricing. The theory of algorithmic collusion maintains that algorithms of automatic pricing could lead to situations of equilibrium with elevated prices, even in the absence of explicit communication among competitors.

The concern has been subjected to rigorous investigation by the OECD and the international academic community.[42] According to the thesis of algorithmic collusion, in the case that an algorithm is programmed with the objective of maximizing enterprise profit and in the case that the algorithm has access to real-time market data that include prices practiced by competitors, the algorithm could undertake to identify the price that permits maximization of profit, taking into account the expected response of competitors. This behavior could lead to a situation of elevated price equilibrium, even in the absence of explicit communication.

In the pharmaceutical context, this dynamic merits particular attention since drug prices are subject to growing automation, especially in the context of dynamic pricing in markets with significant online component. The pricing algorithm could, in theory, learn from observation of competitor prices and adopt a pricing strategy that implicitly coordinates with other competitors. This practice could integrate a violation of Article 101 TFEU if understood as a collusive agreement, although the technology of algorithmic collusion remains technically ambiguous, in so far as there is no explicit communication among algorithms.

A crucial interpretative question concerns whether unintentional algorithmic collusion (that is, the algorithm that autonomously reaches a collusive equilibrium

[42] Calvano et al. (2020).

without explicit instructions to do so) should integrate a violation of antitrust discipline. European antitrust authorities have begun to address this question, considering that where the algorithm has been knowingly programmed so as to reach a collusive equilibrium, there is violation even in the absence of explicit communication.

In the specific context of pharmaceutical prices, the risk of algorithmic collusion merits careful consideration. Pharmaceutical prices are subject to regulation in many European contexts, with reference pricing systems that refer to prices practiced in other countries. This international interconnection of prices creates ideal conditions for algorithmic collusion, in so far as pricing algorithms have access to international real-time information on prices practiced by competitors in different markets. If pricing algorithms were programmed to tacitly coordinate in setting high prices in all markets simultaneously, this would entail a significant reduction in welfare for consumers and for health systems.

The difficulty in proving algorithmic collusion resides in the fact that there is no evidence of explicit communication and the programming of the algorithm could be constructed so as to appear purely oriented toward maximization of local profit, when in reality it implicitly coordinates with competitors. This creates a gap in the capacity of antitrust authorities to address the phenomenon through traditional tools.

8.7.2 Algorithmic Discrimination and Drug Access

A second competition law issue concerns algorithmic discrimination in decisions regarding drug access. The practice of algorithmic discrimination consists in the use of algorithms to differentiate the treatment accorded to different subjects on the basis of personal, demographic, or clinical characteristics.

In the context of pharmaceutical research, algorithmic discrimination emerges in a series of specific contexts. A first contextualization is that of selection of clinical trial cohorts. The algorithms used for identification of patients candidates for clinical trials could contain systematic biases that favor some demographic groups at the expense of others. This

A second contextualization is that of precision medicine based on genetic data. If algorithms for identification of biomarkers for precision medicine have been trained on datasets that underrepresent certain ethnic or demographic groups, the algorithms will be less accurate for those groups, with the consequence that patients belonging to those groups will receive less effective treatment as compared to patients of other groups.

An intersection between algorithmic discrimination and competition law emerges when algorithmic discrimination is practiced by dominant operators for purposes of exclusion of competitors.[43] Suppose for example that a dominant operator that controls a deposit of health data uses a machine learning algorithm for identification of patients candidates for clinical research, but configures the algorithm so as to favor

[43] Obermeyer et al. (2019).

patients that will participate in clinical trials conducted by the same dominant enterprise, excluding or marginalizing patients that will participate in trials of competitors. This practice would entail abuse of dominant position for exclusion.

8.8 Concluding Remarks

The proximity between personal data protection and competition law is not merely accidental.[44] Both orders of rules pursue objectives of protection of fundamental interests. Data protection law aims to protect individual personality and the privacy of subjects; competition law aims to protect the functioning of the market and the interests of competitors. In the algoraceutical context, these two objectives intersect in so far as control of data confers market power and market power permits extension of control of data.

A first significant precedent is represented by the decision of the Bundeskartellamt of February 6, 2019, against Facebook, which addressed the problem of the excluding practice of massive collection of personal data to the detriment of the privacy protection of users. Such decision was subsequently confirmed and systematized by the Court of Justice of the European Union with the judgment C-252/21, Meta Platforms v. Bundeskartellamt, of July 4, 2023, which recognized to the national authorities responsible for competition the power to establish, in the context of examination of abuse of dominant position, the violation of the GDPR by the dominant enterprise, on condition that the principle of loyal cooperation with the authorities responsible for personal data is respected. The Court also clarified that consent obtained by a dominant operator through the imposition of conditions of collection particularly intrusive cannot be presumed freely given within the meaning of Article 4, point 11) GDPR. The judgment surpasses the precedent of 2019 in the part in which it roots the foundation directly in the law of the Union, rather than in domestic legislation alone, and constitutes the first formal recognition, at the supranational level, of the welding together of antitrust discipline and the discipline of personal data protection. Extended to the algoraceutical context, the pronouncement offers a clear legal basis for evaluating as excluding conduct the contractual clauses by means of which a dominant operator in the market of health data imposes on patients or clinical partners conditions of processing that exceed what is strictly necessary to the provision requested.[45]

The analysis we have conducted reveals the complexity of questions that emerge from the intersection between competition law, personal data protection, and

[44] Bundeskartellamt, decision of 6 February 2019, B6-22/16, Facebook (exploitative business terms under § 19(1) GWB for inadequate data processing). In doctrine, see Osti and Pardolesi (2019) and Pardolesi et al. (2020).

[45] Court of Justice, judgment of 4 July 2023, Case C-252/21, Meta Platforms and Others v Bundeskartellamt, paras. 43–62 (concurrent competence of competition authorities to find GDPR infringements in the context of abuse of dominance) and paras. 148–154 (value of consent given to a dominant undertaking). In doctrine, see d'Ippolito (2023).

computational pharmaceutical research. This complexity derives from the fact that data, in the algoraceutical context, is not merely an economic resource, but rather a constitutive element of the structure of the pharmaceutical research market itself.

Several fundamental teachings emerge from our investigation. In the first place, the algoraceutical market is characterized by structural barriers to entry, due to the joint necessity to have massive and granular data, sophisticated computational infrastructure, and highly qualified specialized competencies. In this market condition, the dynamic of perfect competition has no reason to operate and the configuration of a few dominant operators remains stable over time, except for regulatory intervention.

In the second place, contemporary European regulation of data and digital markets, represented by the DMA,[46] the DSA, the Data Act, and the EHDS, represents a significant step toward addressing these phenomena, but remains still incomplete. It is necessary to develop normative tools specifically calibrated for the pharmaceutical sector, which recognize the peculiar importance of computational research for therapeutic innovation, but at the same time ensure that this research is not conducted at the expense of competition, protection of individual personality, and equitable access to drugs for all patients.

In the third place, the affirmation of a right of access to data for alternative innovators must not be configured merely as a constraint imposed on data holders, but rather as a constitutive element of the definition of a fair and sustainable algoraceutical market in the long term.

In the fourth place, data governance in the algoraceutical context requires a multilevel and integrated approach, which combines tools of personal data protection, tools of competition law, tools of regulation of digital markets, and tools of governance of scientific research. None of these orders of tools is sufficient alone. A regulation that addresses only antitrust questions, without at the same time addressing personal data protection questions, would create a situation in which computational pharmaceutical research proceeds at the expense of privacy protection. Reciprocally, a regulation that addresses only personal data protection questions, without addressing antitrust questions, could cement the dominant position of operators that already control data and infrastructure.

A fifth teaching concerns the importance of algorithmic transparency. In the context of computational pharmaceutical research, machine learning algorithms used for data analysis and for selection of research cohorts generate decisions that have significant consequences for patients and for innovation in the sector. The transparency of these algorithms, understood both as transparency regarding the data used for training as well as transparency regarding the decision-making logic of the algorithm, is an essential precondition for effective regulation. However, complete transparency of proprietary algorithms entails risks of disclosure of trade secrets. Finding a balance between transparency and protection of intellectual property remains an open challenge.

[46] Regulation (EU) 2022/1925 (Digital Markets Act).

A sixth teaching concerns the role of data as a public good and the role of solidarity in pharmaceutical research. In the traditional context, patients contribute clinical data as part of their search for treatment and cure. In the context of computational research, these data acquire significant economic value for operators that control them. A question of distributive justice emerges, in the sense that it is necessary to ask whether patients who contributed to data should participate in economic benefits deriving from their use. The concept of data altruism introduced by the European legislator represents an attempt to address this question.

A seventh teaching concerns the phenomenon of killer acquisitions and their peculiar application in the algoraceutical market. The judgment of the Court of Justice of September 3, 2024, in the joined cases C-611/22 P and C-625/22 P, Illumina and Grail, resized the scope of the mechanism of referral of which Article 22 of Reg. 139/2004/EC applies, excluding that the Commission can accept referrals from member states lacking competence according to their respective national legal systems. This pronouncement has reopened a gap in European enforcement of below-threshold concentration operations, particularly dangerous in sectors in which, like the algoraceutical one, the strategic value of an operator is measured by the data and talents it controls more than by its turnover. In this light, operations such as that, already cited, between Anthropic and Coefficient Bio, and more generally the acquisition of stealth startups whose principal assets are proprietary models, data repositories, and research teams, risk escaping both ordinary concentrative control and the most recent mechanisms under Article 22. The identification of new tools, founded for example on thresholds based on the value of the transaction (transaction value thresholds) or on alternative criteria that valorize the informational and computational intensity of the operation, thus constitutes one of the principal open frontiers in the construction of an antitrust framework equal to the algoraceutical market.[47]

Finally, computational research for drug discovery represents one of the most advanced frontiers of contemporary scientific and clinical innovation. The legal regulation of this research must not constitute an impediment to innovation, but rather a framework that permits innovation for the benefit of all market operators and, above all, for the benefit of patients awaiting new and effective therapeutic tools. An adequate balance among these diverse interests remains a crucial challenge for the legislator and for European regulatory authorities in the coming years. Only through constructive involvement among stakeholders (researchers, pharmaceutical operators, antitrust authorities, data protection authorities, patients) is it possible to construct a normative framework that recognizes simultaneously the requirement of innovation, the requirement of competition protection, the requirement of privacy protection, and the requirement of equitable access to drugs.

[47] Court of Justice, judgment of 3 September 2024, Joined Cases C-611/22 P and C-625/22 P, Illumina and Grail v Commission, annulling the decisions by which the Commission had accepted Art. 22 referrals (Regulation (EC) 139/2004) from Member States lacking domestic competence over the transaction. On value-based thresholds to capture killer acquisitions, see Police (2025).

References

Angiolini C (2020) Lo statuto dei dati personali: uno studio a partire dalla nozione di bene. Giappichelli, Torino

Barney J (1991) Firm resources and sustained competitive advantage. J Manag 17(1):99–120

Calvano E, Calzolari G, Denicolò V, Pastorello S (2020) Artificial intelligence, algorithmic pricing, and collusion. Am Econ Rev 110(10):3267–3297

Colangelo G (2023) DMA begins. J Antitrust Enforc 11(1):116–122

d'Ippolito G (2023) Data economy: la Corte di giustizia precisa il rapporto tra concorrenza e protezione dei dati personali e le norme sulla pubblicità personalizzata. Rivista di diritto dei media 2(2023):323–342

De Franceschi A, Schulze R (2024) The EU Data Act. Eur Rev Contract Law 20

Ezrachi A, Stucke ME (2016) Virtual competition: the promise and perils of the algorithm-driven economy. Harvard University Press, Cambridge

Libertini M (2014) Diritto della concorrenza dell'Unione europea. Giuffrè, Milano

Lycett M (2013) Datafication: making sense of big data in a complex world. Eur J Inf Syst 22(4):381–386

Malgieri G, Comandè G (2017) Why a right to legibility of automated decision-making exists in the General Data Protection Regulation. Int Data Priv Law 7(4):243–265

Obermeyer Z, Powers B, Vogeli C, Mullainathan S (2019) Dissecting racial bias in an algorithm used to manage the health of populations. Science 366(6464):447–453

OECD (2017) Algorithms and collusion: competition policy in the digital age. OECD, Paris

Osti C, Pardolesi R (2019) L'antitrust ai tempi di Facebook. Mercato Concorrenza Regole 2(2019):195–217

Ottolia M (2017) Big data e innovazione computazionale. Quaderni di AIDA 28. Giappichelli, Torino

Pardolesi R, Van den Bergh RJ, Weber F (2020) Facebook e i peccati da "Konditionenmissbrauch". Mercato Concorrenza Regole 3(2020):507–537

Police C (2025) The Illumina/Grail case and the redefinition of EU merger control: between procedural flexibility and legal certainty. Eurojus

Prahalad CK, Hamel G (1990) The core competence of the corporation. Harv Bus Rev 68(3):79–91

Rubinfeld DL, Gal MS (2017) Access barriers to big data. Ariz Law Rev 59(2):339–381

Sokol DD, Comerford RE (2016) Antitrust and regulating big data. George Mason Law Rev 23:1129–1161

Wernerfelt B (1984) A resource-based view of the firm. Strateg Manag J 5(2):171–180

The Regulatory Ecosystem: FDA, EMA, AIFA

9

Abstract

This final chapter of the legal analysis turns from legislation to regulatory governance, examining how the agencies that authorise medicines, the United States Food and Drug Administration, the European Medicines Agency and the Italian Medicines Agency, are translating the general rules on artificial intelligence into operational practice. The FDA January 2025 draft guidance introduces a risk-based, seven-phase pathway for assessing the credibility of an AI model in its declared context of use, a framework whose roots lie in the engineering standard ASME V&V 40. The EMA Reflection Paper and the joint EMA-FDA Guiding Principles of January 2026 articulate a risk-based and human-centric approach, while the AIFA guide of 2021 anchors the Italian position. The chapter compares the convergences and divergences among these frameworks, considers the credibility framework as a legal parameter that interacts with the development-risk defense and the AI Act, and proposes a public registry of predictive models to render the state of technological knowledge knowable before litigation. It closes on the International Coalition of Medicines Regulatory Authorities and on the regulatory deadlines that, after the Digital Omnibus, will govern the algoraceutical sector.

9.1 Introduction: From Legislative Regulation to Regulatory Governance

In the pharmaceutical sector, the distinction between legislative regulation and regulatory governance represents a structural element fundamental to understanding the governance of innovation.[1] The former refers to instruments of a legislative

[1] Chiti (2018), pp. 342 ff.; on soft law in regulatory agencies, see Snyder (1993).

G. Rotino, *Algoraceutics - Legal Perspectives on Artificial Intelligence in Drug Discovery and Development*, Law for Professionals,
https://doi.org/10.1007/978-3-032-38537-6_9

nature, such as directives and regulations, which establish general principles and compliance obligations. The latter denotes the set of documents and practices adopted by regulatory agencies to operationalize those general principles into concrete standards, specific procedures and implementing guidelines. Regulatory governance lacks the force of binding law, but possesses considerable practical authority, as it constitutes the framework within which operators are effectively required to work to obtain authorizations.

In the 2024–2026 biennium, the pace of regulatory production underwent extraordinary acceleration.[2] The United States Food and Drug Administration (FDA) issued in January 2025 a draft guidance dedicated specifically to the use of artificial intelligence in support of regulatory decision-making in pharmaceutical matters. Simultaneously, the European Medicines Agency (EMA) finalized, in September 2024, a comprehensive reflection document on the lifecycle of artificial intelligence in medicines. On January 14, 2026, the two agencies jointly published a document containing the guiding principles of good practice in the use of artificial intelligence throughout pharmaceutical development. In Italy, the Italian Medicines Agency (AIFA) disseminated in May 2021 a technical guidance for the authorization of clinical trials with artificial intelligence and machine learning systems, still in force and not subject to substantial updates. This regulatory flourishing is not coincidental. It reflects the recognition, by international agencies, that the pace of technological innovation requires an accelerated response from the regulatory apparatus.

The regulatory ecosystem described in the paragraphs that follow operationalizes the general principles contained in Regulation (EU) 2024/1689 (AI Regulation or AI Act) and in Directive (EU) 2024/2853 on liability for defective products (PLD Directive).[3] As already addressed in Chap. 5, the AI Regulation establishes crosscutting obligations relating to data quality, documentation, human oversight and risk management. The present chapter analyzes how pharmaceutical agencies have implemented these general principles in the specific context of drug discovery and development. This is not a simple reworking. Rather, the chapter addresses how the guidelines and reflection documents of agencies represent, simultaneously, practical orientation instruments for enterprises and legal parameters for evaluating regulatory compliance.

9.2 The Food and Drug Administration

9.2.1 The January 2025 Draft Guidance

In January 2025, the FDA issued a draft guidance titled "Considerations for the Use of Artificial Intelligence To Support Regulatory Decision-Making for Drug and

[2] Permanand (2006).

[3] Regulation (EU) 2024/1689 (Artificial Intelligence Act); Directive (EU) 2024/2853 on liability for defective products, replacing Directive 85/374/EEC.

Biological Products."[4] The document represents a fundamental moment of transition in United States pharmaceutical regulation and inaugurates a new phase, in which artificial intelligence is no longer confined to the sphere of manufacturing and quality control, but is explicitly extended to support regulatory decision-making throughout the drug lifecycle, from nonclinical evaluation to post-approval pharmacovigilance.

The draft is inscribed within a broader regulatory trajectory, initiated by the FDA with the Action Plan on Software as a Medical Device in 2021 and continued with the Discussion Paper on artificial intelligence-assisted pharmaceutical manufacturing in 2023.[5] The 2025 Draft Guidance represents, however, a qualitative break from the preceding documents. It establishes a general principle of crosscutting scope, applicable to any use of AI that contributes to supporting a regulatory decision, namely that the credibility of the model must be established before the model itself can support the decision.[6]

This principle carries a direct and profound consequence, as it reverses the burden of proof. It is no longer sufficient to demonstrate that an artificial intelligence model works in the laboratory. It must be demonstrated that it works reliably in the specific context in which it will be employed, a context that the FDA document defines as "context of use," namely the declared scope of application of the computational tool.

The paradigm shift cannot be underestimated. Traditionally, the FDA evaluated the drug on the basis of data generated from chemical experiments, biological assays, toxicology studies and clinical trials conducted according to predetermined protocols. The reliability of such data was guaranteed by adherence to established experimental protocols such as Good Laboratory Practice and Good Clinical Practice. In the new paradigm, the FDA is called upon to evaluate not only the drug and clinical data, but also the artificial intelligence model that supported the development of the drug itself. The extension of the object of regulatory evaluation imposes on the FDA the development of new competencies, relating to data science, machine learning and validation of computational models. At the same time, it imposes on pharmaceutical enterprises the obligation to document not only the results of traditional experimentation, but also the characteristics, performance and limitations of the models that contributed to generating those results.

---

[4] FDA, *Considerations for the Use of Artificial Intelligence to Support Regulatory Decision-Making for Drug and Biological Products*, Draft Guidance for Industry, January 2025.

[5] FDA, *Artificial Intelligence in Drug Manufacturing*, Discussion Paper, 2023; FDA, *Artificial Intelligence/Machine Learning (AI/ML)-Based Software as a Medical Device (SaMD): Action Plan*, January 2021.

[6] FDA Draft Guidance (January 2025), Section III: the credibility of the model output must be established before the model can support a regulatory decision. The notion of computational credibility derives from the engineering literature on verification and validation; see ASME, *V&V 40: Assessing Credibility of Computational Modeling through Verification and Validation. Application to Medical Devices*, 2018.

9.2.2 The Seven-Phase Pathway for Assessing Credibility

The heart of the Draft Guidance is a seven-phase pathway that the developer must follow to demonstrate the credibility of the model with respect to the specific regulatory context in which its application is envisioned.[7] The framework is not an original discovery of the FDA. It is grounded in the engineering literature on verification and validation of computational models, applied for decades in sectors such as aerospace and nuclear, as well as in the ASME V&V 40 standard on credibility assessment of models employed in medical devices.[8] The FDA has adapted it to the pharmaceutical context and transformed it into a regulatory standard applicable to all models that contribute to supporting an agency decision.

The first phase consists of defining the question of interest, that is, the specific scientific or clinical question to which the model is called upon to respond.[9] This step is not merely administrative. It requires that the developer articulate the question with precision in terms that make possible, in the next phase, its regulatory qualification.

The second phase imposes defining the context of use, that is, the placement of the model in the agency's decision-making process and the weight that its output will have on the final decision.[10] A model trained to estimate the solubility of a molecule in an early phase of development does not have the same context of use as a model intended to support a decision on therapeutic efficacy. The definition of context of use must specify the degree of confidence required in the prediction, the types of patients for whom the model will be applicable and the risks associated with an incorrect prediction.

The third phase is the assessment of model risk, a parameter that the FDA constructs as the product of two factors, namely the influence of the model on the regulatory decision and the consequence of a decision error, the intersection of which determines the level of rigor required in the subsequent phases.[11] A model whose prediction weighs marginally on a low-risk decision for the patient will require less stringent evidence than a model whose output enters directly into a clinical safety assessment.

The fourth phase imposes the preparation of a credibility assessment plan, a document that specifies in advance the evidence, metrics and acceptance criteria that will be employed to demonstrate the adequacy of the model.[12] The FDA attaches

[7] FDA Draft Guidance (January 2025), Section V.A, articulating the risk-based credibility-assessment pathway in seven sequential phases.

[8] ASME, V&V 40 (2018): the Draft Guidance applies to the pharmaceutical sector a scheme already consolidated for medical devices, with adaptations reflecting the drug lifecycle.

[9] FDA Draft Guidance (January 2025), Section V.A.1 (Define the question of interest).

[10] FDA Draft Guidance (January 2025), Section V.A.2 (Define the context of use of the AI model).

[11] FDA Draft Guidance (January 2025), Section V.A.3 (Assess the AI model risk): model risk is a function of the model's influence on the regulatory decision and of the consequence of an erroneous outcome.

[12] FDA Draft Guidance (January 2025), Section V.A.4 (Develop a plan to establish the credibility of the AI model output).

significance to the fact that this plan is prepared before the execution of the tests, so that there is no room for *ex post* construction of criteria on the basis of the results actually obtained.

The fifth phase is the execution of the plan, with systematic collection of the envisioned evidence.[13] The sixth phase requires complete documentation of the results and, in a particularly significant way, of deviations from the plan originally prepared.[14] The seventh and final phase is the determination of the adequacy of the model with respect to the declared context of use, a determination that the FDA reserves the right to verify within the authorization process.[15] Continuous monitoring of performance over time, often invoked as an activity related to the employment of models subject to data drift, is treated by the FDA as a post-deployment activity, separate from but functionally connected to the initial credibility assessment.

9.2.3 Scope of Application

The scope of application of the Draft Guidance is delimited with precision and does not coincide with the entire lifecycle of the drug.[16] The document covers uses of artificial intelligence that directly support a regulatory decision on the safety, efficacy or quality of the product, typically including the nonclinical phase of toxicological evaluation, the clinical phase (study design, patient selection, endpoint analysis), the manufacturing and quality control phase and the post-approval phase, in particular for pharmacovigilance and safety signal detection.

In contrast, uses of artificial intelligence in so-called drug discovery in the strict sense, namely the identification of the biological target, lead optimization and molecular design preceding the evaluation of safety and efficacy, as well as purely operational uses internal to the developer, remain expressly outside the scope of the Draft Guidance. This delimitation is consistent with the mission of the agency, whose mandate is exhausted in the evaluation of the product and does not extend to the free research activities that precede the authorization process. The distinction is not without practical consequences, given that much of the investment of pharmaceutical enterprises in artificial intelligence concentrates precisely in the discovery and molecular optimization phases, which nonetheless remain, at least formally, outside the perimeter of the Draft Guidance.

---

[13] FDA Draft Guidance (January 2025), Section V.A.5 (Execute the plan).

[14] FDA Draft Guidance (January 2025), Section V.A.6 (Document the results of the credibility-assessment plan and discuss deviations).

[15] FDA Draft Guidance (January 2025), Section V.A.7 (Determine the adequacy of the AI model for the context of use). Post-adoption monitoring is treated as a distinct activity, connected to but separate from the initial pathway.

[16] FDA Draft Guidance (January 2025), Section III (Scope): the guidance covers uses of AI that directly support a regulatory decision on safety, efficacy or quality, expressly excluding drug-discovery uses (target identification, lead optimization, molecular design prior to safety and efficacy assessment) and internal operational uses.

It will be observed that, within the clinical phase included in the Draft Guidance, one of the applications on which FDA and EMA have developed a more articulated regulatory position concerns the use of external control arms and synthetic control arms to reduce the sample size of the control arm in randomized trials on rare diseases or high-mortality conditions. The FDA, through the CDER, published in February 2023 a Draft Guidance dedicated specifically to the design and conduct of studies with external controls, in which the credibility framework of computational models is called upon to operate in combination with the requirements of representativeness and comparability of the control population with respect to the experimental arm.[17] The EMA, for its part, qualified in 2022 the PROCOVA methodology, which employs a prognostic covariate constructed with machine learning techniques to increase the statistical power of the study without altering the randomization structure.[18] For the technical analysis of these methodologies, reference is made to Chap. 3, Sect. 3.5, of the present volume, where the TwinRCT is discussed as an advanced use of generative adversarial networks, as well as to Chap. 6, where the Digital Twin represents the fourth case-study application of defective product liability.

The crosscutting approach that the FDA adopts with respect to the phases included within the perimeter of the document represents nonetheless a significant novelty. Before the Draft Guidance, the role of artificial intelligence in pharmaceutical regulation had been considered primarily in the context of tools used by manufacturers for quality control or quality assurance. The Draft Guidance, by contrast, places artificial intelligence at the center of all activities that contribute to a regulatory decision of the agency, requiring that the credibility framework be satisfied in each of them. The integration of the manufacturing phase reflects growing awareness, namely that artificial intelligence is not only a research tool, but a structural component of the entire lifecycle of the drug.

9.2.4 The Elsa Case and the Irony of the Regulator Relying on Generative Artificial Intelligence

Reflection on model credibility assumes further significance when one considers that the FDA itself has begun to rely, for its own internal processes, on generative artificial intelligence systems. On June 2, 2025 the agency announced the launch of Elsa (Electronic Language System Assistant), a conversational assistant based on a large language model, built on Anthropic's Claude platform in a secure cloud

[17] FDA, *Considerations for the Design and Conduct of Externally Controlled Trials for Drug and Biological Products*, Draft Guidance for Industry, CDER, February 2023; on external control arms, see Chap. 3, Sect. 3.5.

[18] EMA, CHMP, *Qualification opinion for Prognostic Covariate Adjustment (PROCOVA™)*, EMADOC-1700519818-907465, adopted 15 September 2022 and published 20 September 2022. See also EMA, *Reflection paper on the use of artificial intelligence in the lifecycle of medicines*, EMA/CHMP/CVMP/83833/2023, 9 September 2024, Section 4. On the Digital Twin as a case study on product liability, see Chap. 6.

environment.[19] Elsa was designed to accelerate the daily activities of FDA personnel, from review of clinical trial protocols to search of scientific literature, from comparison of labeling to synthesis of adverse event reports.

The experience of the first months of deployment, however, made manifest the fragility of the approach. Some reviewers at the agency reported episodes of hallucination in which the system generated nonexistent bibliographic references, imprecise regulatory citations and factually incorrect syntheses of documents loaded into the environment.[20] The FDA's reaction was twofold, as on one hand a principle of human review (human-in-the-loop) was adopted according to which every output of Elsa must be verified by a reviewer before flowing into an instructional act and on the other hand a cycle of continuous improvement of the system was initiated with monitoring of performance and structured collection of feedback.

The Elsa case presents a significant regulatory irony. The same agency that in the January 2025 Draft Guidance imposes on applicants to submit their models to a credibility assessment before using them to support a regulatory decision now finds itself in the position of applying an analogous principle to itself, to the extent that the outputs of Elsa can influence, albeit indirectly, its own decisions. From this arises an empirical confirmation of the theoretical intuition of the Draft Guidance, namely that the problem of model credibility is not an industrial problem but a structural problem of the relationship between artificial intelligence and evidence-based decision-making, which concerns both the developer of the drug and the entity authorizing it. The episode opens moreover an interrogative, thus far little investigated, concerning the standard of care applicable to a regulator that delegates portions of its work to an artificial intelligence system, with possible consequences for the legitimacy of authorization acts and the agency's liability.

9.3 The European Medicines Agency

9.3.1 The Reflection Paper (Final Version, September 2024)

The European Medicines Agency adopted, on September 9, 2024, the final version of the "Reflection paper on the use of Artificial Intelligence (AI) in the medicinal product lifecycle."[21] The document represents the fruit of a consultation process that involved experts from regulatory agencies throughout Europe, representatives of the pharmaceutical industry and academics.

[19] FDA, *FDA Launches Agency-Wide AI Tool to Optimize Performance for the American People*, press release, 2 June 2025. The system (Elsa), built on Anthropic's Claude platform in a GovCloud environment, was subsequently the subject of internal reports of hallucination incidents and inaccurate bibliographic citations.

[20] On the functioning of Elsa, see the reports circulated in the second half of 2025 documenting hallucination incidents involving citations of scientific literature and regulatory references; see also FDA, *Elsa Implementation Update*, September 2025, adopting the human-in-the-loop principle for every use of the system in investigative documents.

[21] EMA, Reflection paper (2024), cited above.

Unlike the FDA's Draft Guidance, the Reflection Paper adopts a distinct methodological approach. It does not articulate a rigid seven-phase pathway. Rather, it proposes a risk-based approach, already consolidated in the tradition of European pharmaceutical regulatory practice.[22] According to this approach, the level of documentation and analysis required for an artificial intelligence model must be proportionate to the risk that the model poses to the patient and to the regulatory system. With respect to the 2023 draft submitted for public consultation, the final version clarifies that the concept of "high risk" must be understood in a dual sense, namely as "high risk to the patient" and as "high regulatory impact," a distinction that permits calibrating with greater precision the documentary response required of enterprises.

The final version has moreover extended the roster of responsible subjects, explicitly including, in addition to the marketing authorization holder, also the sponsor of the clinical trial and the manufacturer of the medicine. The Reflection Paper establishes then a series of documentation requirements that developers of artificial intelligence models must satisfy, which include a complete description of the model's architecture, a detailed characterization of training data, documentation of validation metrics and a plan for monitoring the model over time.[23] Although formulated in a less prescriptive manner than the FDA, these requirements substantially converge with those of the American framework.

9.3.2 The Joint EMA-FDA Principles of January 2026

On January 14, 2026 the European Medicines Agency and the Food and Drug Administration published a joint document entitled "Guiding principles of good AI practice in drug development."[24] The document represents the first structured bilateral exercise on pharmaceutical artificial intelligence and follows from the FDA-EU meeting of April 2024, in which the need emerged to coordinate the approaches of the two agencies on the topics of data, artificial intelligence and software quality. It is situated within the broader joint HMA/EMA Data and AI Workplan and the European Medicines Agencies Network Strategy to 2028 (EMANS 2028). Health Canada, an agency also active on the topic, does not appear among the signatories of the document, a circumstance that should not be read as misalignment, but rather as a choice to concentrate the first formal exercise of convergence on the areas of greatest quantitative weight of the respective authorizations.

[22] EMA, Reflection paper (2024), Section 4.1; on the risk-based approach in pharmaceutical regulation, see Permanand and Mossialos (2005).

[23] EMA, Reflection paper (2024), Section 4.2, listing the documentation requirements for AI models (architecture, characterization of training data, validation metrics, monitoring plan).

[24] EMA and FDA, *Guiding Principles of Good AI Practice in Drug Development*, 14 January 2026: the first structured bilateral exercise on pharmaceutical AI, following the FDA-EU meeting of April 2024, within the joint HMA/EMA Data and AI Workplan and the European Medicines Agencies Network Strategy to 2028 (EMANS 2028).

The joint document identifies a set of principles organized around four fundamental pillars, namely transparency, data quality, human oversight and risk management.[25] It is significant that the two agencies reached consensus on these pillars, as this indicates that, beyond the structural differences between the American and European regulatory systems, there exists a common foundation of principles upon which pharmaceutical enterprises can build their compliance strategies. The principle of proportionality requires that the level of rigor in evaluating a model be commensurate with the risk associated with the decision that the model supports. The principle of transparency imposes that developers make available complete and understandable descriptions of the models. The principle of human oversight establishes the primacy of human decision. The principle of data quality addresses requirements of completeness, representativeness and absence of systematic bias in training data. The further principles address more specific questions, such as management of model changes over time, organizational governance, collaboration with regulators, documentation of known limitations of the model, protection of personal data and incident management.

The principle relating to human oversight merits particular attention. According to the joint formulation, the use of artificial intelligence and machine learning must enhance, not replace, human decision-making in regulatory instances. This principle asserts that technology must expand the decision-making capabilities of the human reviewer, not supplant them. This is a direct corollary of the principle of human oversight established by Regulation (EU) 2024/1689 at article 14.[26]

9.3.3 The Risk-Based and Human-Centric Approach

The EMA's Reflection Paper and subsequent instruments developed by European agencies have consolidated a specific regulatory approach, which combines two methodological elements, namely risk analysis and consideration of human needs.

The risk-based approach entails that documentation requirements, validation metrics and post-approval monitoring modalities be scaled based on the risk profile of the model. A model used to support patient population selection in a clinical trial has a different risk profile from a model used for quality control management in a production line. The EMA has progressively developed a methodology for risk assessment based on dimensions such as the type of decision supported, the number of patients involved and the irreversibility of the consequence of a model error.

The term "human-centric," which recurs frequently in European regulatory instruments, denotes a general orientation according to which technology must be a tool in service of human decision-making capacity and can never replace it. This

[25] EMA and FDA, Guiding Principles (2026): the principles turn on transparency, data quality, human oversight and risk management, and stress that AI/ML should augment, not replace, human decision-making in regulatory submissions.

[26] Art. 14, Regulation (EU) 2024/1689 (effective human oversight throughout the lifecycle of high-risk AI systems).

principle is reflected in a series of concrete obligations, in that it imposes transparent communication to human reviewers of the limitations and uncertainties associated with models, the availability of appeal mechanisms in the event that the model produces unexpected results and the possibility for the human operator to disable or disregard the model's recommendations when appropriate.

In 2024, the EMA issued a supplementary document denominated "Draft Guideline on the Quality of Data Used in the Development of Artificial Intelligence/ Machine Learning Models for the Medicinal Product Lifecycle,"[27] which deepens the standards of data quality in even greater detail than the Reflection Paper.

9.4 The Italian Medicines Agency

9.4.1 The AIFA Guidance of May 2021 for Authorization of Clinical Trials with AI/ML

The Italian regulatory landscape equipped itself, already in May 2021, with a specific instrument dedicated to clinical research employing artificial intelligence and machine learning systems, namely the "Guidance on the presentation of the application for authorization of clinical trials with artificial intelligence and machine learning systems" issued by the Italian Medicines Agency (AIFA) in version 1.0 of May 24, 2021.[28] The guidance represents the first document of a properly administrative nature adopted by a national pharmaceutical agency dedicated specifically to artificial intelligence systems.

The AIFA guidance addresses a fundamental problem that emerges frequently in clinical trial authorization practices, namely the distinction between two typologies of systems, that is, artificial intelligence systems used as tools for research support and systems that intervene directly in clinical decision-making.[29] This distinction is significant for regulatory classification. The former, if they do not modify clinical information, do not fall within the definition of medical device according to Regulation (EU) 2017/745 (MDR).[30] The latter, by contrast, potentially do.

The AIFA guidance establishes a series of specific documentary requirements that applicants must satisfy in submitting an application for authorization of clinical

[27] EMA, *Draft guideline on the quality of data used in the development of artificial intelligence/ machine-learning models for the medicinal product lifecycle*, 2024.

[28] AIFA, *Guide to the submission of clinical trial authorization applications involving artificial intelligence and machine-learning systems*, version 1.0 of 24 May 2021, published on the Agency's website on 28 May 2021. The Guide had not been substantially updated as at the date of this volume.

[29] AIFA, Guide (2021), Section 3, distinguishing AI systems used as research support tools (not classified as medical devices) from systems intervening directly in clinical decision-making (potentially medical devices under Regulation (EU) 2017/745).

[30] Regulation (EU) 2017/745 on medical devices (MDR); on software as a medical device, see Art. 2(1) and Annex VIII, rule 11.

trials using artificial intelligence systems.[31] These requirements include the description of the methodology of training and validation of the model, documentation of training data, assessment of the risk associated with the model and the monitoring plan.

A significant aspect of the guidance is the attention devoted to the quality of data used for training the model in the specific context of the Italian and European population. The document recommends that developers demonstrate that training data are representative of the population for which the drug is intended. This recommendation is particularly relevant, as many datasets available internationally have been constructed predominantly on North American or Anglophone populations and might not adequately reflect the genetic, epidemiological and environmental characteristics of the European population. The guidance further emphasizes the necessity of documenting the data chain of custody, from collection to processing, to guarantee traceability and reproducibility of results produced by the model.

The circumstance that the AIFA guidance has not been subject to substantial updates in the 5 years following its initial publication, despite the adoption of the AI Regulation, the publication of the EMA's Reflection Paper and the evolution of the MDR framework, constitutes a weakness in the Italian regulatory ecosystem. The necessity of aligning the document with the subsequent European sources represents today an operational priority that awaits a response.

9.4.2 Coordination with the European Framework

AIFA, while preserving decision-making autonomy in the authorization of clinical trials, operates within a European regulatory framework that progressively constrains its decisions. Pursuant to Regulation (EC) No. 726/2004, which establishes the centralized procedure, certain categories of medicines must necessarily be authorized at the European level by the EMA.[32] In these cases, AIFA performs the role of rapporteur or co-rapporteur agency, participating in review of the dossier and risk assessment. This architecture implies that the evaluation criteria applied by AIFA in the context of clinical trials must be consistent with those applied by the EMA in the context of authorization for marketing.

While the FDA's Draft Guidance represents a regulatory standard specific to the United States, the EMA's Reflection Paper and related documents, including AIFA guidance, constitute a predominantly European normative framework, in which AIFA assumes a role both as operator and as coordinator.

---

[31] AIFA, Guide (2021), Section 4 (documentation requirements for clinical trial authorization applications involving AI/ML systems).

[32] Regulation (EC) 726/2004 establishing the centralized authorization procedure for medicinal products; see also d.lgs. 24 April 2006, n. 219 (Codice del farmaco).

9.5 Convergence and Divergence Among Regulatory Frameworks

9.5.1 Points of Convergence

Despite methodological differences and divergent wording of the documents, the three regulatory frameworks (FDA, EMA, AIFA) display a remarkable degree of convergence on certain fundamental principles.[33] The first is the necessity of transparency. All three frameworks require that developers fully document how the model was constructed, on which data it was trained and how it was validated. The second is the importance of data quality. All three recognize that bias in training data inevitably propagates to model results. The third is the central role of human oversight. None of the three frameworks permits artificial intelligence to completely replace human decision-making in the matter of drug authorization or design of clinical trials.

9.5.2 Points of Divergence

There are, however, also significant differences among the three frameworks.[34] The principal divergence concerns the degree of prescriptiveness. The FDA, through the Draft Guidance, provides an articulated and sequential framework (the seven phases) that developers are effectively required to follow. This is a characteristic typical of the American regulatory approach, which tends to privilege prescriptive and detailed standards.

The EMA, by contrast, adopts an approach more grounded in principles. The Reflection Paper emphasizes general principles and a proportionate risk analysis, but provides less concrete guidance on how to implement such principles. This approach reflects a European regulatory tradition more oriented toward flexibility and adaptation to specific circumstances.

AIFA occupies an intermediate position. Its guidance is more prescriptive than the EMA's Reflection Paper, but less rigid than the FDA's Draft Guidance. This reflects the structural role of AIFA as a national agency situated within a European normative framework.

9.5.3 Implications for Multi-jurisdictional Enterprises

The divergences among the three regulatory frameworks have concrete implications for pharmaceutical enterprises operating at the international level.[35] An

[33] The convergence on transparency, data quality and human oversight is documented in EMA and FDA, Guiding Principles (2026), and analysed in Lenarczyk et al. (2025).

[34] Vogel (2012), framing the divergence between a prescriptive approach and a principles-based approach as reflecting a structural difference between regulatory systems.

[35] Drexl et al. (2021).

enterprise that intends to develop and commercialize a drug supported by an artificial intelligence model in the United States, in the European Union and in Italy must perform a careful assessment of the documentary obligations specific to each jurisdiction.

An efficient strategy can in large part overlap the requirements of the three frameworks, for instance by producing documentation that simultaneously satisfies the seven FDA phases and EMA principles, but areas of potential divergence persist. A medium-sized enterprise might find it economically difficult to make the dual effort of compliance, with the result of generating, indirectly, a competitive advantage for larger enterprises, which can afford large compliance teams.

A further complication concerns timing. The different agencies proceed at different rates in updating their own guidelines. The FDA's January 2025 Draft Guidance was followed, approximately 1 year later, by the joint EMA-FDA principles of January 14, 2026. The EMA finalized the Reflection Paper in September 2024, but the implementing documents are still in the phase of elaboration. AIFA operates on the basis of a 2021 guidance never updated. This asynchrony generates uncertainty for enterprises, which cannot rely on a stable and final regulatory framework in all jurisdictions simultaneously.

It must furthermore be considered that smaller pharmaceutical enterprises, biotechnology start-ups and computational research enterprises operating at the intersection of technology and pharmaceuticals generally have limited resources for regulatory compliance. For these enterprises, the necessity of navigating a fragmented regulatory ecosystem represents not only a cost, but a genuine barrier to entry. This observation refers to the anticoncerted competition profiles discussed in Chap. 8, where it was highlighted how the concentration of computational resources and data in the hands of a few dominant operators generates conditions of natural oligopoly. Regulatory fragmentation strengthens this tendency, as it increases the fixed costs of compliance that only large enterprises can easily sustain.

9.6 The Credibility Framework as a Legal Parameter

9.6.1 FDA Credibility and the Development Risk Defense

One of the most significant contributions of the present chapter to the overall thesis of the volume concerns the function that the FDA credibility framework assumes as a legal parameter in the context of civil liability for defective products.[36] As already discussed in Chap. 6, Directive (EU) 2024/2853 on liability for damage caused by defective products introduces the right for the manufacturer to prove that the damage is attributable to a circumstance that the state of scientific and technical knowledge did not make possible to discover at that historical moment. This element,

[36] On the relationship between regulatory compliance and civil liability, see Directive (EU) 2024/2853 on liability for defective products.

known as the development risk defense, represents the principal legal protection for pharmaceutical enterprises in the context of defective product liability.[37]

The central question can be formulated in the following terms. In the case of a drug developed with the support of an artificial intelligence model, how is it to be evaluated whether the state of scientific and technical knowledge made possible the discovery of the defect? How does the FDA credibility framework integrate into this evaluation?

It is held that the FDA credibility framework can be usefully employed as a reference parameter to evaluate whether the state of scientific and technical knowledge at the moment of drug development was such as to permit the discovery of the defect.[38] Consider the scenario of an artificial intelligence model used for the prediction of the toxicity of a molecule that produced an incorrect prediction, which then had repercussions on the safety of the drug in the clinical phase. In evaluating whether the manufacturer should have discovered the risk, a court might reasonably ask whether the developer of the model satisfied the seven phases of credibility assessment at the moment of development. If it did, this provides robust evidence that the developer acted in conformity with the declared context of use and the best practices of the sector. If it did not, this is indicative of negligence that could exclude the applicability of the defense.

In other words, the FDA credibility framework performs a dual function. First, it is an instrument of regulatory compliance, which enables pharmaceutical enterprises to demonstrate compliance with agency guidelines. Second, it is a legal parameter, which a civil court can use to evaluate whether the manufacturer acted in conformity with the state of the art of the sector.

The inverse scenario merits equal attention. Consider the case in which a pharmaceutical enterprise developed a drug without making use of available and validated artificial intelligence models and such drug subsequently caused damage that an artificial intelligence model could have predicted with reasonable accuracy. In this case, the FDA credibility framework assumes a different function, no longer that of a defense but of a diligence parameter. If the state of the art of the sector included artificial intelligence models validated according to the FDA phases for the prediction of toxicity and if the enterprise did not employ such tools without adequate justification, a court might reasonably hold that the enterprise did not act in conformity with the state of scientific and technical knowledge available. The FDA credibility framework thus operates as a bidirectional parameter, which protects those who follow it but which at the same time raises the threshold of diligence required of those who do not.

This bidirectionality of the parameter has significant implications for the risk management strategy of pharmaceutical enterprises.[39] It suggests that the adoption

[37] The development-risk defense is governed by Art. 11, Directive (EU) 2024/2853; see Chap. 6, Sect. 6.3.5.

[38] Bertolini (2025), on the context of use as a parameter for assessing the state of scientific and technical knowledge within the meaning of Art. 11, Directive (EU) 2024/2853.

[39] Pagallo (2024), on the shift from formal compliance to qualified diligence in the integration between sectoral frameworks and the AI Act.

of validated artificial intelligence models is not only a matter of operational efficiency, but becomes progressively an implicit obligation of professional diligence. As regulatory agencies consolidate their reference frameworks and models achieve levels of documented and reproducible accuracy, the non-use of such tools could constitute a form of negligence by omission, in particular in cases where the model could have identified a risk that traditional methods did not detect.

9.6.2 EMA Compliance and AI Regulation Requirements

A parallel reasoning can be developed in the European context. As addressed in Chap. 5, Regulation (EU) 2024/1689 articulates a series of technical obligations for high-risk artificial intelligence systems, relating to data, documentation, human oversight and risk monitoring.[40] The EMA's Reflection Paper performs an operationalization of such obligations in the specific context of pharmaceutical development.

It is asserted that systematic compliance with the EMA's Reflection Paper and the joint EMA-FDA principles provides strong presumption of compliance with the requirements of the AI Regulation for artificial intelligence systems used in pharmaceutical development. The Reflection Paper is explicitly designed to integrate the general principles of the Regulation into the specific pharmaceutical context.[41] Consequently, a pharmaceutical enterprise able to demonstrate that it has followed the EMA guidelines has simultaneously provided proof of compliance with the general requirements of the AI Regulation.

This approach permits a simplification of the compliance strategy for enterprises. Rather than addressing separately the compliance with the AI Regulation and compliance with specific pharmaceutical guidelines, enterprises can focus on compliance with pharmaceutical regulatory frameworks, knowing that it assures simultaneously compliance with the more general requirements of the Regulation.

It is, however, necessary to signal a limitation of the presumption of equivalence. The AI Regulation contains obligations that do not find a direct correspondence in EMA documents. Article 13, for example, imposes transparency obligations that extend beyond the scientific documentation provided for by the Reflection Paper, reaching communication toward end users and the public.[42] Similarly, article 9 requires a risk management system that operates throughout the entire lifecycle of the artificial intelligence system, with periodic and documented updates, according to a logic that is not exhausted in the authorization process for the drug but extends to the post-approval phase and continuous monitoring of the model. For these reasons, compliance with the Reflection Paper constitutes a necessary but not always sufficient condition for full compliance with the AI Regulation. Enterprises must integrate specific pharmaceutical

[40] Arts. 10 and 11, Regulation (EU) 2024/1689 (data governance requirements and technical documentation for high-risk AI systems).

[41] EMA, Reflection paper (2024), Section 2, recognizing the AI Act as the reference framework for the sectoral operationalization of general principles in pharmaceutical development.

[42] Art. 13, Regulation (EU) 2024/1689 (transparency enabling deployers to interpret and use the system's output appropriately).

requirements with an autonomous assessment of the residual obligations arising from the Regulation that are not covered by sector-specific guidelines.

9.6.3 Proposal for a Public Registry of Predictive Models

Section 9.6.1 has shown that the FDA credibility parameter operates bidirectionally, as a shield for the enterprise that follows it and as a diligence parameter for the enterprise that omits it. Section 9.6.2 has shown how compliance with the Reflection Paper operates as a presumption of compliance with the general requirements of the AI Regulation. Both mechanisms presuppose, however, that the existence, characteristics and level of validation of predictive models are knowledge accessible to the civil court and to the injured party. In current practice, the credibility documentation deposited with the FDA and the Qualification Opinions issued by the EMA remain kept in regulatory dossiers, subject to the commercial and procedural confidentiality that protects the authorization dossier. The injured party is unaware which model existed at the moment of drug development, which model was validated by the regulatory agency and which would have been exigible in light of the state of scientific art. This information asymmetry evacuates of practical content the bidirectional function of the credibility parameter, as the legal parameter becomes justiciable only to the extent that its technical substance is knowable by the subject who intends to invoke it in court.

It is proposed to establish a public registry of predictive models used in pharmaceutical development, maintained jointly by regulatory agencies with the EMA as lead agency for the European Union and with national nodes at AIFA, fed by pharmaceutical enterprises at the moment of submission of the application for marketing authorization. The registry would contain, for each model, the unique identifier with the version, the context of use declared by the manufacturer, the outcome of the credibility assessment conducted according to the seven phases of the FDA Draft Guidance, any qualification opinion released by the EMA pursuant to the Scientific Advice procedure, the reference scientific literature for the computational architecture adopted and the date of the most recent documented validation. The proposal is situated within the European tradition of public regulatory registries, of which notable examples constitute the European portal for clinical trials established by Regulation 536/2014 and the European database of medical devices established by Regulation 2017/745, of which it reprises the logic of transparency applied to technical data, with the adaptation of three new elements specific to the algorithmic context.[43] The first element is the dynamic dimension of the model, which requires versioned rather than static registration. The second is the probabilistic nature of the output, which requires specification of the confidence interval and domain of applicability. The third is the industrial ownership of the model, which opens the question of balancing regulatory transparency and protection of know-how as trade secret.

[43] On the EudraCT-CTIS model, see Regulation (EU) 536/2014 on clinical trials, Arts. 80–81; on EUDAMED, see Regulation (EU) 2017/745, Art. 33. On public registries of high-risk AI systems (Art. 71, Regulation (EU) 2024/1689), see Veale and Zuiderveen Borgesius (2021) and Ebers (2022).

The registry operates as an instrument of *ex ante* transparency. It renders public the state of the art of available models for each area of pharmaceutical development and permits researchers, industry and agencies to know in real time the validated technological frontier. From this function three concrete consequences derive. First, the reduction of duplication of validation efforts, given that a model already qualified need not be reconstructed de novo by each developer and can be reused following a new Scientific Advice procedure limited to change of context of use. Second, the incentive to adopt validated models in place of unverified proprietary models, as public evidence of the state of the art aligns commercial interest with reduction of regulatory risk. Third, the comprehensibility of the technological perimeter for subjects called upon to pronounce themselves in pharmaceutical disputes, foremost among them civil judges, to whom the registry provides an autonomous cognitive foundation that does not constrain them to rely entirely on the court-appointed technical expert designated in the individual proceeding.

The second function is one of facilitation of proof *ex post* and restores concrete operativity to the bidirectionality of the credibility parameter discussed at Sect. 9.6.1. In civil proceedings, the party injured by the defective drug does not possess the technical instruments to prove that an artificial intelligence model could have predicted the risk avoiding the damage, nor is aware which models were accessible to the enterprise at the moment of development. The public registry, by rendering knowable *ex ante* the characteristics of models available at the moment of authorization application, furnishes the judge an objective parameter to evaluate whether the manufacturer acted in conformity with the state of scientific and technological art. The proof of negligence by omission, introduced by the bidirectionality of the credibility parameter discussed at Sect. 9.6.1, thus becomes effective rather than disclosure provided for by Directive 2024/2853 on liability for damage caused by defective products, reducing the disclosure burden on the individual manufacturer and broadening the cognitive foundation of the injured party from the preliminary stages of the dispute. On the qualification of explainability as an autonomous probative instrument reference is made to Chap. 4, Sect. 4.6, while for the concrete illustration of the functioning of the credibility parameter in a case of damage caused by a drug assisted by artificial intelligence reference is made to Chap. 6, Sect. 6.6.4, dedicated to the Digital Twin case study.[44]

9.7 The International Coalition of Medicines Regulatory Authorities

The International Coalition of Medicines Regulatory Authorities (ICMRA) is a coordination body that brings together the pharmaceutical regulatory agencies of the world's principal countries, including the FDA, EMA, Health Canada, AIFA and the agencies of countries such as Japan, Australia, Brazil and India. Lacking direct

[44] On evidential facilitation for defective products generated through AI, see Arts. 9 (disclosure of evidence) and 10 (presumptions), Directive (EU) 2024/2853. On strict liability, see Wendehorst (2020) and Bertolini (2020).

normative power, ICMRA operates as a forum through which the various agencies share experiences, identify shared concerns and develop documents of a consultative and collaborative nature.

The only structured document that ICMRA has devoted to artificial intelligence is the "Horizon Scanning Assessment Report - Artificial Intelligence," published on August 6, 2021, in which the dedicated working group had identified the principal risks emerging from the employment of artificial intelligence throughout the drug lifecycle, among which algorithmic bias, decision opacity, cybersecurity risks and overfitting of models to training data.[45] The document anticipated with remarkable prescience themes that national and European agencies would address systematically only in the years following. At 5 years' distance, the failure to publish a formal update of the document represents a significant gap in the landscape of global regulatory convergence, in light of a production of norms and soft law that has in the interim become substantial.

The report identifies systematically the list of risks considered priorities by international agencies. Among them are algorithmic bias, understood as the tendency of an algorithm to systematically discriminate groups of patients based on characteristics such as sex, age or ethnic origin, decision opacity, which concerns models with respect to which it is not possible to understand their decision mechanisms, cybersecurity risks that affect artificial intelligence systems vulnerable to cyberattacks and overfitting, with which is meant the tendency of the model to memorize training data rather than to extract generalizable regularities.[46]

ICMRA performs a crucial role in promoting international regulatory harmonization, not through the imposition of binding standards, but through the progressive construction of convergence in best practices.[47] The fact that FDA, EMA, AIFA and other agencies collaborate through ICMRA provides a guarantee that standards emerging from individual agencies will not diverge excessively and that enterprises operating at the global level will not have to face excessive regulatory fragmentation.

A particularly significant element of ICMRA's reflection concerns the explicit recognition that artificial intelligence is no longer a peripheral technology in the pharmaceutical context.[48] International agencies take note that pharmaceutical enterprises already use artificial intelligence extensively and routinely in drug development, independent of the state of completion of regulation. Artificial intelligence is a consolidated reality, not a future prospect. This finding strengthens the urgency of regulation and motivates the acceleration of regulatory activity observed in the 2024–2026 biennium.

---

[45] ICMRA, *Horizon Scanning Assessment Report - Artificial Intelligence*, 6 August 2021, the only structured ICMRA publication specifically dedicated to AI in the medicinal product lifecycle.

[46] ICMRA, Horizon Scanning Assessment Report (2021), Section 3, identifying the priority risks of AI in pharmaceutical development.

[47] Breckenridge and Jacob (2019), on the role of ICMRA in promoting international regulatory harmonization.

[48] Cohen et al. (2020).

A further contribution of ICMRA to international reflection concerns the question of early interaction between developers and regulators (the so-called early dialogue). ICMRA recommends that pharmaceutical enterprises undertake dialogue with regulatory agencies already in the initial phases of development of an artificial intelligence model, without waiting for the phase of formal submission of the authorization application. This preventive dialogue permits the timely identification of any regulatory criticalities and the orientation of model development in a manner consistent with the expectations of regulators. This is a recommendation that, while lacking binding force, reflects a consolidated trend in contemporary pharmaceutical regulation, in which the relationship between enterprise and regulatory authority is conceived as collaborative rather than merely inspective.

9.8 Concluding Observations

The present chapter has analyzed the regulatory ecosystem of artificial intelligence in the pharmaceutical sector, focusing on documents issued by FDA, EMA, AIFA and ICMRA. Three conclusions of synthesis emerge from this analysis.

The first conclusion concerns the operational function of pharmaceutical regulatory frameworks. They are not mere documents of general guidance, but represent concrete operationalizations of the general principles contained in Regulation (EU) 2024/1689 and Directive (EU) 2024/2853 in the specific context of drug discovery and development. Regulatory frameworks transform abstract principles, such as transparency and risk management, into applicable technical prescriptions.

The second conclusion concerns the role of the FDA as an author of *de facto* global standards. Although the Draft Guidance is formally binding only on enterprises seeking authorization of drugs in the United States, the seven-phase pathway has achieved a position of reference at the international level. Even enterprises operating exclusively in Europe find it convenient to refer to the FDA framework, as it provides a proven and transparent methodology for evaluating the credibility of models. The EMA has progressively recognized this convergence, incorporating into its own documents references to FDA principles and participating, on January 14, 2026, in the formulation of joint principles on best practice in the use of artificial intelligence in pharmaceutical development.

The third conclusion concerns the dual function that regulatory frameworks assume in the context of civil liability. They are simultaneously instruments of regulatory compliance, that is, documents that permit enterprises to demonstrate compliance with administrative rules, as well as legal parameters, that is, standards that civil courts can use to evaluate whether the manufacturer acted in conformity with the declared context of use, the state of the art of the sector and the state of scientific and technical knowledge at the moment of product development. This dual function amplifies the practical importance of regulatory frameworks and underlines the necessity of compliance that is not merely formal, but substantive.

Looking toward the near future, it is necessary to recall the deadlines of the AI Regulation that will mark the transition of the entire pharmaceutical sector. The provisions on prohibited practices became applicable on February 2, 2025. The obligations relating to general-purpose AI models apply from August 2, 2025. The full regime for high-risk systems will enter into force on August 2, 2026, a deadline subsequently postponed by Omnibus Regulation VII of March 2026 to December 2, 2027 for standalone high-risk systems and to August 2, 2028 for embedded ones.[49] A significant portion of the artificial intelligence systems described in the present chapter will fall into this latter category through Annex III, with substantial consequences for the documentary, governance and post-market surveillance obligations that pharmaceutical enterprises will be required to respect in addition to sector-specific requirements.

A further reflection is imposed, in closing, on the relationship between regulatory compliance costs and concentration of the pharmaceutical market. As highlighted in Chap. 8, the stratification of credibility, validation and documentation requirements imposed by regulatory frameworks strengthens the position of integrated operators, who possess the resources necessary to sustain simultaneously authorization instances and internal artificial intelligence governance processes, at the expense of smaller entities. The regulatory governance of artificial intelligence in the pharmaceutical sector reveals itself thus to be terrain on which administrative law, civil law, antitrust law and computer engineering meet and mutually condition each other.

An aspect destined for deepening in the coming years concerns the question of shared responsibility among the various actors in the chain of algorithmic pharmaceutical development. The traditional model of pharmaceutical liability assigns responsibility to the marketing authorization holder. However, when drug development avails itself of artificial intelligence models provided by third parties (technology enterprises, computational research centers, AI as a Service platforms), the causal chain fragments. The current regulatory framework, both in the United States and in Europe, does not address in an organized manner the question of allocation of responsibility between the marketing authorization holder and the provider of the artificial intelligence model.[50] This gap will need to be filled, presumably through a combination of regulatory interventions and contractual practice, before resort to artificial intelligence in pharmaceutical development can be considered fully governed by law.

---

[49] Art. 113, Regulation (EU) 2024/1689, on the progressive entry into application of the Regulation: the prohibited practices apply from 2 February 2025, the general-purpose model rules from 2 August 2025, and the high-risk system rules from 2 August 2026, a deadline subsequently postponed by the Digital Omnibus on AI (proposed November 2025) to 2 December 2027 for standalone high-risk systems and to 2 August 2028 for embedded ones.

[50] On the fragmentation of the causal chain in healthcare AI, see Price II (2017); Aboy et al. (2024), anticipating a specific regime allocating responsibility between the marketing-authorization holder and the model provider.

References

Aboy M, Minssen T, Vayena E (2024) Navigating the EU AI Act: implications for regulated digital medical products. NPJ Digit Med 7(1):237

Bertolini A (2020) Artificial intelligence and civil liability. Study PE 621.926, European Parliament, Policy Department for Citizens' Rights and Constitutional Affairs, Brussels. https://www.europarl.europa.eu/RegData/etudes/STUD/2020/621926/IPOL_STU(2020)621926_EN.pdf. Accessed 7 June 2026

Bertolini A (2025) Artificial intelligence and civil liability: a European perspective. Study PE 776.426, European Parliament, Policy Department for Citizens' Rights and Constitutional Affairs, Brussels. https://www.europarl.europa.eu/thinktank/en/document/IUST_STU(2025)776426. Accessed 7 June 2026

Breckenridge A, Jacob R (2019) Overcoming the legal and regulatory barriers to drug repurposing. Nat Rev Drug Discov 18:1–2

Chiti MP (2018) Diritto amministrativo europeo. Giuffrè, Milano

Cohen IG, Evgeniou T, Gerke S, Minssen T (2020) The European artificial intelligence strategy: implications and challenges for digital health. Lancet Digit Health 2(7):e376–e379

Drexl J, Hilty RM, Desaunettes-Barbero L, Globocnik J, Gonzalez Otero B, Hoffmann J, Kim D, Kulhari S, Richter H, Scheuerer S, Slowinski PR, Wiedemann K (2021) Artificial intelligence and intellectual property law. Position statement of the Max Planck Institute for Innovation and Competition of 9 April 2021 on the current debate. Max Planck Institute for Innovation and Competition Research Paper No 21-10

Ebers M (2022) Regulating explainable AI in the European Union: an overview of the current legal framework(s). In: Nordic yearbook of law and informatics 2020–2021, Stockholm, pp 103–132

Lenarczyk G, Minssen T, Price WN, Rai AK (2025) The future of AI regulation in drug development: a comparative analysis. J Law Biosci 12(2):lsaf028

Pagallo U (2024) Dismantling four myths in AI & EU law through legal information "about" reality. In: Sousa Antunes H, Freitas PM, Oliveira AL, Martins Pereira C, Vaz de Sequeira E, Barreto Xavier L (eds) Multidisciplinary perspectives on artificial intelligence and the law. Springer, Cham

Permanand G (2006) EU pharmaceutical regulation: the politics of policy-making. Manchester University Press, Manchester

Permanand G, Mossialos E (2005) Constitutional asymmetry and pharmaceutical policy-making in the European Union. J Eur Public Policy 12(4):687–709

Price WN II (2017) Artificial intelligence in health care: applications and legal implications. SciTech Lawyer 14

Snyder F (1993) Soft law and institutional practice in the European Community. EUI Working Paper, European University Institute, Florence

Veale M, Zuiderveen Borgesius F (2021) Demystifying the draft EU Artificial Intelligence Act. Comput Law Rev Int 22(4):97–112

Vogel D (2012) The politics of precaution: regulating health, safety, and environmental risks in Europe and the United States. Princeton University Press, Princeton

Wendehorst C (2020) Strict liability for AI and other emerging technologies. J Eur Tort Law 11(2):150–180

FSC
www.fsc.org
MIX
Papier | Fördert
gute Waldnutzung
FSC® C083411

Kolibri 360 GmbH
Ferdinand-Jühlke-Straße 7
99095 Erfurt, Deutschland
produktsicherheit@kolibri360.de